THE PHONOLOGICAL STRUCTURE OF THE VERBAL ROOTS
IN ARABIC AND HEBREW

STUDIES IN SEMITIC
LANGUAGES AND LINGUISTICS

EDITED BY

T. MURAOKA AND C.H.M. VERSTEEGH

VOLUME XXXIV

THE PHONOLOGICAL STRUCTURE OF THE VERBAL ROOTS IN ARABIC AND HEBREW

TUTA SUB AEGIDE PALLAS

· 1683 ·

THE PHONOLOGICAL STRUCTURE
OF THE VERBAL ROOTS
IN ARABIC AND HEBREW

BY

BERNARD N. BACHRA

BRILL
LEIDEN · BOSTON · KÖLN
2001

This book is printed on acid-free paper.

Library of Congress Cataloging-in-Publication Data

Bachra, Bernard Nehemia, 1926-
  The phonological structure of the verbal roots in Arabic and Hebrew / by
Bernard N. Bachra.
      p. cm. — (Studies in Semitic languages and linguistics, ISSN
  0081-8461 ; 34)
  ISBN 9004120084(alk. paper)
      1. Arabic language—Verb. 2. Hebrew language—Verb. 3. Hebrew
language—Phonology, comparative—Arabic. 4. Arabic language—Phonology,
comparative—Hebrew. I. Title II. Series
PJ6351 .B33 2000
492.7'5—dc21   00-063108
                                                                       CIP

Die Deutsche Bibliothek-CIP-Einheitsaufnahme

Bachra, Bernard N.:
The phonological structure of the verbal roots in Arabic and Hebrew /
by Bernard N. Bachra. - Leiden ; Boston ; Köln : Brill, 2000
  (Studies in Semitic languages and linguistics ; Vol. 34)
  ISBN 90-04-12008-4

                                            _PJ_
                                            _6351_
                                            _.B33_
              ISSN   0081-8461   _2001_
              ISBN   90 04 12008 4

PRINTED IN THE NETHERLANDS

CONTENTS

CHAPTER 4. Methodology used in this study

CHAPTER 5. Co-occurrence restrictions which act on the consonants in the verbal root patterns of Arabic and Hebrew

CHAPTER 6. Co-occurrence preferences for verbal roots in Arabic and Hebrew

CHAPTER 7. Co-occurrence restrictions and co-occurrence preference in Arabic and Hebrew. Refinement and summary of the findings

CHAPTER 8. Theoretical implications

ACKNOWLEDGEMENTS

This book was originally prepared as a doctoral thesis. During the time when I was studying for my Master's degree in Semitic languages and linguistics and during the period of the work for this thesis, many people have contributed to my progress in knowledge and to my maturity as an investigator in this field. I thank them all, but I want to single out some of them here.

Prof. J. Hoftijzer (formerly in the Dept. of Hebrew, Aramaic, Ugaritic and Phoenician) has been my teacher of Biblical Hebrew ever since at an advancing age I started out as a 'young' student. I have learned a great deal from his meticulous and careful way of analyzing the syntax of Biblical texts. I greatly benefitted from his critical remarks at various stages of my work.

Dr. Harry G. van der Hulst (Dept. of General Linguistics, at present Univ. of Connecticut, U.S.A.) introduced me to the field of generative phonology of which I hardly had any prior knowledge. He stimulated me continuously and enthusiastically to get familiar with the recent developments in his field. His provocative suggestions concerning my subject of investigation often induced me to follow as yet untrodden paths.

Prof. J.G. Kooij (Dept. of General Linguistics) served as the advisor for my doctoral thesis during a number of years. Due to his critical influence the text became more lucid and more flowing. He kept me on the track by his decisiveness and by his matter of fact approach.

Dr. P.K. Doorn (Dept. of General History) and *Dr. A.H. Zwinderman* (Dept. of Medical Statistics) both advised me on the choice of a suitable statistical test.

Mr. P.M. Hijzelendoorn, B. Eng. (Dep. Of General Linguistics) gave invaluable advice to me in the early phases of this work on the use of PROLOG-2. I am greatly indebted to him for this. He kindly and patiently pulled me out of the mire whenever, as a beginner in the field, I threatened to get bogged down in the intracacies of MS-DOS or of PROLOG-2.

Dr. J.M.. van de Weijer corrected my English. Being a major in English and in generative linguistics he anglicized, in particular, my word order and my interpunction.

Above all I want to express my gratitude to my beloved wife Nettie, who patiently and with great understanding let me perform the painstaking chore of finishing my doctoral thesis without ever complaining about the time consuming effort I had to devote to it. Unfortunately, she did not live long enough to be present when I received my PhD degree nor to see the appearance of this book.

Abbreviations for the languages which are used in the text

CA   =   Classical Arabic
AR   =   Modern Standard Arabic
BH   =   Biblical Hebrew
HEB   =   'Whole Hebrew' which is defined as the whole collection
               of verbal roots from all stages of the Hebrew language
MIH   =   Modern Israeli Hebrew

Explanation of technical terms

Autosegmental representation = the morphological representation of a word in which the consonants of the root of a verbal form, its vowels and its affixes are present on separate tiers

Binyan = one of the conjugations of a Semitic verbal root

Root pattern = a collection of verbal roots which have in common a consonant or a phonological consonant group in two or more of their root positions

Co-occurrence relationships = co-occurrence restrictions or co-occurrence preferences which hold with respect to the consonants in a root pattern

Observed frequency = the frequency with which a root pattern occurs in the language

Expected frequency = the frequency with which a root pattern is expected to occur for statistical reasons

Avoidance = a situation in which the observed frequency of a root pattern is significantly lower than its expected frequency

Preference = a situation in which the observed frequency of a root pattern is significantly higher than its expected frequency

Feature = a phonological property of a phoneme

Manner = the manner of articulation of a phoneme, such as stop, fricative or its sonority

Place = the place of articulation of a phoneme

Combinatory constraint = a constraint on co-occurrence which is independent of the order of the consonants in a root pattern

Ordering constraint = a constraint on co-occurrence which is dependent on the order of the consonants in a root pattern

The symbols used for the consonant groups and for the individual consonants are explained in *Table 2.1*.

CHAPTER ONE

GENERAL INTRODUCTION, PURPOSE AND SCOPE OF THIS STUDY

1.1 *General Introduction*

During the years 1974 and 1975 a graduate student and I were involved in a research project involving the messenger RNA (mRNA) of collagen, which is the major structural protein of connective tissues, such as skin, tendons and bone. This project concerned the putative folding of this messenger RNA as a consequence of its high content of the nucleotide bases guanosine and cytosine. mRNA's which code for proteins consist of a sequence of building blocks, the nucleotide bases guanosine, cytosine, adenosine and uridine, which are symbolized by the capitalized initial letters of their names: G, C, A and U. A codon, which is a sequence of three nucleotide bases, codes for one of the twenty different amino acids and for certain functions in the process of protein synthesis. The theoretical number of codons is 64 and they are all used in protein synthesis. Our approach to this biochemical problem was based on calculations with a computer program (Bachra 1976).

Already in the seventies it occurred to me that there is a striking formal correspondence between the functioning of the amino acid codons in biochemical genetics, as symbolized by their capital letters, and some of the properties of the verbal roots in the Semitic languages, which roots usually consist of three consonant phonemes. Below some examples of these similarities are shown. This correspondence suggested to me that the study of certain aspects of the phonology of the triliteral verbal roots in the Semitic languages by means of computer methods might well yield interesting information on the phonological properties of these roots. Of course, I realized right from the start that this striking correspondence is nothing more than a strictly formal one.

Biochemical Genetics	Semitic languages
nucleotide alphabet (4 different nucleotide bases, symbolized by G, C, A and U)	alphabet of consonant phonemes (28 in Arabic, 23 in Hebrew)
codons consisting of 3 nucleotide bases	verbal roots consisting of 3 consonant phonemes
codon library consisting of 64 different codons (all in use) for 20 amino acids	very large theoretical verbal root library (used only to a very limited extent)
mutations: transformation of a nucleotide base into another one and of one codon into another one	phonological change affecting one of the consonant phonemes and resulting in a different root

In the course of 1988 and 1989 I took note of some of the earlier studies which dealt with the restrictions on the co-occurrence of consonants in the verbal roots (see ch. 3). This stimulated me to do some preliminary work on this subject, which resulted in a master's thesis in 1989. Further studies made it possible to write a doctoral thesis which dealt with the co-occurrence relationships of the consonants in the verbal roots of Arabic and Hebrew (Bachra 1999). This thesis resulted in the publication of the present book.

1.2 *Purpose and scope of this study*

The purpose of this work was to study the co-occurrence restrictions on consonant pairs in the verbal roots of Arabic and Hebrew and to evaluate my findings against the background of the literature on this subject. In addition, I have looked into the possibility that the verbal roots may show preferences for certain consonant pairs. While other authors have also studied co-occurrence restrictions (see ch. 3), to the best of my knowledge nobody has systematically investigated preferred consonant pairs (co-occurrence preferences). For this reason, I have also performed a systematic study of such preferences. My study of the avoided and preferred consonant pairs was carried out within the framework of generative phonology and an autosegmental approach was used. Since neither avoidance nor preference is absolute, I decided to subject the material to appropriate tests for statistical significance.

I have studied Arabic and Hebrew, which both belong to the family of the Semitic languages, but which show important differences in their consonant inventories and syntax. This implies that both similarities and differences may exist for these languages with respect to both co-occurrence restrictions and co-occurrence preferences which operate on consonant pairs.

I decided to study both Biblical Hebrew (*BH*) and 'Whole Hebrew' (*HEB*). *HEB* represents the combined verbal files of *BH*, Mishnaic, Mediaeval Hebrew and also of Modern Israeli Hebrew (*MIH*). This latter form of Hebrew has evolved from *BH*, Mishnaic and Mediaeval Hebrew. For lack of a better term I have chosen to use *HEB* in this study in order to symbolize this whole collection of verbal roots which have been attested in written Hebrew from the period of *BH* up to present-day *MIH*. It should be borne in mind that *HEB*, as defined in this study, does not necessarily reflect all aspects of the synchronic phonology of the verbal roots that are used in present-day spoken *MIH* (see § 2.1.2). The corpus of verbal roots of *BH* is considerably smaller than that of *HEB*, because the latter has incorporated not only the roots of *BH* but has also absorbed those of Mishnaic Hebrew. Moreover, many denominal verbs arose after the period of *BH* and, in particular, in *MIH*. Considerable differences exist between the syntactic structure of *BH*, Mishnaic Hebrew and later forms of Hebrew, for example with respect to the functions and temporal aspects of the various forms in the verbal paradigm (see Kutscher 1982). For this reason, one cannot safely decide whether the phonology of co-occurrence restrictions and co-occurrence preferences of consonant pairs in the verbal roots is similar or different in *BH* and *HEB* without having studied both.

In addition, I have studied Modern Standard Arabic (*AR*) and compared it to both *BH* and *HEB*. The study of Classical Arabic is still incomplete, in particular, as far as its lexical aspects are concerned. As a consequence, the number of verbal roots which occur in this language is unclear. *AR* is better documented in this respect. For this reason, I chose to study *AR* and not Classical Arabic, following in this McCarthy (1979, 1981). This problem is discussed in somewhat greater detail in § 2.2.

At this point a few general remarks will have to be made on some of the reasons why certain roots may either be accidentally absent from a language or rather that they will occur by accident. This is discussed in some detail in the next section.

1.3 *Accidental absence or presence*

All languages possess a limited number of consonant phonemes. As a consequence, the theoretically possible maximum number of tri-literal verbal roots in a Semitic language is also limited. This number can easily be calculated. It equals N^3, in which N is the number of different consonant phonemes in the language, that is 28 in Arabic and 23 in Hebrew. This then would amount to a total of 21,952 theoretical roots in AR and to 12,167 in BH and *HEB*. If the Mediae Geminatae and roots with three identical consonants are disregarded, this would amount to a theoretical maximum number of 19,628 roots in *AR* and 10,603 in *BH* and *HEB*. These theoretical maximum numbers of roots are considerably larger than the numbers which have actually been attested in the lexicons of these languages (see *Table 2.3*) or in any of the other Semitic languages. Moreover, a sizeable number of roots may occur in one particular Semitic language, but does not in another member of the family. These facts should be taken into account in studies of the frequencies of the verbal roots in a Semitic language which aim at obtaining information on the phonological reasons that may underlie co-occurrence phenomena. In such a study one could compare for a given language the observed frequencies of occurrence of the different phonological sets of consonant pairs or roots with the maximal frequencies with which they can be expected to occur on theoretical grounds. This kind of approach, however, would very likely lead to the conclusion that most of the consonant pairs or roots are avoided. Many such cases of avoidance will then be accidental and the information gathered would hardly lend itself to a phonologically meaningful interpretation. For this reason, calculations of the expected frequencies of the different sets of consonant pairs or of roots should not be based on the maximum numbers of theoretically possible triliteral verbal roots. More meaningful will be a statistical evaluation of the observed frequencies of the consonant pairs or roots within the more limited domain of the triliteral verbal roots which have actually been attested in the language. Such considerations will be even more compelling when one studies the quadriliterals, because the observed frequencies of occurrence of the different types of quadriliteral roots are extremely small as compared to the frequencies which one could expect for them on theoretical grounds. In ch. 3 I will discuss the work of a number of investigators who have taken such considerations into account in studying the co-occurrence restrictions on pairs of consonants in the triliterals (Greenberg 1950, Koskinen 1964, Kurylowicz 1972, Yip 1989, McCarthy 1994). This approach is also in line with remarks by Fronzaroli (1973) on the use of statistical methods in linguistic research. He stated that the 3775 roots of CA which Greenberg (1950) has investigated, should be considered as a complete corpus. This should follow from the fact that the verbal root morphemes have not been built by a random selection of the phonemes, because their shapes have been influenced by the following factors:

1) The preceding historical situation,
2) Phonetic developments,
3) The entry of loanwords into the language,
4) Onomatopoetic formations.

In addition, another investigator (Herdan 1962) noted that the file of roots used by Greenberg contained only 3775 roots. According to Herdan's calculation, the number of roots which would be allowed by the co-occurrence restrictions, as formulated by Greenberg, should have been 6332, even in case all the so-called 'forbidden' consonant combinations were to be disregarded. This number, according to him, would constitute only a minimum, because in most cases the prohibitions on certain consonant pairs are not absolute. The implication then would be that at most only 60% of the possible roots are actually present in the lexicon. In addition, Herdan stated that it is to be expected that the differences between the relative frequencies with which the individual consonants occur in the three root positions should have a measurable effect on the results. This latter point, in fact, has been taken into account by the authors who used the χ^2-test in their work, because the possible effects of the skewed consonant distribution are inherently neutralized in this test. These effects are also neutralized in the statistical method which I have used in my work.

In view of all these considerations it is clear that one should be aware of the fact that if certain sets of consonant pairs or roots are avoided or preferred, this may be due to factors which are not phonological. It could, for example, also be caused by accidental gaps or by accidental preference. Moreover, co-occurrence restrictions and co-occurrence preference usually are not absolute. Rather they are of a stochastic nature. For this reason, statistical methods have been employed in the relevant literature on this subject and this was also done in my study (see § 4.2 and 4.3). I will clarify my views on these matters in ch. 5 to 8 when describing my findings and when attempting to provide phonological interpretations for them.

1.4 *Outline and Organization of the Presentation*

The presentation of the work in this book is organized as follows:

Ch. 1 contains an outline of this study and also a discussion of some of the reasons which may cause the wide discrepancy between the number of verbal roots which are theoretically possible in a Semitic language and their actual numbers as attested in its lexicon.

Ch. 2 contains a description of the consonant inventories and of the types of verbal roots which exist in Arabic and Hebrew. Some of the arguments are discussed which favor the autosegmental representation, as proposed by McCarthy for the morphological processes that these roots and their derivatives undergo.

Ch. 3 consists of a critical evaluation of the earlier pre-generative and generative literature concerning the co-occurrence restrictions on the presence of certain consonant pairs in the verbal roots of the Semitic languages. The OCP, which was introduced by McCarthy, is discussed. It is used in this book as a tool to explain the co-occurrence restrictions. The findings of the various authors are compared.

Ch. 4 gives a detailed description of the methodology employed in this work. The term 'root pattern', as used in this study, is defined. A description is given of the methods used to calculate the observed and expected frequencies for the different root patterns and of the statistical test which was employed to determine whether the differences between these two frequencies are statistically significant or not. This test of binomial proportions was used to determine whether the root patterns are subject to co-occurrence restrictions or to co-occurrence preferences. In the closing section the subdivision of the consonants into phonological groups classified on the basis of Manner or on that of Place is described in detail.

Ch. 5 describes the co-occurrence restrictions on consonant pairs (avoided consonant pairs) in Arabic and Hebrew triliteral verbal root patterns. The consonants were grouped either on the basis of Manner or on that of Place. In addition, the co-occurrence restrictions on quadriliterals, on Mediae Geminatae and on triliteral root patterns with three specified root positions are described.

Ch. 6 describes the co-occurrence preferences for consonant pairs (preferred consonant pairs) in the triliteral verbal root patterns, again with the consonants grouped either on the basis of Manner or of Place. Also descibed are the co-occurrence preferences for the quadriliterals, for the Mediae Geminatae and for the triliteral root patterns with three specified positions.

Ch. 7 consists of a refinement and a detailed summary of my findings which are described in chs. 5 and 6 and some preliminary conclusions are drawn.

Ch. 8 contains a discussion of the theoretical implications of some of my findings. Where possible, phonological explanations are given.

CHAPTER TWO

THE VERBAL ROOTS OF ARABIC AND HEBREW AND THEIR AUTOSEGMENTAL REPRESENTATION

2.1 *Aspects of the phonology of Arabic and Hebrew*[1]

There are 28 consonant phonemes in Arabic and 23 in Hebrew. These two inventories have much in common, but the number of voiceless and voiced fricatives in Arabic is larger than it is in Hebrew (see *Tables 2.1 and 2.2*)[2]. Certain consonants occur as separate phonemes in Arabic, but they have merged in Hebrew (see § 2.1.2).

A number of consonants are traditionally called 'emphatic'. They are said to be velarized or pharyngealized: in Arabic *ṭā'* (T), *ḍād* (D), *ẓa'* (Z) and *ṣād* (S) and in Hebrew *ṭēt* (T). In Ethiopic Semitic the corresponding consonants occur as ejectives. This has often been ascribed to the influence of the Cushitic languages in the region, but many investigators now hold the opinion that this ejective character may well represent an old heritage of the precursor languages of attested Semitic (see among others Joüon and Muraoka 1991, p.25). According to some investigators (see Versteegh 1997, p.21) the *ḍād* (D) perhaps originally had a lateral component, like the Hebrew *śīn* (see § 2.1.2).

---

[1] See the explanatory list at the beginning of this book for the abbreviations used for some of the languages.

[2] I have not tried to use IPA symbols for these consonants. This perhaps may have been feasible for *AR*, because of its rather standardized pronunciation, although it is affected by the influence of the dialect used in daily speech by a particular speaker (see § 2.1.1). Using the IPA symbols for the Hebrew consonants throughout this book would have been impossible, because the pronunciation of the consonants of Hebrew has been subject to drastic changes throughout its history (see § 2.1.2). For this reason, only the major Manner and Place class nodes of the consonants can be specified with a sufficient degree of certainty. It would have been impractible to employ the IPA only for *AR* and not for Hebrew. The symbols used in my investigation for the consonants of Arabic and Hebrew deviate in part from those commonly used in Semitic studies. The reason for this is that these symbols had to be compatible with PROLOG-2. They are rather similar to those used by McCarthy (1994). To facilitate reading this book, one should refer to *Table 2.1* in which all consonants and the symbols which were used for them are listed (see also § 4.5).

2.1.1 *The consonant phonemes of Arabic*

In my study I investigated Modern Standard Arabic (*AR*). The pronunciation of its consonants follows rather closely the traditional pronunciation of Classical Arabic (the Quran and the pre-Islamic poetry), but there is some regional variation in the pronunciation of *AR* which is due to the influence of the local dialects (Al-Ani 1970). The bilabial *fā'* (f) in Arabic is traditionally pronounced as a fricative, while a bilabial stop is absent. It corresponds to /p/ in Hebrew (see *Tables 2.1 and 2.2*). In many of the current forms of Arabic which are used in daily speech (usually called dialects) the pronunciation of the consonants may diverge considerably from that in Classical and Modern Standard Arabic (see for more details and for references Fischer and Jastrow 1980 and Versteegh 1997). In Classical Arabic the *jim* (G) is pronounced as a voiced laminoalveolar affricate (Al-Ani 1970), but in a number of current dialects it is a velar stop, as it is in Hebrew (*gimel*) and in other Semitic languages. The *jim* appears to have been pronounced in Arabic as a stop, also in the early centuries of Islam (Moscati et al. 1969, § 8.4.2). According to many investigators this corresponds to its original pronunciation (Fischer and Jastrow 1980). It should be noted that Al-Ani (1970) ranges *ḫā'* (x) among the velars, while McCarthy (1994) places it among the uvulars (see *Table 2.2*).

2.1.2 *The consonant phonemes of Hebrew*

The phonetic realization of both the consonant and the vowel phonemes of *BH* is known only by approximation (see e.g. Joüon and Muraoka 1991, p.23 and Kutscher 1971 and 1982, p.120). This is the case for the period during which its records were orally transmitted, as well as for the time when these texts were written down and edited during the first millennium B.C. The phonetic characteristics of these phonemes can be surmised to some extent, however, from the lexical correspondences with other Semitic languages and from the transcription of Hebrew names into Greek and Latin.

The following consonants are separate phonemes in Arabic but have merged in Hebrew:

Arabic	Hebrew
ḍād (D), *ẓāʾ*(Z), and *ṣād* (S)	*ṣade* (S)[3]
ḥāʾ (x) and *ḫāʾ*(H)	*ḥet* (H)[4]
ʿayn (9) and *ghayn* (g)	*ʿayin* (9)[5]
ṭāʾ (F)	*šin* (c)[6]
ḏāl (v)	*zayin* (z)

For some other consonants no straightforward correspondence exists between Arabic and Hebrew. The Arabic *sīn* (s) corresponds with the Hebrew *samek* (s). It also corresponds with part of the Hebrew *šīn* (C), while another part of the latter corrsponds to Arabic *ṭāʾ* (F) (see for this and related problems e.g. Moscati et al. 1969, § 8.28 to 8.37 and Brovender 1971).

The canonical written consonant text of the Hebrew Bible was established during the first millenium B.C. Its vocalization, however, was formalized in Tiberias by the Masoretes only between 600 and 900 A.D. (see Dotan 1971). This Masoretic text and its vocalization were based on the traditional pronunciations of those days, but it appears to have preserved many of the original phonological characteristics of *BH*. During the historical period, however, the pronunciation of both consonants and vowels has varied considerably. It differed from region to region and also with the type of liturgy (see Morag 1971).

To complicate matters further the *šīn* (C) and the *šīn* (c) were represented by the same sign already in *BH* and thus it represented two different consonant phonemes. The diacritical dot to differentiate between these two phonemes was not added before the time of the Masoretes. The *šīn* (C) in Hebrew may have been a lateral coronal fricative, as it still is in Modern South Arabic (see Moscati et al. 1969). Already before the time of the Masoretes the phonetic difference between the *samek* (s) and the *šīn* (C) was lost and the sign of the former consonant is sometimes used in *BH* for the latter one. This became even more common in Mishnaic Hebrew. The velarized (pharyn-

---

[3] One coronal stop and two coronal fricatives in Arabic merged into a coronal affricate in Hebrew. See Steiner 1982 for a thorough discussion of this subject and for references.

[4] Two gutturals in Arabic merged into one guttural in Hebrew.

[5] As in [4]).

[6] *ṭāʾ* and *ḏāl* have merged with the in Hebrew already existing *šin* and *zayin*, respectively.

gealized) consonants *ṭēt* (T) and *qof* (q) had lost this trait, already in the traditional pronunciation of *BH*. Usually, the *ṣade* in Hebrew (S) was pronounced as a coronal affricate at a period later than *BH*. In *MIH* the loss of the phonetic differences between these consonants continued and some other phonetic changes also arose, but its spelling remained traditional in order to avoid complications with the interpretation of the older texts. This phenomenon has hardly any effect on the results of my study. In addition, it should be noted that the mergers of Arabic consonant phonemes in Hebrew occur within the groups of the coronals and the gutturals, while the variation in the pronuncation of Hebrew phonemes all concern coronal fricatives. It is clear therefore that these hardly affect the subdivision of the consonants into the phonological groups which I have used for the purpose of the present study (see § 2.1.3 and *Tables 2.1 and 2.2*).

In the North-West Semitic languages and in many of the dialects of Arabic, stops can be spirantized under certain conditions (Moscati et al. 1969 § 9.5, Fischer and Jastrow 1980). In the Masoretic tradition of *BH* the stops bet (b), gimel (G), dalet (d), kaf (k), pe (p), and taw (t) are spirantized in a number of specific phonological contexts. This phenomenon may have developed already around the 4th century B.C. or even before that time. The rules for spirantization can be stated in a somewhat simplified manner as follows. It will generally occur in any of the three root positions in all forms of the paradigm of the verb and the noun wherever these consonants either are syllable final or are preceded by an open syllable. Present-day Israeli Hebrew has maintained the spirantization only of bet (b), kaf (k) and pe (p) (see Joüon and Muraoka 1991, § 5o-s for further details and references). It seems fair to assume, however, that the vast majority of the triliteral verbal roots of *BH* and of later forms of Hebrew had already been in use for a long time before the development of spirantization took place. The implication is that at this early period these consonants still behaved entirely as stops, as they still do in many other Semitic languages, such as *AR*. In any case, it can safely be postulated for the purpose of the present study that spirantized stops in Hebrew are still stops underlyingly.

This discussion of the consonant phonemes in Hebrew shows that the phonetic realization of the consonant and vowel phonemes in Mishnaic Hebrew and in *MIH* deviates in a number of important respects from that of *BH* as it was recorded in the tradition of the Masoretes. This has considerably influenced the phonology of *MIH* (see e.g. Weinberg 1966, Bolozky 1978). In spite of this, many of the ancient phonological characteristics of *BH* have still been preserved up to the present day and virtually all the verbal roots of *BH* and of Mishnaic Hebrew are used in *MIH* and the latter has largely maintained the traditional spelling of the consonantal skeleton of the words. Since in this study the verbal roots are considered to be an old heritage of Semitic, I have assumed that my analysis of *BH* and *HEB* (the latter of which, as defined in § 1.2 represents the verbal roots of *BH,* Mishnaic, Mediaeval Hebrew and *MIH*) is not affected by the differences in the phonological characteristics which exist between *BH* and *MIH* and other forms of Hebrew.

2.1.3 *Subdivision of the consonants into phonological groups*

I described in § 2.1.2 some of the uncertainties which exist with respect to the phonetic realization of the consonants in the older phases of Hebrew. This problem, of course, also applies to pre-Classical Arabic. It follows, therefore, that one should avoid trying to characterize the consonants of the verbal roots from the older stages of the Semitic languages by using the finest distinctions of their phonological features. For these reasons, I have grouped the consonants on the basis of either Manner or Place, using Manner features such as [α cont] and only major articulatory class nodes, such as [coronal], as dependents of the Place node. I did not attempt to use finer phonological distinctions (see *Tables 2.1 and 2.2*) in order to reduce the effects of the phonetic uncertainties. At the same time, this also made it possible to study the co-occurrence relationships with sufficiently large groups of consonants, so that a meaningful statistical analysis could be performed (see § 4.2).

2.2 *Types of verbal roots*

It seems fair to assume that the large majority of the triliteral verbal roots of Arabic and Hebrew constitute an old heritage, which dates back to before the oldest written records of these languages. I studied these triliterals, irrespective of the fact that there is suggestive evidence that biconsonantal precursors have existed (see Hurwitz 1966, Kurylowicz 1972, ch. 1, Conti 1980 and Voigt 1988, ch. 2). My assumption is that if at a certain stage third consonants were added to these precursors they should have been subject to the co-occurrence restrictions and preferences like the precursor biconsonantal roots (see also § 8.9.3, 8.9.4 and 8.10).

The written records of the Semitic language family span a period of about 4500 years, making it is one of the few language groups in the world for which written records are available which cover such an extensive period. Yet, it is only in relatively recent times that linguists have begun to realize that the morphology of most of the verbs in the Semitic languages is based on the existence of consonantal roots which consist of three consonants (see e.g. Fischer 1972, p.33, Kutscher 1971 and 1982, § 30 and Joüon and Muraoka 1991). This concept of triliterality of the verbal roots of Arabic arose in the early Middle Ages among the Arab grammarians (Bohas 1982) and later also for Hebrew in the 10th or 11th century, during the period of Arab-Jewish cultural symbiosis (see for references Colin 1939, Greenberg 1950, Barr 1971).

The purpose of my investigation was to determine the co-occurrence relationships of the consonants in the verbal roots of Arabic and Hebrew. The great majority of these roots constitute an old heritage. But a number of denominal verbs arose, in particular in *MIH*, and probably also in *AR* which have phonological properties which deviate from those of the old heritage of triliteral verbs in that their morphology and phonology are governed by syllable structure (see § 8.9.2). My study is based on the concept that the morphology of the great majority of the verbs in Semitic is based on the traditional concept of the triliteral structure of their consonantal roots.

At the present time, no comprehensive lexical study seems to be available which covers the whole corpus of Classical and Middle Arabic (Monteil 1960, p.162). Many of the verbal roots of *CA* occur only once in pre-Islamic Classical poetry and their status is unclear. For these reasons, the number of verbal roots which are present in *CA* and Middle Arabic is controversial. For example, in his study of *CA* Greenberg (1950) has used a file of 3775 triliteral verbal roots which was based on the dictionaries of Classical Arabic by Lane (1863) and Dozy (1881). On the other hand, Baccouche (1974) used in his study the dictionary of Al Munjid: 'Lisan al'arab', which contains 5978 triliteral verbal roots. Other dictionaries of *CA* contain intermediate numbers of roots. Modern Standard Arabic (*AR*), however, is well documented in recent dictionaries. It seemed therefore preferable to study this form of Arabic in the present work. This was

done also by McCarthy (1979, 1981, 1994). I studied the verbal roots
of *BH* and those of *HEB* in separate files[7].

Triliteral verbal roots contain three and quadriliterals four consonants. The numbers of roots of these two types and also the numbers of some special groups of roots (see below) are shown in *Table
2.3*. The number of attested triliteral roots of *HEB* is considerably
larger than that of *BH*. One reason for this is that *BH* was a literary
language which dealt with only a limited number of subjects and,
moreover, hardly with those of daily life (Ullendorff 1971). It probably was rather far removed from the language spoken in the period that *BH* was used in its written form (presumably not much earlier
than about 600 B.C.). Most of the roots in *HEB* also occur in Mishnaic Hebrew. The latter form of the language must have developed
as a language employed for writing at some time during the period
of the Second Temple (from about 500 B.C. onwards). It may well
have been closer to the spoken language of that period (see Kutscher
1971 and 1982, p.115).

The number of quadriliterals is very small in *BH*, but it is considerable larger in Mishnaic Hebrew and *HEB*, and also in *AR* (see *Table
2.3*). These roots may have arisen at a relatively late time.

The large majority of the verbal roots of Arabic and Hebrew are
triliterals with three different consonants in root positions C1, C2
and C3. A special group of roots are the Mediae Geminatae (MG),
which contain the same consonant in C2 and C3. In the paradigm
of the MG's in Arabic there often is no vowel present between these
consonants which then form geminates. However, this never occurs
in *MIH*[8].

A number of verbal roots in certain Semitic languages has a glide
/w/ or /y/ in one of the three root positions (*Table 2.3*). In many
forms of the verb these glides behave as weak consonants, which
implies that they are replaced by vowels: /w/ by u or o and /y/ by
i, e, or a. This occurs particularly often in Hebrew, but also in Arabic.
In Hebrew the glides are still present in a part of the verbal paradigm, such as in the hif'il, the nif'al and in the participium of the

---

[7] See § 4.1 for my sources for the verbal roots of *AR*, *BH* and *HEB*.

[8] Gemination was probably still present in *BH* and it is still marked in the
Masoretic text, although it has disappeared from later forms of the language, in
particular from *MIH*. For further details on this point and on other points discussed in this section see also Fischer 1972, Kutscher 1971, p.1580 and 1600, Joüon
and Muraoka 1991, § 82.

qal of the Tertiae Infirmae, (see Fischer 1972, Joüon and Muraoka 1991, §79). Most of the investigators assume that in the earliest stages of these languages /w/ and /y/ were present as consonants and that their replacement by vowels must have occurred at later stages of their evolution. Already before the oldest known records of early Hebrew, Phoenician and Aramaic, such as the Hebrew Bible and inscriptions from the first millenium B.C., the group of the Primae W (roots with the /w/ in C1) had merged with that of the Primae Y and the group of the Tertiae W (roots with the /w/ in C3) with that of the Tertiae Y. Moreover, in these old records the weak consonant /y/ is no longer found as a consonantal segment in root position C3 in most of the verbal paradigm. In the dictionaries of Hebrew the C3 of these roots is traditionally symbolized by an 'h' (serving as a mater lectionis for 'a'). The laryngeal fricative /h/, however, is present as a consonant in root position C3 in five of the verbal roots in *BH* and in seven in seven of these in *HEB*[9]. It further occurs in many roots as a laryngeal fricative in positions C1 or C2. In Arabic the /w/ and the /y/ can still easily be identified as root consonants in positions C1 and C3, although also in this language they have been replaced by vowels in a considerable part of the paradigms of the verb and of the noun. For the purpose of the present study I have assumed that in the period that Arabic and Hebrew acquired their triliteral verbal root inventories, the glides still functioned as consonants. I have included in my analyses of the verbal roots those with glides. Because of the complicated problems presented by the roots with glides (see above) I decided, however, not to study the co-occurrence relationships of the glides as a separate group.

In many of the verbal roots of both Arabic and Hebrew /w/ and /y/ may alternate in one particular root position and this does not result in a difference in the meaning of the root. This, in particular, is the case for the Mediae Infirmae (roots with a /w/ or a /y/ in position C2). Such roots, therefore, have been entered in my files only once and not twice. The root numbers which are shown in *Table 2.3* have been corrected for this phenomenon.

Both in Arabic and Hebrew a large number of quadriliterals exists which have four root positions C1, C2, C3 and C4 (see *Table 2.3*.

---

[9] These roots are 'blh', 'jbh', 'mhh', 'njh' and 'tmh' in *BH* and *HEB* and '?hh' and '?lh' in *HEB*. '?lh' occurs also with a glide in C3 in *BH* and *HEB* and 'blh' does so in *HEB*.

Most of these roots contain four different consonants). A special group of roots is of the type C1C2C1C2. In these roots positions C1 and C3 contain the same consonant and so do root positions C2 and C4. Many members of this group of roots have an iterative meaning. Another special group is that of the type C1C2C3C3 in which the consonants in root positions C3 and C4 are identical. This group occurs rather frequently in *HEB*. In *AR* it is rare.

   Many quadriliterals are denominal verbs in which the consonant from an affix of a noun functions as an additional consonant in the new verbal stem. A number of quadriliterals is based on loanwords from outside the realm of Semitic. In such cases four consonants have been extracted from the loanword to create new verbs according to the requirements of syllable structure[10].

2.3 *Autosegmental representation of phonological features*

In classical structuralist phonology phonemes were defined as distinct phonological units which may form the basis for semantic differences between words. In this view, phonemes consist either of one single sound (phone) or of several related sounds (allophones) which together function in the phonology of the language as a unit (phoneme). In the early days of generative phonology the series of sounds (segments) which constitute a word were represented as linear strings of bundles of phonological features (Chomsky and Halle 1968). The further development of the theory resulted in a number of nonlinear models for the features of the segments. Characteristic for many of these later models is that they are based on a hierarchical relationship between the features (many such models are discussed in Den Dikken and van der Hulst 1988, McCarthy 1988, Durand 1990 and Kenstowicz 1994).

2.3.1 *Autosegmental representation of tonal features*

One of the first nonlinear models in generative phonology was that of the autosegmental representation of tonal features. The earliest proposal for such a type of representation was presented by Goldsmith (1976) in order to provide an adequate explanation for the phonological behavior of the tones in tone languages. His represen-

---

[10] See for this and for verbs with five or more consonants § 8.9.2.

tation was nonlinear in that it placed the tonal features on a tier separate from that of the skeletal tier which contained the consonants and the vowels. Goldsmith connected the tonal tier to the vowels on the skeletal tier by means of association lines. The association of the tonal and the skeletal tiers was considered to be subject to what was termed a Wellformedness Condition and to association conventions which would prevent the surfacing of illformed structures. These were summarized in Van der Hulst and Smith (1982) and they are given below in a slightly modified form (see Goldsmith 1990, ch.1 for a more detailed discussion of this subject).

Wellformedness Condition

a) Association lines do not cross.
b) All Tone Bearing Units (TBU's) are associated to at least one tone.
c) All tones are associated with at least one TBU.

Association Conventions

a) *Mapping.*
Association lines are inserted between one tone and one TBU, going from left to right (or from right to left) and starting with the leftmost (or rightmost) tone and TBU.

b) *Dumping.*
Left over tones are associated to the nearest TBU which is on their right (or left).

c) *Spreading.*
Left over TBU's are associated to the nearest tones to their right (or left).

In his work, Goldsmith also made use of the Obligatory Contour Principle (OCP), a concept which had been introduced in tonal phonology a few years earlier by Leben (1973). According to this Principle, adjacent autosegments on an autosegmental tier cannot be underlyingly identical. To avoid this situation, a pair of adjacent identical tones is reduced to a single tone which is associated with two TBU's by spreading.

In the mid-eigthies it became clear that many phonological features presuppose the presence of other features. In addition, it was shown that certain sets of features will undergo phonological rules as a unit. This has given rise to a variety of models in which the phonological features are arranged in hierarchical sets of tiers. Some of these proposals will be discussed in §8.5. An autosegmental model for the verbal paradigms of Arabic and Hebrew is discussed in the next two sections.

2.3.2 *Autosegmental representation of the Arabic verb*

McCarthy (1979, 1981) was the first author to propose an autosegmental model for the morphological structure of the verb in the Semitic languages. In his view, this verbal morphology is non-concatenative[11]. In the morphology of Semitic, the verbal roots were considered to function as discontinuous morphemes which consist of three or four consonants. In the paradigm of the verb the patterns of the vowels which occur between the root consonants and the affixes characterize the different morphological conjugations or stem formations of the verb. The vowel patterns and the root consonants in McCarthy's model function as separate entities and the vowels are placed on a separate tier. Affix morphemes, which may consist of both consonants and vowels, are represented on tiers of their own and are distinct from the tier of the root consonants and from that of the stem vowels. This concept is known as the Morpheme Tier Hypothesis. McCarthy called these separate tiers of root consonants and vowels 'melody tiers'. He used association lines to associate these tiers with the skeletal tier which contains the C and the V slots. This association should conform to the following conditions, some of which are very similar to those formulated by Goldsmith for tonal phonology:

1) Every unit on one level must be associated with at least one unit on every other level.
2) The association must proceed from left to right.
3) Many-to-one Association (that is: more than one 'melodic'slot associated with one skeletal element) is prohibited but the reverse of this is allowed (spreading).

---

[11] See for a summary of this work also Goldsmith 1990, ch. 2 and Spencer 1991, ch. 5.

4) Association lines may not cross. The association should observe the Obligatory Contour Principle (OCP)[12].

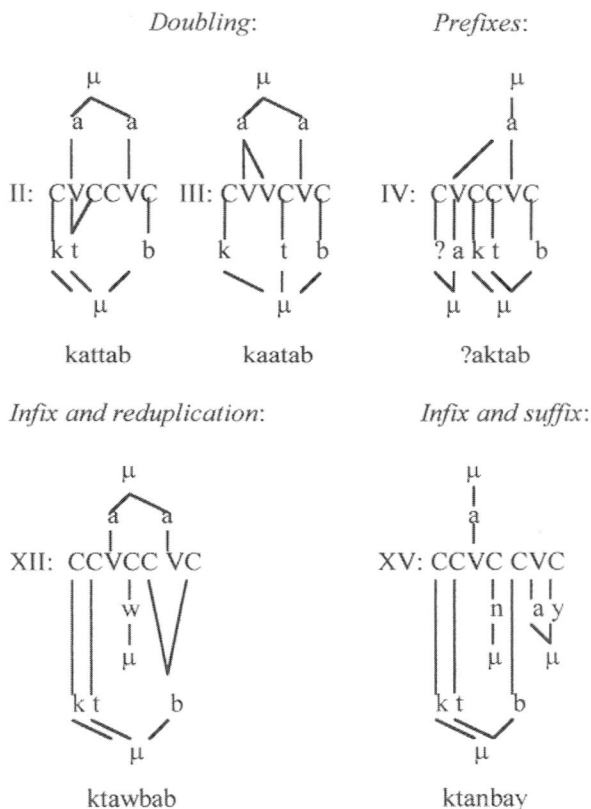

Fig. 2.1 Selection of the autosegmental representations for some of the binyanim of the verb in Arabic as proposed by McCarthy

Shown are: the skeletons (templates), which consist of a string of C's and V's, the tiers which contain the autosegments (consonants, vowels and affixes), the morphemes μ of which they are a part and the association lines.

Basic to McCarthy's model is a skeletal tier consisting of a string of C and V positions. In Arabic a triliteral verbal root may, in principle, have 15 different conjugations, for which McCarthy used the

---

[12] According to McCarthy this Principle should apply to all languages and it is part of UG (Universal Grammer).

term binyanim[13]. Each of these conjugations of the Arabic verb may have a perfective and an imperfective tense (alternatively also called suffix and prefix conjugations), an imperative, an active and passive participle, an infinitive, a subjunctive and a jussive. The perfective and imperfective tenses may also have forms for the passive. *Fig. 2.1* shows examples of the representations for the third person masculine singular of the perfective of some of these binyanim for the root /ktb/ (to write).

The 15 different binyanim of Arabic are:

I	katab	IV	ʾaktab	VII	nkatab	X	staktab	XIII	ktawwab
II	kattab	V	takattab	VIII	ktatab	XI	ktaabab	XIV	ktanbab
III	kaatab	VI	takaatab	IX	ktabab	XII	ktawbab	XV	ktanbay

Binyanim XI-XV are very rare, but IX occur frequently, although one particular verbal root rarely has all of these ten binyanim. To facilitate the description of the morphological shapes of the binyanim in Arabic and Hebrew the three root consonants of the verb are indicated as C1, C2 and C3 and the vowels as V1, V2 and V3. The following phenomena are to be noted:

1) *Doubling of the middle consonant (C2):* in II and V and of V1 in III and VI.
2) *Prefixes:* /ʾ/ in IV, /t/ in V and VI, /n/ in VII and /st/ in X.
3) *Infixes:* /t/ in VIII and /w/ in XII and XIII (a doubled /w/ infix in the latter) and /n/ in XV (and also the suffix /ay/).
4) *Reduplication of the rightmost consonant (C3):* in IX, XI, XII and XIV.

McCarthy postulated that in this way for each of these 15 different binyanim a specific prosodic template can be defined:

I:	CVCVC	VI:	CVCVVCVC
II,IV:	CVCCVC	VII,VIII,IX:	CCVCVC
III:	CVVCVC	XI:	CCVVCVC
V:	CVCVCCVC	X,XII,XIII,XIV,XV:	CCVCCVC

---

[13] Following general practice in the study of Hebrew McCarthy called the fifteen conjugations of the Arabic verb binyanim. The meaning of 'binyan' in Hebrew is 'building'.

Complications exist for some of the binyanim, because the root consonants are the first to associate with the slots of the template from left to right, leaving the appropriate slot to which a particular infix should associate unoccupied (e.g. in binyan VIII). In other cases the doubling of a root consonant by spreading will occur on the right side of the template, because association is from left to right, although it should have occurred on the inside of the template (e.g. in binyan V). To solve these problems McCarthy proposed special flop and erasure rules. Since these rules do not seem to play a role in my investigation, the reader is referred to the cited literature for further discussion.

In subsequent work, McCarthy (1986) extended his model in order to include phonological processes which occur at later stages of the derivation. He suggested that many of these processes which affect the verb should occur already in lexical phonology, when the various morphemes are still present on separate tiers (1). Ultimately, however, as is shown in (2) these separate morphological tiers will collapse by 'conflation' into one single tier, at a later stage of the derivation. According to McCarthy 'conflation' will occur postlexically and after that further phonological processes may take place, in particular, those which involve syllable structure. The OCP is supposed to operate at all levels of the derivation, both before and after conflation (see also Yip 1988a).

McCarthy derived the Mediae Geminatae from biconsonantal roots. Shown as an example is the representation of the underlying form of the third person singular of the perfective of the root rdd 'to hand back' before 'conflation' (3) and also after it (4). In order to avoid violation of the OCP the consonant /d/ has spread to the right and is doubly linked to the skeleton. McCarthy stated specifically that this derivation is meant to be a morphonological process and not necessarily a historical interpretation.

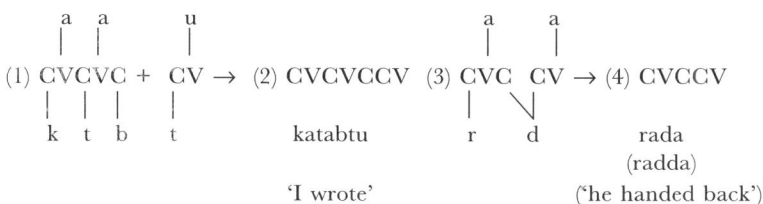

$$
\begin{array}{ll}
\text{(1)} & \overset{\displaystyle a \quad a \quad\ \ \ u}{\text{CVCVC} + \text{CV}} \rightarrow \text{(2) CVCVCCV} \quad \text{(3)} \overset{\displaystyle a \quad\ \ a}{\text{CVC CV}} \rightarrow \text{(4) CVCCV} \\
 & \ \ k\ \ t\ \ b\ \ \ \ \ t \qquad\qquad\qquad \text{katabtu} \qquad\qquad r\ \ \ \ d \qquad\qquad\ \ \text{rada} \\
 & \qquad\qquad\qquad\qquad\qquad \text{'I wrote'} \qquad\qquad\qquad\qquad\qquad \text{(radda)} \\
 & \qquad\qquad\qquad\qquad\qquad\qquad\qquad\qquad\qquad\qquad\qquad\quad \text{('he handed back')}
\end{array}
$$

2.3.3. *Autosegmental representation of the Hebrew verb*

As in the case of Arabic, the verbal root /ktb/ is used for the description of the binyanim of the Hebrew verb. In Hebrew, each binyan may also have a perfective and an imperfective tense, an imperative (except in the case of the binyanim IV and VI), active and passive participles, an infinitive and jussive forms, the latter in particular in the case of the Tertiae Infirmae. In Hebrew, like in Arabic, not all of the binyanim will occur for each of the roots. The binyanim are symbolized below, again by the third person masculine singular of the perfective. For simplicity, spirantization of /k/ and /b/ is neglected here and gemination of /t/ in the binyanim III and VII is shown as it occurs in the Masoretic text of *BH*.

I	kaatab	III	kitteeb	V	hiktiib	VII	hitkatteeb
II	niktab	IV	kuttab	VI	hoktab		
					huktab		

In addition, a set of specialized binyanim exists for a number of verbs, which have the following forms:

1) šakteeb	2) koobeeb	5) kabkeeb	7) hitkatbeeb
	3) koobab	6) hitkabkeeb	
	4) hitkoobeeb		

Most of these additional binyanim are relatively rare, but binyanim nubers 2, 3 and 4 occur frequently in the case of the group of the verbs which contain w or y in C2[14]. Some cases of passive and reflexive binyanim derived from a binyan of type number 1 are known, which are not listed here. In many cases the autosegmental representations of the binyanim of Hebrew are rather similar to those proposed by McCarthy for Arabic.

In *Fig. 2.2* representations are shown only for stem number 5 and 6, which are also given in McCarthy (1981), but in a slightly modified form. The root gl is also used here. The root which underlies these two binyanim belongs, in fact, to the special group of quadriliteral roots of the type C1C2C1C2. This type of root occurs rather

---

[14] These stem are also known as Mediae Infirmae or hollow roots in which the second consonant of the root is a glide (see *Table 2.3*).

frequently not only in Mishnaic Hebrew and *MIH* but also in *AR* (see *Table 2.3*).

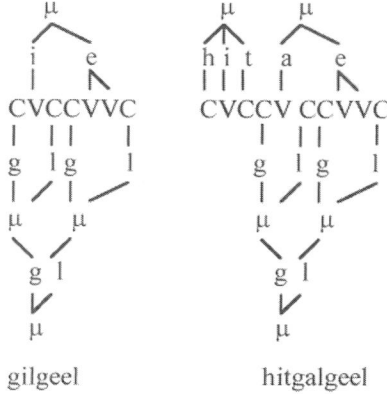

Fig. 2.2 Autosegmental representation of two of the specialized binyanim in Hebrew
    The two binyanim, which correspond to the numbers 5 and 6 of the text, are derived here from the biconsonantal root gl by a process of reduplication.

2.3.4 *Further developments and criticisms of McCarthy's model*

In subsequent work by McCarthy and by others the autosegmental model has been applied to a variety of languages which belong to the family of the Semitic languages and also to many members of other language families. It soon became clear that it cannot be maintained that the C and V slots are unchangeable, because in certain phonological processes a vowel may replace a consonant in its slot position in the skeleton and vice versa (see e.g. Durand 1990, §§ 7.3 and 7.4). For this reason a neutral timing unit (skeletal position) X was introduced to replace the fixed C and V slots.

    McCarthy's approach has met with some criticism (for reviews see Den Dikken and van der Hulst 1988, Goldsmith 1990). McCarthy's concepts have been rejected altogether in some of the papers on this subject (BatEl 1988, 1994, 1995, Odden 1988), but in others they were confirmed or modified (e.g. by Hoberman 1985, Prince 1987, Sagey 1988a, Yip 1988a and b, Paradis and Prunet 1990, Bohas 1997). This controversy is discussed in more detail in § 8.9.

    McCarthy's nonlinear approach in his study of co-occurrence restrictions has led to a meaningful interpretation of this phenom-

enon on the basis of Place. For this reason, I decided to use his model
of nonconcatenous morphemes for my study of the co-occurrence
restrictions on the consonants in the verbal roots of Arabic and
Hebrew not only on the basis of Place, as was done by him, but also
on that of Manner. In addition, I also studied the co-occurrence
preferences which apply to these consonants, with the aim to eluci-
date the phonological basis for both of these types of co-occurrence
relationships.

CHAPTER THREE

EARLIER WORK ON CO-OCCURRENCE RESTRICTIONS IN SEMITIC

3.1 *Phonological constraints on pairs of consonants*

Only a relatively small proportion of the large number of triliteral verbal roots which, in principle, could occur in the lexicon of the Semitic languages is attested (see § 1.3). In addition, it has been known for already quite some time that the co-occurrence of certain consonant pairs in these roots is restricted. A series of authors has dealt with this problem. However, only some investigators have reported that certain consonant pairs may show co-occurrence preferences (see § 3.4.2.1).

Already in the Middle Ages, Arab and Jewish grammarians had noted that pairs of certain consonants either do not co-occur or rarely do so in the verbal roots of Arabic and Hebrew (see Colin 1939, Greenberg 1950, Barr 1971 for references). It is rather surprising, therefore, that this phenomenon is not even mentioned in two of the standard grammars of the beginning of the 20th century by Brockelman (1908) and Bauer and Leander (1922) of the Semitic languages in general and of *BH*, respectively. During the past forty or fifty years, however, a number of investigators have studied this phenomenon in a more systematic fashion in a variety of Semitic languages: in *CA* (Cantineau 1946, Greenberg 1950, Petráček 1963, Kurylowicz 1972), in *BH* (Koskinen 1964, Kurylowicz 1972, Weitzman 1987), in *AR* (Yip 1989, McCarthy 1994), in Akkadian (Reiner 1966), and in *MIH* (Morgenbrod and Serifi 1981, Tobin 1990). These studies which are summarized in this chapter, differ in the phonological frameworks used and also in the way in which the consonants were subdivided into groups. In my evaluation of the earlier work on this subject attention is paid to the following aspects:

1) The phonological framework used in these studies,
2) The types of Morpheme Structure Conditions (MSC's) postulated,
3) The type of statistical analysis, if employed at all.

The MSC's to which I shall refer in the summary of these studies are of the following three types: Positional, Combinatory or Ordering. In § 5.2 I will characterize them in detail. Separate descriptions of the pregenerative and the generative approaches are given below in § 3.2 and § 3.3.

3.2 *The pregenerative approach*

This section summarizes the structuralist studies of the co-occurrence restrictions on pairs of consonants in the verbal roots of Semitic.

3.2.1 *The work of Cantineau on Classical Arabic*

Cantineau (1946) was the first investigator in the structuralist tradition who made a systematic study of the co-occurrence restrictions on consonant pairs in the verbal roots of *CA*. He characterized the different consonant and vowel phonemes of *CA* by means of their oppositions. He subdivided the consonant phonemes mainly according to their places of articulation into what he termed 'classes de localization' (which in this section is indicated by the term 'class of localization'):

1) labials (f, b, m),   6) postpalatals (k, q),
2) interdentals (F, v),   7) velars (x, g),
3) sibilants (s, z, S, Z)[1]   8) pharyngeals (H, 9),
4) alveolars (t, d, D, T),   9) laryngeals (h, ?).
5) prepalatals (c, G),[2]

Two additional groups of consonants were distinguished by him beside these nine 'classes of localization':

liquids (l, n, r)[3], and emphatics (S, D, T, Z).

After making some remarks about the roles played by the degree of closure and by what in generative phonology are now called Manner features, the author discusses consonant gemination in relation

---

[1] Of course, the sibilants do not form a 'class of localization' according to Cantineau's definition.
[2] See *Table 2.1* for the symbols used for the consonants.
[3] The reason why Cantineau chose to call /n/ a liquid will become clear below.

to syllable structure and morae. He then deals with the incompatibility of certain consonant phonemes.

Cantineau notes that most cases of incompatibility refer to adjacent consonants which are present in root positions C1 and C2 or in C2 and C3 (see *Table 3.1*). He finds that consonants in root positions C1 and C2 cannot be identical, nor can they belong to the same 'class of localization'. In root positions C2 and C3 identical consonants can occur. Different consonants can be in adjacent positions, but they should not belong to the same 'class of localization' and quite often not to 'classes of localization' which are close to each other. The following consonants which belong to two different 'classes of localization' were found quite generally to be incompatible in adjacent root positions:

1) an interdental with a sibilant, an alveolar or a prepalatal,
2) a prepalatal with a velar,
3) a postpalatal with a velar,
4) a velar with a pharyngeal or laryngeal,
5) a pharyngeal with a laryngeal,
6) the liquids /l/ and /r/.

Cantineau also observes that combinations of /n/ with /l/ and /r/ are excluded in root positions C1 and C2, but that they do occur in positions C2 and C3. Since the nasal /n/ occurs frequently also with alveolars he concluded that /n/ does not function as an alveolar in consonant incompatibility. This may be the reason why he decided to call it a liquid.

Cantineau studied combinatory constraints only on adjacent root positions. He gives little information on the frequencies of occurrence of the different types of roots and he did not subject his findings to a statistical evaluation. In spite of these shortcomings, this work forms the first attempt to study this problem with the tools of structuralist phonology.

3.2.2 *The work of Greenberg on Classical Arabic*

Greenberg's (1950) line of approach was rather similar to the one taken by Cantineau (1946). Stimulated by Cantineau's work, he studied a file of 3775 verbal roots which was based on the dictionaries of *CA* by Lane (1863) and Dozy (1881). In addition to adjacent consonant pairs, he also investigated nonadjacent pairs and he was the first investigator to use a statistical test to evaluate his results. To carry out this test he determined the frequencies of occurrence of pairs of individual consonant in two of the three root positions. He tabulated the frequencies of these consonant pairs in three tables for root positions C1 and C2, C1 and C3, and C2 and C3. An entry in these tables indicates the number of roots in which a specific consonant pair occurs in two of these positions. He then determined for each entry per consonant pair in the tables the total frequency of occurrence of the whole collection of roots in a column of the table (C). This value corresponds to the total number of roots which contain this pair in a specific order. He did the same for the row (R) in which the entry for this pair is present in the reverse order. For each pair of individual consonants he calculated CR/n, in which n is the total number of verbal roots: 3775. He called this value the 'coefficient of probability'. It corresponds to the expected frequency of occurrence for the consonant pair in the entry, irrespective of order. The author then subjected these 'coefficients of probability' to a standard χ^2-test in order to see whether the actual frequencies which were observed for the different consonant pairs deviated significantly from their expected frequencies of occurrence[4]. He followed this procedure not only for the pairs of individual consonants, but also for the phonological groups of consonants by determining the sum of both the observed and the expected frequencies of the consonants which belong to such a group. Subsequently, he again used the χ^2-test to determine whether there were significant differences between their observed actual frequencies of occurrence and the calculated expected frequencies of these consonant groups.

Greenberg grouped the consonants in the following way:

1) Back consonants:
   velars (k, G, q), postvelars (x, g,), pharyngeals (H, 9) and laryngeals (?, h),
2) Front consonants:
   sibilants (c, s, z, S), dentals (D, t, d, T) and interdentals (F, v, Z),
3) liquids (l, n, r)[5],
4) labials (f, b, m).

---

[4] For levels of significance >5% the differences between the observed and expected frequencies were considered to be not significant.

[5] It seems likely that Greenberg called /n/ a liquid for the same reason as Cantineau. See for this the text further down.

The author studied not only *CA* but he also compared the situation in *CA* with that in other Semitic languages, such as Syriac, Hebrew, Ugaritic, South Arabic, Ethiopic and Assyrian. He did not present detailed statistical calculations for these other languages, but he concludes from his findings that the results of this semiquantitative inspection justifies the conclusion that the general tendencies with respect to the co-occurrence restrictions on consonant pairs in these other languages are rather similar to those shown by *CA*. This led him to speculations on what types of co-occurrence restrictions might have operated in Proto-Semitic. I shall limit myself here to a description of his findings for *CA*. These findings are summarized in *Table 3.2.*

Greenberg observes, as did Cantineau, that it is extremely rare for the same consonant to occur in root positions C1 and C2. This is somewhat less rare in root positions C1 and C3. But Mediae Geminatae occur frequently. These contain geminates in positions C2 and C3 (which are pairs of the same consonant except laryngeals). The following groups of consonant groups are subject to combinatory constraints:

1) Extremely rare are pairs of pharyngeals, of postvelars or of velars.
2) Pairs of adjacent liquids are extremely rare in root positions C1 and C2, but some what less so in C2 and C3. But the sequence /r/-/n/ has an expected frequency in C1 and C2. In the non-adjacent root positions C1 and C3 a pair of /r/ and /l/ is absent.
3) Two sibilants co-occur very rarely. Where they do, /c/ precedes the other sibilant.
4) Two adjacent dentals co-occur with a significantly low frequency. They are absent in root positions C1 and C2 and rare in C2 and C3, but in the nonadjacent positions C1 and C3 they occur with an expected frequency.
5) Pairs of adjacent labials are absent and nonadjacent labials are virtually absent.

Pairs of consonants which belong to two different consonant groups are subject to the following combinatory constraints:

1) Mixed pairs of a pharyngeals and laryngeals occur with low frequency. Most of the pairs which exist are either /H/ with /?/ or /9/ with /h/.

2) Postvelars have a marked tendency not to combine with velars,
    pharyngeals or laryngeals in adjacent positions. When present
    in nonadjacent positions /x/ is found in C1 and /9/ in C3 and
    these roots occur with a frequency which is to be expected. Al-
    most all pairs of a postvelar and a laryngeal contain /?/ and
    /x/.
3) Two adjacent consonants show a tendency not to co-occur in a
    root, if both of them belong to one of the sets of back conso-
    nants (velars, postvelars, pharyngeals and laryngeals). This is also
    the case if the two adjacent consonants belong to two different
    sets of back consonants. However, a velar will co-occur freely
    with a laryngeal or a pharyngeal.
4) Velars, postvelars, pharyngeals and laryngeals will occur freely
    with all consonants which are more forward in their points of
    articulation. This fact and their tendency to exclude each other
    led Greenberg to place these four sets of consonants together in
    the section of the back consonants.
5) The relationships within the section of the front consonants are
    very complex. There is a marked tendency for sibilants not to
    co-occur with interdentals.Their relationship to the dental stops,
    however, is more complicated. Dental stops and sibilants co-occur
    rarely. In most of the roots in which they co-occur, a sibilant in
    C1 precedes a dental stop in C2, but the reverse order is
    rare.There are no roots which contain /z/ and dental stops in
    root positions C1 and C2. Pairs of members of these two conso-
    nant groups in positions C2 and C3 have significantly lower
    frequencies than expected and, again, roots of this type which
    contain /z/ and dental stop are absent. But roots which con-
    tain a sibilant and a dental stop in positions C1 and C3 have
    expected frequencies.
6) The relatively rare consonant Z co-occurs with postvelars far
    more frequently than expected, while its co-occurrence with sibi-
    lants is extremely low and it is low with /l/, interdentals and
    dental stops[6].

---

[6] A pair consisting of a sibilant and an interdental consonant tends to co-occur only rarely. Greenberg concludes from his findings that Z may behave in co-
occurrence either as a sibilant or as an interdental, but in view of what is known
about other Semitic languages he tends to accept the former option. The phonetics of Z is a subject on which much controversy exists in the literature.

7) The co-occurrence of dentals with interdentals in adjacent positions is significantly low, but in nonadjacent positions it is as expected.
8) Liquids (/n/,/l/ and /r/) show free co-occurrence with all other consonants which have their points of articulation either more to the front or more to the back. For this reason and because of their strong tendency to exclude each other Greenberg concludes that the liquids (that is /n/,/l/ and /r/) behave as a separate group.

Greenberg draws the following conclusions from his findings:

1) Besides the 'semivowels' /w/ and /y/, there are four sections of consonants: back consonants, liquids, front consonants and labials. Consonants from any one of these sections occur freely in the verbal roots with those from any other section.
2) Two consonants from the same section show a tendency not to co-occur with the following exceptions:
a. velars co-occur freely with pharyngeals and laryngeals.
b. sibilants co-occur fairly freely with dentals in the adjacent positions C1 and C2, but the sibilant then always precedes the dental.
3) The restrictions on the co-occurrence of consonants from the same section apply with considerable rigor to adjacent positions, but less markedly so or even not at all to nonadjacent positions.
4) The above restrictions act on the verbal root morphemes of *CA*, but they are frequently violated in nouns.

3.2.3 *The work of Koskinen on Biblical Hebrew*

Koskinen (1964) was stimulated to study *BH* by the work of both Cantineau and Greenberg. He composed a file of roots of *BH* from the dictionaries of Koehler-Baumgartner and Gesenius-Buhl. He excluded the Mediae Geminatae and also roots that contain a glide in root positions C2 or C3 (Mediae and Tertiae Infirmae). He included, however, roots with a glide in root position C1 (Primae Infirmae) and also nominal roots, because many denominal verbs exist. The frequency tables which he produced were similar to those of Greenberg, but apparently he did not use a statistical method to evaluate his findings. He notes the following combinatory constraints:

1) In *BH* roots with the same consonant in positions C1 and C2
   are very rare.
2) Two consonants occur only rarely in the same root if both of
   them are laryngeals-pharyngeals (?, h, H, 9), velars (G, k, q),
   dentals (d, T, t), sibilants.(z, s, C, c), liquids (r, l, n) or labials (b,
   m, p)[7].

The author hardly mentions the mutual incompatibility of two homorganic consonants which belong to different groups.

3.2.4 *The work of Reiner on Akkadian*

With her book 'A Linguistic Analysis of Akkadian' Reiner (1966) was
the first author to give a thorough structuralist analysis of a Semitic
language other than Arabic and Hebrew. Her analysis dealt with its
phonology, phonotactics, morphology and also with the morphopho-
nemic and phonotactic alternations which occur in that language.
    A great deal of uncertainty exists with respect to the precise pho-
netic characteristics of the consonants in Akkadian. What is known
about this is based mainly on correspondences of the lexicon with
that of other Semitic languages and on the transcription of Akkadian names into Greek and other languages. In view of this problem
her findings should be evaluated with great care. Yet, it is of interest to discuss her results for the co-occurrence restrictions on consonant pairs in Akkadian, because of the similarities between these
results and those which have been reported elsewhere for Arabic and
Hebrew.
    Reiner subdivides the consonants according to what in generative
phonology would now be called Manner groups:

stops: (b, p, t, T, G, k, q)
spirants: (z, s, S, c, h)
sonants: (m, n, r, l)

In her study of co-occurrence restrictions she groups the consonants
according to a structuralist framework based mainly on Place:

---

[7] See footnote 20 for the reason why Koskinen considered /n/ to be a liquid.

	lab.	dent.	liq.[8]	groovealv.	Velar	palat.	Tongue base
voiceless	p	t		s	k	c	H
voiced	b	d		z	G		
emphatics	T			S	q		
nasals	m		n				
			r				
			l				

She referred to the work of Greenberg (1950), but she did not subject her findings to a statistical evaluation. Only adjacent consonant pairs were studied and she described the restrictions on their co-occurrence under the heading of consonant clusters. Her reason for this was that in some inflectional forms the first and second or the second and third consonants of a verbal root will appear as a consonant cluster without an intervening vowel. She did not give the source of the lexicon which she used for her work, but most probably she employed standard dictionaries of Akkadian.

Reiner also made an attempt to characterize the consonants on the basis of the early distinctive feature system of Jakobson and Halle (1956). In view of the many uncertainties which are known to exist in Akkadian with respect to the phonetics of the consonants (see above) it does not seem to be justified to even make an attempt to characterize the consonants by anything more than their major Manner and Place features. For this reason, I have limited here my survey of her work to her analysis of adjacent clusters of consonants which belong to the phonological groups shown above.

Reiner notes that some of the consonant clusters which do not occur in Akkadian are reversible, while others are nonreversible. In the former case, the order of the consonants in the pair is immaterial (combinatory constraint). In the latter case order is one of the determining factors (ordering contraint). She concludes from her study that in Akkadian the following consonants do not occur in adjacent positions:

1) Reversible homorganic clusters which consist of two dissimilar labials, dentals, velars, sibilants (groove-alveolars), liquids or emphatics.

---

[8] See footnote 20 for the reason why Reiner considered /n/ to be a liquid.

2) Non-reversible non-homorganic clusters consisting of pairs of dentals followed by sibilants, dentals followed by palatals, sibilants followed by palatals or /n/ followed by the liquids /l/ or /r/.

Reiner notes furthermore that the incompatibility rules in Akkadian are rather similar to those found in Arabic and Hebrew. But in these two languages the rules only apply within the root morpheme. In Akkadian they apply only within the root morpheme if the affix is a grammatical morph, such as a personal or a morph which occurs in derived stems. However, they straddle the morpheme boundary when the affix is derivational, such as in the case of the prefix ma/me, which becomes na/ne in front of a root which contains a labial. In Arabic and Hebrew the incompatibility rules do not apply between the root and any of the affixes.

3.2.5 *The work of Kurylowicz work on Classical Arabic and Biblical Hebrew*

Kurylowicz (1972) provides in his book a rather extensive structuralist analysis of a considerable portion of the grammar of a number of different Semitic languages. I shall limit myself here to a summary of the part that deals with the co-occurrence restrictions on consonant pairs. The author studied the restrictions which apply to the adjacent root positions C1 and C2 of the triliteral verbal roots of *CA*. He collected his root material from the Arabic-German dictionary of A. Wahrmund (1898). He did not include the Mediae Geminatae, the hollow roots (i.e. the Mediae Infirmae which contain /w/ or /y/ in position C2) and those which do not occur in Form I (see §§ 3.2.2 and 3.2.3). He included, however, the triliteral nominal roots which have given rise to denominative verbs of Form I. He used methods which were similar to those of Greenberg, and he noted that his results for *CA* were similar to those of that author, but he did not provide a statistical evaluation of his observations.

Kurylowicz observes that one should be aware of the fact that some groups of roots may be accidentally absent. In addition, one should note that the results may be influenced by the relative rarity of certain consonants in a particular root position. It seems, however, that he did not make an attempt to take these factors into account in his work. He states that he confirmed the findings of Greenberg, who took into account the skewed distribution of the consonants in the three root positions by using the χ^2-test. In addition, Kurylowicz notes the following combinatory constraints:

1) Adjacent dental fricatives or adjacent dental stops are incompatible (the latter with rare exceptions). But dental stops and dental fricatives can co-occur in either order.
2) Two voiceless velars, pharyngeals or laryngeals are mutually incompatible and so are the voiced members of these groups. On the other hand, combinations of voiceless and voiced members of these consonant groups do occur.

Kurylowicz also studied *BH*. He claimes that his findings for this language were rather similar to those for *CA*. He makes the suggestion that one of the reasons for the mutual incompatibility of two consonants in root positions C1 and C2 in *CA* and *BH* could be their immediate contiguity in these positions in the imperfect and in the imperative, where there is no intervening vowel. He also suggests that combinations of consonants which are incompatible in root positions C2 and C3 may well have existed, but that they disappeared by assimilation, giving rise to Mediae Geminatae.

3.2.6 *The work of Morgenbrod and Serifi on HEB*

Morgenbrod and Serifi (1981) studied *HEB*[9]. They collected their file of roots from the lists of verbal roots of Barkali (1972) and of Even-Shoshan (1972). They grouped the consonants on the basis of Place and distinguished the following groups:

1) bilabials/labiodentals: b, w, m, p,   4) palatal: y,
2) dentals/alveolars: d, z, T, l,   5) postpalatals: j, H, k, q,
   n, s, S, r, C, t,   6) laryngeals: ?, h, 9.
3) palato-alveolar: c,

The authors tabulated the verbal roots of *HEB* in a similar way as did Greenberg for *CA* and then determined the frequencies of pairs of consonants from these consonant groups in adjacent and nonadjacent root positions. They made use of a χ^2-test in order to decide

---

[9] For a definition of *HEB* see § 1.2 and § 4.1.

whether pairs of consonants from the same or from different groups
are compatible or not. They did not state specifically whether they
excluded the MG's from their analysis. From the frequencies of roots
with two consonants from the same group in positions C2 and C3
one would conclude, however, that they did so (see their *Fig. 2*). Their
findings are summarized below and in *Table 3.3*. I have added some
of my own observations which are based on the figures in their paper.
It can be seen that there are many cases of co-occurrence restrictions. Most of these cases are ordering constraints (combinatory
constraints are specifically mentioned)[10]. The authors find co-occurrence restrictions on consonants in the following positions:

1) *Positions C1 and C2*:
a. Two consonants from the same group, two palatoalveolars ex-
    cepted. (combinatory constraints).
b. Bilabials/labiodentals followed by dentals/alveolars.
c. Dentals/alveolars followed by bilabials/labiodentals, a postpalatal
    or laryngeals.
d. The palatoalveolar followed by a postpalatal.
e. The palatal followed by bilabials/labiodentals or laryngeals.
f). The postpalatal followed by bilabials/labiodentals, dentals/
    alveolars or laryngeals.
g. Laryngeals followed by dentals/alveolars.

2) *Positions C2 and C3*:
a. Two consonants from the bilabials/labiodentals or from the
    dentals/alveolars (combinatory constraints).
b. Dentals/alveolars followed by postpalatals or laryngeals.
c. Palatal followed by laryngeals.
d. Laryngeals followed by postpalatals.

3) *Positions C1 and C3*:
a. Two consonants from the groups of the bilabials/labiodentals or
    the postpalatals (combinatory constraints).
b. Bilabials/labiodentals followed by postpalatals.

The authors furthermore state that the dentals/alveolars are the

---

[10] See § 5.2 for a definition of these constraints.

most frequently occurring consonant group in any of the three root positions and that palatoalveolars and palatals, (both represented by only one consonant), occur comparatively often.

Another question addressed by Morgenbrod and Serifi is whether there is a correlation between the consonantal structure of the roots and the seven binyanim in which they occur[11]. They report the following results:

1) *Root position C1*:
a. Dentals/alveolars are strongly avoided in the hitpaʿel. The palato-alveolar is preferred in this binyan,
b. The palatal is avoided in the nifʿal,
c. Laryngeals are strongly avoided in the hofʿal.

2) *Root position C2*:
a. Dentals/alveolars are preferred in the nifʿal.
b. The palatal is very strongly avoided in the qal, hifʿil, nifʿal and hofʿal,
c. Laryngeals are strongly avoided in the puʿal.

3) *Root position C3*:
a. Laryngeals are avoided in the piʿel, hifʿil and puʿal.

The authors, however, do not draw conclusions from these findings. Unfortunately, their paper contains only one figure which shows the relative frequencies of the consonants in the three different root positions and, in addition, three tables with such frequencies in the seven binyanim. No examples of occurrences and nonoccurrences are given.

When trying to evaluate their results one should be aware of the following points:

1) Their consonant groups do not take into account the effects of sonority: e.g. all coronal sonorants have been placed in the group of the dentals/alveolars.
2) They neglect the fact that /w/ and /y/ may alternate in one particular root position without resulting in a difference in the meaning of the root.

---

[11] See § 2.3.2 and footnote 14 for a definition of binyanim .

3.2.7 *The work of Weitzman on Biblical Hebrew and Classical Arabic*

Weitzman (1987) investigated the distribution of the individual consonants of *BH* and *CA* in the three different positions of their verbal
roots. His purpose was to determine whether the consonants are
unevenly distributed. To this end he determined the frequency of
occurrence in the three root positions for each of the consonants in
the tables of Koskinen for *BH* with 1099 roots and in the tables of
Greenberg for *CA* with 3775 roots. He then calculated the correlation coefficient for the frequencies of occurrence of the consonant
in the pairs of root positions C1 and C2, C2 and C3, and C1 and
C3. Weitman's findings for *BH* are as follows:

1) Sibilants (z, s, C, c), velars (G, k, q), gutturals (?, H, 9, but not
   h) and /n/ prefer root position C1 over C2 (Type I consonants)
2) Labials (b, m, p), dentals (d, T, t), liquids (l, r, but not n) and h
   prefer root position C2 over C1 (Type II consonants).
3) /S/ is equally distributed over positions C1 and C2.
4) Roots with a Type I consonant in position C1 and a Type II
   consonant in position C2 (a total of 440) occur more than 2.5
   times as frequently as do roots with the reverse sequence (a total of 173). This would imply that this reverse sequence is subject to an ordering constraint.

Weitzman notes that in many forms of the paradigms of the verb
and also of the noun a vowel is lacking between the first two consonants of the root, while this is much less frequently the case between the last two consonants. He suggests that the frequent absence
of a vowel intervening between root positions C1 and C2 may have
been a reason for the uneven distribution of the consonants in these
root positions. This leads him to suggest that in case that such a vowel
was lacking *BH* may have shown a preference for sequences of two
consonants which require a movement of the tongue from back to
front and from a fricative to instantaneous articulation (stop or liquid), rather than the reverse. He postulates that *BH* may also have
shown a preference for an increase in 'clarity' at its syllable boundaries. This would have resulted in a transition from a Type I to a
Type II consonant. He suggests that such factors may also have
played a role in the development of consonant metathesis in the
hitpaʿel of *BH* between a sibilant in root position C1 and the t-in-

fix[12]. In addition, he proposes that this preference for 'clarity' could also have resulted in the spirantization of the consonants from the group {bgdkpt}. The need for 'clarity' would have caused these consonants to become fricatives when they were the first consonant of a pair and to remain stops when they were the second one.

That the dental liquid /n/[13] behaves as a Type I and not as a Type II consonant at first sight seems to disturb the picture. To explain this fact, Weitzman notes that this consonant, when in C1, does not generate clusters, but instead it usually assimilates to the following consonant.

The guttural fricative /h/ may belong to the Type II consonants because, according to Weitzman, it is difficult to pronounce it at the end of a syllable and this may also be a reason why it is found very infrequently in C3.

In *CA* the tendencies were found to be very similar to those in *BH*. The consonants /f/ and /Z/ belong to the group of Type I while the other interdentals and, in *CA* also /z/, are Type II consonants. Like in *BH*, consonant clusters in *CA* seem to exhibit a general preference for movement from back to front articulation.

In addition to his study of consonant distribution in the three root positions of *BH* and *CA*, Weitzman also tried to obtain information on what he called the degree of phonetic dissimilarity of consonant pairs in *BH*. In order to simplify the discussion of this part of his work, I will introduce some symbols in order to characterize the different quantities which he has used in his calculations. For each pair of consonants he determined the value of $(n_i \times n_j)/N$, in which n_i is the frequency of occurrence of consonant C_i in one of the three root positions, n_j that of another consonant C_j in the adjacent position, and N the total number of roots in the file. He then calculated a similar value for the reverse order of this pair of consonants. The average of these two values was termed the dissimilarity index for the pair. The collection of these indexes for all the possible pairs of consonants was then submitted to the method of multidimensional scaling[14]. In the resulting twodimensional map the consonants turned out to be distributed over four different groups:

---

[12] This t-infix normally precedes the first root consonant, so that e.g.' *ktb*' yields '*hitkateb*'. If the first consonant is a sibilant, the infix follows it (metathesis), such as with *šlb* which yields '*hištaleb*' (to simplify matters the spirantization of b is omitted here).

[13] See footnote 20.

[14] This method has also been used in archeological and literary studies.

gutturals/velars, dentals/sibilants, liquids, and labials.

With this technique Weitzman obtains rather similar results for *CA*. The interdentals in *CA* group with the dentals/sibilants. In both languages the emphatic consonants map more closely with the velars than with their nonemphatic counterparts.

3.2.8 *The work of Tobin on Modern Israeli Hebrew*

Using principles of combinatory phonology, Tobin (1990) has studied the co-occurrence restrictions on the consonants in the verbal roots of *MIH*. Proponents of this theory maintain that phonetics and phonology are interrelated and mutually dependent and that these two branches of linguistics should not be studied autonomously and independently from each other, because they together are part of human behavior. The author assumes that for *MIH* the following 'active articulators'exist: the lips, the tongue (divided into apex, antedorsum, and postdorsum), the pharynx, the glottis[15], the vocal folds, and the uvula. He characterized the consonants of *MIH* according to the types of 'active articulators' which are actively involved in their articulation.

Tobin grouped the consonants according to these 'active articulators'and then determined for each of such groups their frequencies of occurrence in the three root positions and also the percentage of the total number of roots in which these groups occur. He notes that consonants which use more than one 'articulator' at the same time are disfavored, in particular in root positions C1 and C3. Also avoided is the use of the same 'articulator' in more than one of the three root positions. Consonants which are produced by the apex and also what he termes 'visible' phonemes are generally favored in root position C1[16]. However, the author does not provide a statistical evaluation of his findings nor does he pay attention to the positive correlation which should exist between the number of consonants in a group which uses a particular 'active articulator' and the frequencies of occurrence of the roots which contain the consonants of such a group. This makes it impossible the carry out calculations

---

[15] To say the least, it is rather strange to consider the glottis as an active articulator.

[16] Presumably, these are consonants which are pronounced in a way which makes them visible to the eye.

which takes such a correlation into account. For this reason, it is difficult to judge Tobin's conclusions.

3.2.9 *The work of Petráček on Classical Arabic*

Petráček (1963) reanalysed the results of Greenberg (1950) for *CA* and used an early version of feature phonology for his analysis, viz. the twelve binary distinctive features, as defined by Jakobson and Halle (1956). Each of the consonant phonemes was characterized by marking its features with +, − or 0. He took the sum of these + and − values for each the phonemes and called this sum its coefficient of relative distinctiveness. Petráček considers the difference between the coefficients for the two consonants of a pair to be a measure of the compatibility of this pair. He furthermore assumes that a consonant pair is incompatible if this difference is 4 or greater, but he does not specify his reasons for this assumption. He claims that the results which he obtains with his method are rather similar to those of Greenberg for the consonant pairs in root positions C1 and C2 or for those in C2 and C3. For root positions C1 and C3, however, his method did not work.

3.3 *The generative approach*

The earliest example of a not strictly structuralist analysis of a Semitic language was Chomsky's master's thesis (1951) 'Morphophonemics of Modern Hebrew'. To my knowledge, only a few studies have been published which used the framework of generative phonology to analyze the co-occurrence restrictions on pairs of consonants in the verbal roots of Semitic.

3.3.1 *The work of Yip on Modern Standard Arabic*

Yip (1988) studied the co-occurrence restrictions on pairs of consonants in a series of languages: Javanese, Cambodian, Yucatec Mayan, Luo, Pomo, Ponapean and Modern Standard Arabic. She assumed that the Morpheme Structure Constraints which cause these co-occurrence restrictions are OCP effects on the underlying representations.

For *AR* she based her study in part on work by McCarthy, which

at that time was still unpublished[17]. In the earlier version of his manuscript, McCarthy comes to the conclusion that pairs of homorganic
consonants in *AR* tend not to co-occur in a verbal root if both consonants belong to one of the following classes:

1) labials (f, b, m),
2) coronal stops (t, d, T, D),
3) coronal fricatives (F, v, s, z, S, Z, c),
4) velars-uvulars (G, k, q, x, g),
5) gutturals (x, g, H, 9, h, ʻ),
6) coronal sonorants (l, r, n).
7) high glides (w, y),

Yip subjected McCarthy's material to a further analysis. She notes
that a number of what she termed identity classes of consonants can
be distinguished which exhibit co-occurrence restrictions. However,
she does not discuss the statistical aspects. Below and in *Table 3.4*
her conclusions are described:

1) *The Labial Node*: This node forms a single identity class with the
    feature [labial].
2) *The Coronal Node*: This node shows a threefold distinction for the
    fricatives between interdental (F), alveolar (s) and palatal (c). Yip
    argues that the coronals form two identity classes for the co-
    occurrence restrictions. The reason for this is that McCarthy's
    findings indicate that there are no restrictions on a pair of coronals
    if one of them is [+cont] and the other is [-cont], while there
    are restrictions if both are either [+cont] or [-cont].
3) *The Dorsal Node*: This node also has a threefold distinction be-
    tween velar (k, G), uvular (q, x, g) and pharyngeal (H, 9). But
    the dorsals form two identity classes. The velar stops (k, G) and
    the uvular stop (q) can co-occur with the pharyngeal fricatives
    (H, 9). The uvular fricatives (x, g) can co-occur neither with the
    pharyngeal fricatives nor with the velars. This implies, accord-
    ing to Yip, that the dorsals form two identity classes and this leads
    her to group the uvular fricatives (x, g) with both the velars in
    the class 4, and with the gutturals in the class 5 consonants.
4) *The uvular stop* /q/: This segment can co-occur with the pharyn-

---

[17] see § 3.3.2 below for a more recent version of McCarthy's work.

geals, whereas the uvular fricatives cannot. Yip tries to explain this by defining the pharyngeal fricatives and the laryngeals (with the possible exception of /ʔ/) as [+cont] dorsals, while the uvular stop /q/ is a [-cont] dorsal.

Yip makes the proposal that the co-occurrence restrictions which act on consonant pairs in the verbal roots of *AR*, should be formulated on the basis of a filter of the type *Place$_i$Place$_i$, and, in addition, of similar filters for the individual Place features. She furthermore suggests that similar filters may well exist for the Manner features [continuant] and [sonorant].

3.3.2 *The work of McCarthy on Modern Standard Arabic*

To my knowledge McCarthy's work is one of the most recent contributions to the discussion of the phonotactics of consonants in the verbal roots of the Semitic languages. For this reason, I will give a summary of this work here, but I shall return to it more extensively when discussing my own work in ch. 7 and 8. In ch. 8 some other very recent work along similar lines will also be discussed.

In a recent publication (circulating already for some years in the form of a number of preliminary manuscripts) McCarthy (1994) analyzed the phonetic properties of a group of consonants in Semitic (g, x, H, 9, ?, h) which he called the gutturals. A number of reasons led him to postulate the existence of such a natural class of gutturals in the Semitic languages which comprises the uvulars, pharyngeals and laryngeals[18]. All members of this class are postulated to possess [phar] as one of their Place features (see *Table 2.2*). According to the author, not only the uvulars, pharyngeals and laryngeals, but also the pharyngealized (or emphatic) coronals (T, D, S and Z) in *AR* are characterized by a pharyngeal constriction, which is why he assignes the feature [phar] also to them. In his model the Place Node has [lab], [cor], [dors] and [phar] as dependents[19].

In his study of the co-occurrence restrictions on pairs of consonants in the verbal roots of *AR*, he grouped the consonants on the

---

[18] These reasons are discussed in greater detail in § 8.3.

[19] This model is discussed in detail in § 8.3. In further, as yet unpublished work, McCarthy attaches the feature [phar] directly to the Place Node, while the features [lab], [cor] and [velar] are attached to an Oral Node which is a dependent of the Place Node.

basis of their Place features (see *Table 2.2*). He compiled his file of verbal roots from the dictionary of *AR* by Wehr and Cowan (1974), omitting the Mediae Geminatae. He used the same methods as Greenberg (1950) to analyze his material and subjected the frequencies of occurrence of the consonant pairs to a χ^2-test.

McCarthy concludes from his results that the roots tend not to contain pairs of two adjacent consonants if both belong to one of the following groups:

labials (f, b, m)
coronal sonorants (l, r, n)
coronal stops (t, d, T, D)
coronal fricatives (F, v, s, z, S, Z, c)
velars (G, k, q)
gutturals (g, x, H, 9, ?, h)

In contradiction to Yip's statement, he concludes that roots which combine a coronal stop and a coronal fricative are also avoided. He finds that the co-occurrence of uvular continuants with either the velars or the low gutturals is strongly restricted. For this reason, McCarthy assigns the feature [phar] to the low gutturals (H, 9, ?, h) and [dors] to the velars (G, k). He postulates that the uvular continuants (x, g) and the pharyngealized uvular stop /q/ possess both of the features [phar] and [dors]. McCarthy lists the stop /q/ among the uvulars in the consonant groups based on Place of articulation, but for the purpose of the co-occurrence restrictions he ranges it among the velars[20].

McCarthy proposes that the co-occurrence restrictions can be explained in two different ways:

1) *The No-branching Condition (NBC)*. This condition prohibits branching from a single Place Node to two root nodes in underlying representations. Branching will be allowed only in derived representations through the application of Place Assimilation.

2) *The Obligatory Contour Principle (OCP)*[21]. According to this Principle, adjacent identical elements are prohibited. In the case of the

---

[20] This contradiction is discussed in greater detail in § 5.6.3 and § 8.3.
[21] Goldsmith (1976, 1990) has used this principle for tones (see § 2.3.1).

co-occurrence restrictions this principle would apply not to whole consonants, but rather to specific features which are present in a particular phonological context.

3.3.3 A gradient model of OCP-Place

In a recent manuscript[22], Frisch, Broe and Pierrehumbert (1997) present an approach to the study of the co-occurrence restrictions in Arabic which differs a great deal from that of McCarthy and mine. Although retaining the concept of the OCP they do not apply it to single features. Rather they extend it to encompass sets of features, which they term natural classes. In addition, they make an attempt to provide a statistical evaluation of co-occurrence in which allowance is also made for consonant distance in the root. They reject the OCP-model of McCarthy with its feature tiers, which they call the categorical OCP-model, since it does not incorporate gradient constraints. The model which they introduce is called by them a stochastic constraint model or a natural class model. In short, their method involves the following steps:

1) Assign Place, Manner and Laryngeal features to the consonants.
2) Construct a lattice based on shared features of the consonants. Consonants which share a set of features form a natural class.
3) Compute O/E, i.e. the ratio of the observed and the expected frequencies of a natural class.
4) Define the similarity of the consonants as the ratio of the number of shared natural classes over the sum of this number and that of the nonshared natural classes.
5) Fit the similarity of the consonants and O/E to a logistic function, which is an S-shaped curve: $y = 1/(1+e^{K+S \cdot x})$.
6) Define the perceived similarity of the consonants as the variable x of this logistic function.
7) Choose for the two constants K and S of this logistic function the values which will yield the best fit.

In § 8.10 I shall discuss this proposal and its consquences in more detail.

---

[22] This manuscript can be obtained from the following website: http//ruccs.rutgers.edu/roa.html.

3.4 *Discussion of the earlier work on co-occurrence restrictions and preference*

3.4.1 *Some general remarks*

The methods of calculation which were used by Greenberg and others have been criticized by two authors (Herdan 1962 and Fronzaroli 1973). These papers were discussed in § 1.3.

There are significant differences between the pre-generative and the generative approaches with respect to the way in which the consonants of Semitic are grouped. However, in both approaches the same group of labials figures. The most important differences in the grouping of the consonants are:

1) Groups such as interdentals, dentals/alveolars, sibilants and palatals are often considered to form separate groups in the structuralist framework. In the generative approach, they are taken together as a single group of coronal obstruents which comprises the coronal stops and fricatives.
2) The three groups of postvelars, pharyngeals and laryngeals of the structuralists are combined into a single group of gutturals by the generativists.
3) The group of the liquids of the structuralists corresponds to that of the sonorant coronals of the generativists[23].

These differences in the grouping of the consonants should be borne in mind when comparing the findings of the two schools. Furthermore, the structuralists consider the consonants to be structural units which they group largely according to their places of articulation. On the other hand, in the original generativist framework, the consonants are considered to be bundles of features. In later versions of this framework these features exhibit dependency relationships and they are represented in some sort of hierarchical structure. This implies that in generative phonology much more attention is paid to the properties of the features than to those of the phonemes.

---

[23] See footnote 20.

3.4.2 *Comparison of the findings in the earlier studies*

There is general consensus in the earlier studies about the following facts:

1) Identical adjacent consonants in root positions C1 and C2 are very rare in Semitic, but they are very common in root positions C2 and C3 (the Mediae Geminatae).
2) There are rather strong combinatory constraints on pairs of non-identical consonants that belong to the same consonant group, whatever the definition of the consonant groups may be. Such pairs occur only rarely in root positions C1 and C2 or in positions C2 and C3, but the restrictions are less strict for such pairs in positions C1 and C3. According to Greenberg, however, laryngeals do not exclude each other.
3) Labials are subject to combinatory restraints which are almost absolute.

On other counts, however, differences exist between the findings reported by the different authors. My discussion of these differences is limited to Arabic and Hebrew, because almost all of the published studies concern these two languages and they also form the subject of the present work. As before, the findings in the structuralist and the generative frameworks will be discussed separately.

3.4.2.1. *The structuralist approach*

Co-occurrence restrictions

1) Cantineau and Greenberg differ in some details in their definitions of the groups of the interdentals, sibilants and dentals/alveolars (which are coronal obstruents in the generalist view). Both noted, however, that in general adjacent pairs of consonants from these groups are avoided in *CA*. In addition, Greenberg noted that sibilants and dental stops in *CA* tended to avoid each other. When they co-occur the sibilant in C1 precedes a dental stop in C2, but /z/ and dental stops are subject to an absolute combinatory constraint.
2) These two authors also noted that in general postvelars[24],

---

[24] Velars in the terminology of Cantineau and uvulars in that of the generativists.

pharyngeals and laryngeals[25] strongly exclude each other in adjacent positions. According to Greenberg, this is also the case if they are in nonadjacent positions. In addition, he found that mixed pairs that consist of a pharyngeal and a laryngeal generally occur with low frequency in *CA* and that most of such pairs, when they do occur consist either of /H/ and /?/ or of /9/ and /h/.

3) A strong mutual exclusion of liquids[26] was observed by all authors, but according to Cantineau this is not the case for pairs consisting of /n/ with /l/ or /r/ in positions C2 and C3.

4) According to Kurylowicz and Koskinen, the situation in *BH* is similar to that found by Greenberg in *CA*. In addition, it was noted by Kurylowicz that in *CA* two adjacent fricatives or two dental stops in root positions C1 and C2 are incompatible, but that dental stops can either be preceded or followed by dental fricatives.

Co-occurrence preferences

Only two papers mention the existence of co-occurrence preferences. In all cases they are ordering preferences.

1) Morgenbrod and Serifi reported a number of such cases for *HEB* (see § 3.2.6). Many of these contain bilabials/labiodentals in the first or the second position of the consonant pair.

2) Weitzman claimed (see § 3.2.7) that in *BH* and *AR* roots with sibilants, velars or gutturals in position C1 and with labials, dental stops or liquids in C2 are considerably more frequent than roots which contain such consonants in reverse order[27].

3.4.2.2. *The generative approach*

Yip and McCarthy interpret the co-occurrence restrictions on consonant pairs in adjacent root positions in *CA* in a rather similar way. There are, however, the following differences:

---

[25] According to McCarthy these three groups together form the group of gutturals.

[26] Coronal sonorants according to the generativists. See footnote 20.

[27] See footnote no. 20.

1) Both authors observed that, in general, adjacent pairs of coronals are avoided. According to McCarthy this is also the case for pairs consisting of a coronal stop and a coronal fricative. Yip, however, stated that such pairs occur relatively frequently and that this implies that according to her not only [coronal] but also [continuant] would be involved in the co-occurrence restrictions on coronals.

2) Yip noted, just like McCarthy did, that the velar stops and the uvular stop co-occur with the pharyngeal fricatives, but that co-occurrence of the uvular fricatives with either the former or the latter is strongly restricted. Yip assigned to all of these consonants the feature [dorsal] and concluded that the feature [cont] may play a role not only in the case of the coronals, but also in that of the dorsals. McCarthy noted, in addition, that a strong restriction exists on the co-occurrence of the velar stops with either the uvular stop or the uvular fricatives. To explain this behavior he as signed the feature [dorsal] to the velar stops, the uvular fricatives and the uvular stop and the feature [pharyngeal] to all gutturals and to the uvular stop.

The differences between the views of Yip and McCarthy and the conclusions which I have drawn from my own work are discussed in greater detail in § 8.2 and § 8.3.

In my opinion, the approach of Frisch et al. has serious shortcomings. Some of the most important ones of these are:

1) It is unclear what is meant by the expected frequency E and this value remains unexplained. It is said to represent random occurrence of adjacent or nonadjacent consonant pairs, but its values deviate considerably from those obtained in the work of McCarthy and in my own study, in which the distribution of the consonant groups in the three root positions is taken into account.

2) A dorso-pharyngeal feature is introduced, while [dorsal] and [pharyngeal] should be considered as separate features, both according to McCarthy's as well as to my own findings (for further discussion see § 8.3).

3) They claim that pairs of the velar stops (including the uvular stop /q/) and the emphatics are underrepresented[28].

---

[28] I have shown in my own work (see § 8.3) that this is not at all the case for pairs of velars with the uvular stop /q/.

4) In order to arrive at what the authors call a OCP-gradient they
    treat all Place features and Voice as if they are of equal strength
    in relation to the co-occurrence restrictions, but no reason is given
    why this should be the case. However, they state specifically,
    without elaborating on this that OCP-Place is weaker for [cor]
    than for [lab].

5) The use of the logistic function and the determination of its
    constants and variable serve the purpose of fitting the calculated
    values. However, the values which are purported to fit this func-
    tion are not given an appropriate phonological interpretation and
    do not clearly identify the natural classes of consonants.

Still, the approach of these authors is of interest, because it apparently constitutes the first serious attempt to provide a quantitative
account of the co-occurrence restrictions on consonant pairs in
Arabic. I shall return to this point in § 8.10.

CHAPTER FOUR

THE METHODOLOGY USED IN THIS STUDY

4.1 *The files of verbal roots*

In my study I used for each of the three languages files comprising the triliterals, the Mediae Geminatae and the quadriliterals. The files of *AR* were based on the dictionary by Wehr and Cowan (1974)[1]. For the files of *BH* I used the dictionary by Koehler and Baumgartner (1958). I added a small number of altogether 14 verbal roots from the collection of ancient Hebrew inscriptions which were listed by Donner and Röllig (1971-1976) and by Gibson (1973). The files of *HEB* were compiled from the tables of Even-Shosan (1968-1970) and Barkali (1972). These tables contain a collection of all the verbal roots of Hebrew which have been attested in the complete corpus of its written records from the period of *BH* up to present-day *MIH*. *HEB* includes *BH*, Mishnaic, Medieval Hebrew and MIH[2].

As was mentioned in § 2.2, /w/ and /y/ may alternate in one particular root position in many of the verbal roots of both Arabic and Hebrew and this does not result in a difference in the meaning of the root. These roots were listed only once and the root numbers shown in *Table 2.3* have been corrected for this phenomenon.

I have collected the Mediae Geminatae and the various types of quadriliterals from the same sources as the triliterals. The Mediae Geminatae represent roots which have the same consonant in positions C2 and C3. Their phonological properties are different from those of the triliterals proper and there are phonological reasons to consider the MG's as biliteral roots in which the consonant in root position C2 has reduplicated in position C3 (see McCarthy 1979, 1981 and §§ 2.3.2 and 2.3.3). I have therefore decided to study these roots separately.

In *AR* and *HEB* many quadriliteral roots are of the type C1C2C1C2 and in *HEB* there also is a fairly large number which

---

[1] The file of *AR* was kindly provided to me by Prof. J.J. McCarthy (University of Massachsetts, Amherst, U.S.A).

[2] For this definition of *HEB*, see also §§ 1.2 and 4.2.

are of the type C1C2C3C3 (see *Table 2.3*). Both types have special phonological properties and I studied them separately.

The aim of my study was to compare the observed frequencies of occurrence for the different groups of triliterals, Mediae Geminatae and quadriliterals with the frequencies with which they are expected to occur on the basis of statistical calculations. Such a comparison should make it possible to decide whether for a groups of roots statistically significant differences between these two frequencies could be due to phonological factors. To this end, I studied groups of verbal roots which contain in two of their three (triliterals) or of their four (quadriliterals) root positions consonants from specific phonological consonant groups and arbitrary consonants in the remaining one position (triliterals) or in the two remaining positions (quadriliterals). In addition, I have studied triliteral groups of verbal roots which contain consonants from specific phonological consonant groups in all of their three root positions. I also studied roots which contain one or two individual consonants. In this book a 'root pattern' is defined as a family of verbal roots with two specified positions in the triliterals or quadriliterals or with three specified positions in the triliterals or Mediae Geminatae.

As is explained in § 1.3 it is advisable not to compare the observed frequencies of root patterns in the files with the theoretically possible maximum frequencies. The calculations of the expected frequencies for the different root patterns in the files of the triliterals were based on the frequencies of occurrence of the different phonological consonant groups in the three root positions (and in some cases also of some of the individual consonants). The calculations for the quadriliterals were based on the consonant frequencies in their four positions. The methods of calculation are described in § 4.2 and § 4.3.

4.2 *Method of calculation for the triliterals*

The procedure used for the triliterals consisted of the following steps:

1) *Generating root patterns in PROLOG-2. Screening of the files*
For the study of triliteral root patterns with two specified root positions I wrote a series of programs in PROLOG-2 which use the list of the consonants of *AR*, *BH* or *HEB*. These programs were designed to generate all the triliteral roots which can possibly exist and which contain a specific consonant in one of their three root

positions and arbitrary consonants in the other two positions. For each of the roots thus generated the programs then screen the roots which actually occur in the file of a particular language. The programs also produce tables. A root with the specific consonant in a particular position is marked in the table with a 1 if it is present in the file. If it is absent it is marked with a 0. For each consonant, three different tables are produced, one table for each of the three root positions. Thus, sets of three different tables for all the members of a specific phonological consonant group will typify the consonant group. An example of such a table is shown in *Table 4.1.* It contains the roots of *AR* which have the consonant /t/ in root position C1. This table belongs to the set of tables which constitute the output of a program for all the roots which contain any of the coronal stops in root position C1.

For triliteral root patterns with three specified root positions the screening was done with computer generated roots which contain specific consonants from the groups in two positions. The resulting tables were analysed in a similar way as in the case of the triliteral root patterns with one specified root position (see below).

The files of the Mediae Geminatae and those of the quadriliterals which are of the type C1C2C1C2 were screened by a method similar to that used for the triliteral root patterns with one specified root position. The screening method for quadriliterals which are not of the types C1C2C1C2 or C1C2C3C3 was different. This is decribed in § 4.3.

2) *Calculation of the observed frequencies of occurrence*
In step 2 the sets of tables obtained in step 1 were used to calculate the observed frequencies of occurrence (No) for all the root patterns which are represented in these tables. This calculation was performed in LOTUS-1-2-3 (and later in EXCEL). To give an example, I shall explain how the observed frequencies in *AR* of the root patterns (cs)(so)(X) and (cs)(X)(so) were calculated.

The root pattern (cs)(so)(X) contains any of the coronal stops in root position C1, it has any of the coronal sonorants in root position C2 and an arbitrary consonant in root position C3[3]. In order to obtain the number of roots which contain /t/ in root position

---

[3] See *Table 2.1* and § 4.5 for an explanation of the symbols which are used for the different consonants and consonant groups.

C1 and any of the coronal sonorants in position C2 the rows in *Table 4.1* marked with /n/, /l/ and /r/ were added up. This yields the value for the observed frequency of occurrence of the root pattern (t)(so)(X). This procedure was followed with similar tables which were obtained for the root patterns with each of the other coronal stops in position C1. After this the observed frequency of occurrence of the root pattern (cs)(so)(X) was calculated by summation of the values for the individual coronal stops.

To obtain the number of roots in *AR* with /t/ in root position C1 and a coronal sonorant in root position C3 the columns marked with /n/, /r/ and /l/ in *Table 4.1* were added up. This yielded the observed frequency of occurrence of the root pattern (t)(X)(so). This procedure was followed again for each of the consonants which belong to the group of the coronal stops and the resulting observed frequency for the whole group was obtained by summation in a way similar to that described in the preceding paragraph. This then yields the observed frequency of occurrence of the root pattern (cs)(X)(so).

This procedure was carried out for all computer generated root patterns and after this the observed frequencies of occurrence of all the specific sets of root patterns were collected in secondary tables in order to compare them with the expected frequencies. The statistical tests were performed in LOTUS-1-2-3 (or EXCEL). In *Table 4.2* are listed the observed frequencies of occurrence for the root patterns in *AR* which contain /t/ in root position C1.

3) *Calculation of the expected frequencies*

For step 3 it was necessary to determine the distribution over the three root positions for the individual consonants and for each of the different consonant groups. The percentage of the total number of roots of the whole file in which a particular consonant or consonant group is present in these positions is a measure for this distribution (see *Tables 4.3.1-3 and 4.4.1-3*)[4]. After this the expected frequencies of occurrence for the root patterns were calculated in the following way. The above percentages for the consonant groups (or for the individual consonants) in the root positions which were relevant for a particular root pattern were multiplied with each other and with the total number of roots in the whole file (Nt). This yield-

---

[4] The values for the individual labials and coronal sonorants, for the velar stops (/k/ and /G/) and for the uvular stop /q/ are also shown in these tables. It will become clear in § 5.6.3 and § 8.3 why this was done.

ed the frequency expected for the root pattern (Ne) on the basis of the distribution of the consonants and of the consonant groups in the whole file. This procedure was followed for all the root patterns which can possibly exist, that is, for all the possible permutations in which the different consonant groups or specific individual consonants can occur. *Table 4.5* gives the values of Ne for the root patterns which contain a coronal stop in root position C1. As an example the calculation of the expected frequency of the root pattern (cs)(la)(X) in *HEB* is given here:

%$_{cs}$ in C1	times	%$_{la}$ in C2	times	Nt	Ne for (cs)(la)(X)
0.1014	×	0.1678	×	2169	= 36.92[5]

This way of calculating the expected frequencies bears some similarities to that used in the χ^2 test which was used by other investigators to study the co-occurrence restrictions on consonant pairs (Greenberg 1950, Koskinen 1964, Kurylowicz 1972, Yip 1988, McCarthy 1994). In the χ^2-test, however, the calculation of the expected frequency of a consonant pair takes into account only the positions of the pairs of consonants in the roots, but it disregards the order in which these consonants occur. This implies that combinations of consonant pairs are studied rather than their permutations. In the method used in my work their order is also taken into account and in this way the expected frequencies for all the possible permutations of the different consonant groups and individual consonants can be obtained. As will be shown in ch. 6 and, in particular, in chs. 7 and 8, this fact turns out to be of great importance for the study of co-occurrence preferences.

In my study of co-occurrence preferences I compared the observed and the expected frequencies not only for triliteral root patterns with two specified root positions but also for those with three specified positions. In the latter cases, the percentages for the consonant groups were calculated for the three root positions and were multiplied with each other and with the total number of roots in the whole file.

---

[5] Calculations in LOTUS-1-2-3 or EXCEL yield nine-place values. To simplify matters the values for Ne have been rounded off to two-place values throughout the text, in *Table 4.5* and in the other tables.

4) *The statistical test to determine avoidance or preference*
In order to determine whether a root patterns has an expected frequency or rather tends to be avoided or preferred I used in step 4 the statistical test for the binomial distribution of proportions: (No-Ne)/√(Ne(1Ne/Nt)). In this formula No and Ne are the observed and the expected frequencies of a root pattern and Nt is the total number of roots in the file. This formula was applied to the difference No-Ne for each of the root patterns by means of LOTUS-1-2-3 (or EXCEL). This yielded a value Z for each of the root patterns. The level of significance to which such a value of Z corresponds (P in the tables in this book) was obtained from a standard statistical table for areas under the curve for the Normal Distribution. The difference No-Ne differs significantly from 0, at a level of significance of 5% or lower, if 1.96 ≤ Z ≥ +1.96. If Z > 1.96 or < +1.96, the difference No-Ne is not significantly different from 0. This means that the No of the root pattern then is within the expected range. In the tables in this book values for Z with '+' and '-' signs indicate avoidance and preference, respectively. Blanks in the P-column's indicate expected frequencies. In the tables the levels of significance were rounded off to the nearest whole per cent (see for examples *Table 4.5*).

I also investigated the Mediae Geminatae in separate files. For this purpose the percentages for the different consonant groups in root positions C1 and C2 in these files were determined (see *Table 4.6*). The expected frequencies were then calculated by using these percentages and the statistical test for the differences between observed and expected frequencies was performed as described for the files of the triliterals.

4.3 *Method of calculation for the quadriliterals*

The quadriliteral roots contain two special groups of root patterns, one of which is of the type C1C2C1C2 and the other of the type C1C2C3C3. There are many root patterns of the former type in *AR* and *HEB*, but there are only three of these in *BH*. In *AR* there are only four root patterns of the type C1C2C3C3 and they are absent from *BH*. In *HEB*, however, there are 131 root patterns of this type (see *Table 2.3*). I studied the files of these two specific types of root patterns separately from those of the file of the other quadriliterals.

The procedure which was followed for the quadriliterals which are

not of the types C1C2C1C2 or C1C2C3C3 differed in certain respects from that used for the triliterals. The number of these roots
in *AR* and *HEB* is considerably smaller than that of the triliteral roots
(see *Table 2.3*). However, running the appropriate programs in
PROLOG-2 for the quadriliterals with their four consonant positions
would be much more time consuming than it is for the triliterals with
three root positions. I decided, therefore, to use the sort function of
WP 5.1 for specific consonants in order to search the files of the
quadriliterals. This method yielded the distribution of the consonants
in the four root positions and also that of the different sets of roots
which contain members of specific consonant groups in two of their
four root positions (see *Tables 4.7.1 to 4.8.2*). The calculation of the
observed frequencies of occurrence of a root pattern (No) was performed in a way similar to that used for the triliterals. This was done
by adding up the observed frequencies for the whole set of roots which
contain consonants from the consonant groups which are present in
the two relevant root positions of the quadriliterals. The statistical
procedure was similar to that used for the triliterals.

In my study of co-occurrence phenomena for the special group
of quadriliterals of the type C1C2C1C2 I assumed that in these root
patterns the consonants in root positions C1 and C2 are reduplicated in positions C3 and C4 (*Fig. 2.2* and McCarthy 1979, 1981). They
were studied in the same way with PROLOG-2 and LOTUS-1-2-
3 (or EXCEL) as the triliterals. I first determined the percentages of
occurrence in positions C1 and C2 for each of the different consonant
groups (see *Tables 4.7.1 to 4.8.2*. Then the expected frequencies were
calculated from these percentages. The statistical test was performed
for the differences between the observed and the expected frequencies, just as described for the triliterals.

There are only 131quadriliterals of the type C1C2C3C3 in *HEB*
and this number is too small for a meaningful statistical study. The
frequencies of occurrence for the different root patterns of this type
are discussed in § 6.9.

4.4 *Possible effects of low frequencies of occurrence*

In analyzing the statistical results one should be aware of the following complications. If both the observed and the expected frequencies of a root pattern are small, the statistical test will become unreliable. It may then indicate that a root pattern is avoided while

this could be due to an accidental gap. Equally, preference for a root pattern could then also be accidental. In such cases avoidance or preference would not be caused by phonological factors but rather by chance. The examples given in *Table 4.9* show how such a situation could blur the picture. If in these cases the observed frequency is arbitrarily raised or lowered by just 1 or 2[6] root patterns which seem to be avoided may then show an expected frequency or even become preferred. In a similar way apparently preferred root patterns may then exhibit expected frequencies or even become avoided. I shall discuss possible effects of this problem in chs. 5 and 6 in the description of my findings for the Mediae Geminatae, the quadriliterals, the root patterns of the type C1C2C1C2 and the triliterals with three specified root positions.

4.5 *The two approaches used in this study*

The symbols used in the PROLOG-2 programs for the different consonants are shown in *Table 2.1*. They are rather similar to those used by McCarthy in his file of the verbal roots of *AR*. Where necessary these symbols were slightly modified. An important reason for the choice of these symbols was that they had to be compatible with PROLOG-2.

As is explained in the discussion in ch. 8, I am of the opinion that the co-occurrence phenomena shown by the verbal roots of Arabic and Hebrew represent an old heritage. I mentioned in § 2.1.3 some of the reasons why it is not possible to give a detailed phonetic characterization of the consonants in the older stages of Semitic. Therefore, I could not use the finer distinctions of the Place features of the consonants, such as [high], [strident] etc. This also precluded the use of the International Phonetic Alphabet, which incidentally, is also not compatible with PROLOG-2[7].

---

[6] The values 1 and 2 have been chosen for demonstrative purposes only.
[7] See for this also footnote 2 in ch. 2.

obstruents		obstruents		high sonority consonants	
		voiceless	voiced		
				nasals	na
stops	st	ls	ds	liquids	li
fricatives	fr	lf	df	glides	gl

For the purpose of my study I subdivided the consonants into phonological groups in two different ways. In the first approach, I distinguished the different groups of consonants on the basis of Manner, in a way similar to that proposed by Clements (1985, 1990). The groups of the stops and the fricatives were subdivided into their voiceless and voiced counterparts. The grouping of the consonants on this basis is shown in *Table 2.1* and it is repeated above in a shortened form.

In the other approach the consonants were grouped on the basis of Place (see *Table 2.2*). These consonant groups are rather similar to those used by Yip (1988) and McCarthy (1994):

la: labials   so: coronal sonorants
cs: coronal stops   ve: velars
cf: coronal fricatives   uv: uvular fricatives
co: coronal obstruents   pl: pharyngeals/laryngeals
   (cs + cf)   gu: uv + pl

In addition, I studied a number of individual consonants both on the basis of Manner and on that of Place:

1) the labials: /b/, /p/(/f/) and /m/,
2) the coronal nasal: /n/,
3) the coronal liquids: /l/ and /r/,
4) the velar stops: /k/ and /G/,
5) the uvular stop: /q/.

In the early phases of my study it became clear that in the co-occurrence phenomena the uvular stop /q/ patterns with the velar stops /k/ and /G/ and not with the uvular fricatives /x/ and /g/. In the course of my further work I decided, therefore, to include this consonant in the group of the velars and not in that of the uvulars (see for more details § 5.6.3 and § 8.3).

The pharyngeals and laryngeals were always combined into one group. As pointed out before (see *Tables 2.3*) the number of roots in the files of the Mediae Geminatae, the quadriliterals and the root patterns of the type C1C2C1C2 are relatively small. The same holds for the number of roots which are represented by a triliteral root pattern with three specified positions. For the purpose of my calculations with these root patterns, I did not subdivide the stops and fricatives into their voiceless and voiced subsets. In addition, I combined the uvular fricatives and the pharyngeals/laryngeals in *AR* into the group of the gutturals. In these cases, the group of the pharyngeals/laryngeals in *BH* and *HEB* is also classed as the set of gutturals.

CHAPTER FIVE

CO-OCCURRENCE RESTRICTIONS ON THE CONSONANTS IN THE VERBAL ROOT PATTERNS OF ARABIC AND HEBREW

5.1 *Introductory remarks*

This chapter describes my findings with respect to the co-occurrence restrictions which hold for the verbal root patterns of *AR*, *BH* and *HEB*[1]. I studied the following types of root patterns:

1) all triliterals and quadriliterals (not of the type C1C2C1C2 or C1C2C3C3) with two specified root positions,
2) triliterals, Mediae Geminatae and quadriliterals of the types C1C2C1C2 with all root positions specified.

The triliteral root patterns with two specified root positions contain members from the same or from different consonant groups or individual consonants in two of their three root positions: C1, C2 and C3. The remaining root position contains arbitrary consonants which is indicated by 'X' in the tables. Triliterals with three specified root positions contain members from the consonant groups in their three root positions.

The quadriliteral root patterns have members from the same or from different consonant groups in two of their four root positions: C1, C2, C3 and C4. The two other root positions contain arbitrary consonants which are indicated in the tables by 'X' and 'Y'.

The consonants were subdivided into phonological groups on the basis of Manner or on that of Place (see § 4.5). The results based on Manner are presented for voiceless and voiced subsets of the stops and the fricatives only in cases where this is advisable on statistical grounds. Otherwise, the results are shown only for the stops and the fricatives, irrespective of voicing. In similar cases the results on the basis of Place are shown only for the coronal obstruents as a group and they were not subdivided into the corresponding stops and fricatives, while the

---

[1] The term root pattern is defined in § 4.1.

the uvular fricatives and the pharyngeals/laryngeals in *AR* were combined as the group of the gutturals.

The observed frequency of occurrence of an avoided root pattern should be significantly smaller than the frequency which is to be expected for it on the basis of the distribution of the consonants in the different root positions in the whole file of verbal roots. The tables show the results of the statistical calculations which were performed to arrive at the levels of significance for the differences between the observed (No) and the expected frequencies (Ne). This is explained in detail in § 4.2.

My findings concerning the preferred verbal root patterns in *AR*, *BH* and *HEB* are described in ch. 6.

5.2 *Types of phonological constraints which can cause co-occurrence restrictions*

In most languages specific phonological constraints exist which limit the occurrence of certain sequences of consonants, e.g. in the onsets or codas of syllables. Such constraints are also involved in the co-occurrence restrictions on pairs of consonants in the verbal roots of Semitic. McCarthy (1979 and 1981) proposed that in the morphology the consonantal roots in this language family function as discontinuous morphemes (see § 2.3.2 to § 2.3.4). This would imply that in these languages the phonological constraints which cause the co-occurrence restrictions should have the characteristics of Morpheme Structure Conditions (MSC). In principle, the following types of MSC's can be expected to act on the Semitic verbal roots:

1) *Positional constraints.* These will cause a consonant or a consonant group to be either absent from a particular root position or to be present there only relatively infrequently.

2) *Combinatory constraints.* These will prevent or disfavor the occurrence of a consonant pair in adjacent or in nonadjacent root positions or in both. Combinatory constraints will act on a pair of consonants irrespective of the order in which they occur in the pair. This implies that combinatory constraints are bidirectional.

3) *Ordering constraints.* These will prevent or disfavor the occurrence of a certain sequence of consonants in a particular order in adjacent or in nonadjacent positions. Ordering constraints are unidirectional.

An important fact which must be taken into account is the strength of a constraint. A constraint can be either absolute or relative (statistical). The co-occurrence restrictions on consonant pairs are usually relative rather than absolute. It was necessary, therefore, to subject my findings to a statistical evaluation in order to obtain information on the extent to which the restrictions act on the avoided root patterns (for more details see § 4.2). If both the observed and the expected frequencies of a consonant pair happen to be small, a statistical evaluation may be of limited value (see § 4.4). To the preferred root patterns similar considerations will apply (see ch.6).

5.3 *The consonant distribution in the three root positions of the triliterals*

5.3.1 *Positional constraints*

In this section the positional constraints are discussed which were found to hold with regard to the different consonant groups and the individual consonants in the three root positions of the triliterals. The cases of positional preference are described in § 5.3.2. The effects of positional constraints and of positional preference should manifest themselves in a significant skewing of the distribution of the individual consonants and of the consonant groups.

In § 4.2 the method used to calculate the expected frequencies of the root patterns was discussed. This involved the use of the percentage of the total number of roots in a file in which the relevant consonant groups or individual consonants occur in the two or the three different root positions which define a root pattern. This method neutralizes possible effects on the statistical evaluation of a skewed distribution of the consonants in the three root positions in the files of the verbal roots. Nevertheless, it was considered to be important to obtain some information also on the distribution of the individual consonants and consonant groups. For this purpose, for each of the three root positions the percentage of the total number of roots in the files of the triliterals was calculated in which the individual consonants or the different consonant groups occurred. This, in fact, corresponds to their actual distribution in the files. These percentages were then compared with those which were to be expected on the basis of an assumed even distribution of the consonant groups and of the individual consonants in the three root positions. In this comparison the number of the different consonants which belong to a particular consonant group was taken into account. In order to determine the statistical significance of the difference between the observed and expected frequencies the test of the binomial distribution of proportions was used (see § 4.2). This procedure for determining the distribution of the individual consonants and of the consonant groups was followed only for the triliterals, but not for the Mediae Geminatae, the quadriliterals or the root patterns of the type C1C2C1C2. The files of these root patterns are relatively small and it is doubtful whether this procedure would yield meaningful results for these files. The results for the triliterals are shown in *Table 5.1*.

On the basis of Manner, voiced fricatives in C3 in *AR* are significantly less frequent than is to be expected. Fricatives not specified for Voice are so in C2 and C3 in *AR* and only in C3 in *BH*. On the basis of Place, coronal fricatives in C2 are siginificantly less frequent than expected in *AR* and in C3 in *AR* and *BH*. Coronal obstruents are less frequent in *AR* in all three root positions and in *BH* only in C3. None of the consonant groups in *HEB* is subject to positional constraints and none of the individual consonants (including those which are not shown in *Table 5.1*) exhibits positional constraints in any of the three languages.

5.3.2 *Positional preferences*

Table 5.1 also shows which of the different consonant groups and individual consonants exhibit positional preferences. In *AR*, *BH* and *HEB* liquids in C2 and C3 are significantly more frequent that expected on the basis of Manner, and so are nasals in C1 and glides in *AR* in C2. On the basis of Place, coronal sonorants in *AR*, *BH* and *HEB* are significantly more frequent than expected in C3 and in *AR* also in C1 and C2. In *AR* this is also the case for glides in C2 and labials in C2 and C3.

Among the sonorants /m/, /n/, /r/, and /l/, the labial sonorant /m/ does not deviate from the expected values. Among the coronal sonorants /n/ is significantly preferred in C1 in *AR* and *BH*, /r/ in C2 and C3 in *AR*, *BH* and *HEB* and /l/ in C3 in *AR*. It seems therefore that the significant preference for the liquids and for the coronal sonorants in C2 and C3 is particularly due to /r/, but in *AR* /l/ also contributes to this in C3. None of the other consonant groups or individual consonants exhibits positional preference.

The facts described in § 5.3.1 and § 5.3.2 lead to the following conclusion:

Conclusion 1. *In a statistical evaluation of the co-occurrence relationships of the consonants in the verbal roots of Arabic and Hebrew it is necessary to take into account the distribution of the consonants in the three root positions.*

5.4 *Combinatory constraints acting on triliterals*

The absolute combinatory and ordering constraints (for which No = 0) are discussed in § 5.4.1 and the relative ones (for which No > 0) in § 5.4.2.

5.4.1 *Absolute combinatory and ordering constraints*

Table 5.2 lists the observed and the expected frequencies (No and Ne) of the consonant pairs which do not occur in triliteral root patterns and which are therefore subject to absolute combinatory constraints. This implies that in these cases No = 0. Also listed are the levels of significance of the differences between No and Ne (P). In most cases, P is considerably smaller than 1%. For the avoided root patterns which are shown in the table, No equals 0 in at least one of the three languages. If in such cases the values of No for the root patterns are larger than 0 in the other languages, these values are also listed in the table. In all such cases, however, these root patterns in the other languages are subject to relative combinatory constraints. The avoided root patterns which are subject to absolute combinatory constraints, constitute only a very small proportion of the total number of avoided root patterns. The overwhelming majority of the avoided root patterns are subject to relative combinatory or ordering constraints (see § 5.4.2).

Table 5.2 shows that the majority of the root patterns which exhibit absolute combinatory or ordering constraints contain, in two adjacent root positions, either consonants from the same group or an individual labial or coronal sonorant adjacent to members of the consonant group to which it belongs The following root patterns with sonorants are subject to absolute combinatory constraints in at least one of the three languages:

In adjacent or nonadjacent positions:
1) /m/ and labials,
2) the velar stops (/k/ and /G/) ('ve' in the table).

In adjacent positions:
1) /l/ or /r/ and liquids,
2) the uvular stop /q/ and velar stops,
3) /n/ followed by nasals or liquids.

In *AR* the uvular stop /q/ and uvular fricatives are subject to absolute combinatory constraints in the adjacent positions C1C2.

   The co-occurrence relationships between the velar stops, the uvular stop /q/ and the uvular fricatives will be discussed in detail in § 8.3.

5.4.2 *Relative (statistical) combinatory constraints*

Tables 5.3 and 5.4 show the relative combinatory constraints on pairs of consonants from the same or from different consonant groups. Also shown are such constraints on consonant pairs which contain, in one of their positions, members of one of the consonant groups and in another position the individual consonants /f/ in Arabic, /S/ in Hebrew or /q/ in both languages. In *Table 5.3* are shown the findings for consonant groups classified on the basis of Manner and in *Table 5.4* for those classified on that of Place.

5.4.2.1 *Relative combinatory constraints on consonants from the same group*

a) *Consonant groups classified on the basis of Manner*

When the consonants are grouped according to Manner, the following pairs of consonants which belong to the same group are usually avoided in all three languages:

1) stops, fricatives or liquids in adjacent and in nonadjacent root positions[2],
2) nasals or glides in the adjacent positions C1C2 and C2C3[3].

   When the obstruents are subdivided into their voiceless and voiced subsets the following pairs are avoided in all three languages:

---

[2] However, stops are not avoided in the nonadjacent positions C1C3 in *AR*.
[3] However, in *BH* nasals are not avoided in the adjacent positions C2C3.

1) voiceless stops (ls) in the adjacent positions C2C3[4],
2) voiceless fricatives (lf) in adjacent positions[5],

Only in *AR* voiced stops are avoided in the nonadjacent positions C1C3.

b) *Consonant groups classified on the basis of Place*

In all three languages, pairs of consonants which belong to the same consonant group classified on the basis of Place are subject to combinatory constraints in both adjacent and nonadjacent positions. But not avoided is a pair of glides in positions C1C3. In *AR* a pair of uvular fricatives is avoided only in positions C1C2.

5.4.2.2 *Relative combinatory constraints on consonants from different groups*

a) *Consonant groups classified on the basis of Manner*

On the basis of Manner the only root patterns with two different consonant groups which are subject to relative combinatory constraints contain pairs of voiceless and voiced fricatives in the adjacent positions C1C2 in *AR* and *HEB* and, in addition, in *HEB* also in C2C3.

b) *Consonant groups classified on the basis of Place*

The following root patterns which are subject to combinatory constraints and which contain a pair of consonants from two different consonant groups classified on the basis of Place are found only in *AR*:

1) coronal stops and coronal fricatives in adjacent positions,
2) velars and uvular fricatives in adjacent positions,
3) pharyngeals/laryngeals and uvular fricatives in adjacent or in nonadjacent positions.

---

[4] In *AR* also in the adjacent positions C1C2 and in *BH* and *HEB* in the nonadjacent positions C1C3.
[5] In *HEB* also in the nonadjacent positions C1C3.

5.5 *Ordering constraints acting on triliterals*

The root patterns noted below are subject to such constraints in all
three languages, unless mentioned otherwise.

a) *Consonant groups on the basis of Manner*

1) voiceless stops in C1 followed by voiced fricatives in C2 in *AR*,
2) voiceless fricatives in C1 followed by voiced fricatives in C2 and
    in *HEB* the.same sequence in C2C3 and C1C3,
3) nasals in C1 followed by liquids in C2,
4) glides in C1 followed by nasals in C2 in *AR*.

b) *Consonant groups on the basis of Place*

The following root patterns which contain sequences of consonants
from different groups classified on the basis of Place are subject to
ordering constraints:

1) coronal stops in C1 followed by coronal fricatives in C2 in the
    three languages and the same sequence in C2C3 in *AR*,
2) glides in C1 followed by coronal obstruents in C2 in *AR*.

5.6 *Co-occurrence restrictions on specific consonants*

I also studied the co-occurrence restrictions on a number of specific
consonants. These consonants were:

1) in the three languages: the individual labials and coronal
    sonorants and the uvular stop /q/,
2) in *AR*: the jim and the fa',
3) in *BH* and *HEB*: the sade.

5.6.1 *The labials and the coronal sonorants*

A variety of root patterns were studied which contain these consonants in the following combinations:

1) two labials (see *Table 5.5*) or two coronal sonorants (see *Table 5.6*),
2) a labial and a coronal sonorant (see *Table 5.6*),

3) a labial or a coronal sonorant and representatives of one of the different consonant groups (see *Tables 5.7 and 5.8*).

In all these root patterns the remaining position contains an arbitrary consonant, symbolyzed by (X).

5.6.1.1 *Root patterns with two labials, two coronal sonorants or one labial and one coronal sonorant*

The root patterns with two labials are subject to virtually complete combinatory constraints in both adjacent and nonadjacent positions, but only in *AR* and *HEB* (see *Table 5.5*). This is also the case for the root patterns with two coronal sonorants, but to a somewhat smaller extent (see *Table 5.6*). Most of the root patterns which contain both of the liquids /l/ and /r/, are strongly avoided in all three languages when present in adjacent and, in part, in nonadjacent positions. The labial /m/ patterns more with the labials than with /n/, while the latter patterns with the liquids.

Some of the root patterns which contain a nasal and a liquid in nonadjacent positions are preferred rather than avoided.

5.6.1.2. *Root patterns with a labial or a coronal sonorant and one of the consonant groups*

a) *Consonant groups classified on the basis of Manner* (see *Table 5.7*)

Combinatory constraints apply to the following root patterns:

1) /l/ or /r/ and liquids[6].
2) /n/ and liquids in adjacent positions[7].

Ordering constraints apply in all three languages to the adjacent positions of the following root patterns:

1) /n/ followed by nasals[8],
2) nasals followed by /m/.

---

[6] However, the root pattern (li)(X)(l) has an expected frequency in *BH*.
[7] However, the root patterns (li)(n)(X) in *BH* and (X)(li)(n) in *HEB* have expected frequencies.
[8] And also in nonadjacent positions in *AR*.

There are no avoided root patterns which contain /m/ and liquids. A few avoided root patterns contain /m/ and stops in adjacent positions:

1) /m/ followed by voiced stops in C1C2 in *AR* and *BH*,
2) /m/ followed by stops as such in C1C2 in *BH* and the same sequence in C2C3 in *HEB*.

b) *Consonant groups classified on the basis of Place* (see *Table 5.8*)

All root patterns which contain a pair of /m/ and labials in adjacent positions exhibit strong combinatory constraints in each of the three languages. A strong ordering constraint exists for /m/ followed by labials in the nonadjacent positions C1C3.

Another combinatory constraint exists for pairs which consist of coronal sonorants as a group and one of the individual coronal sonorants /n/, /l/ and /r/ in adjacent positions and for /r/ also in nonadjacent positions.

Some of the root patterns in *BH* and *HEB* which contain the coronal sonorant /l/ and coronal obstruents are subject to ordering constraints. They are of the following types:

1) /l/ in C1 followed in *BH* by coronal stops or fricatives or coronal obstruents in C2,
2) coronal fricatives in C1 in *BH* and *HEB* or coronal obstruents as a group in C1 in *BH* followed by /l/ in C3.

In addition, a pair of coronal sonorants followed by /m/ in positions C1C2 is subject to an ordering constraint in *BH*.

Many of the above constraints are absolute (see *Table 5.2* and § 5.4.1). The properties and mutual relationships of /m/, /n/, /r/ and /l/ are discussed in greater detail in § 8.6.

5.6.2. *The status of the fa' and the jīm in Arabic and of the ṣade in Hebrew*

As was noted in § 2.1.1. the fa' is a labial fricative in Classical and Modern Standard Arabic, while it is a labial stop in most of the other Semitic languages. The ṣade in Hebrew is classified as an affricate. It probably constitutes a merger of a number of coronal obstruents (see § 2.1.2.). It seemed to be of interest, therefore, to investigate whether these consonants behave as stops or as fricatives in their co-occurrence relationships in the verbal roots. For this purpose the root patterns which contain one of these consonants were studied separately.

Table 5.3 shows my findings for the co-occurrence restrictions on the fa' and on the sade and *Table 6.1* shows the co-occurrence preferences for these consonants. The total number of triliteral verbal roots which contain these consonants is relatively small. This number is 388 for the fa' in *AR* and for the sade it is 140 in *BH* and 220 in *HEB*. As a result, in many cases, the number of root patterns which contain one of these consonants in one root position and members of one of the consonant groups in another position is rather small. For this reason, no conclusion can be drawn as to the status of either the fa' or the sade. Since this phonological evidence is inconclusive I decided to range the fa' of *AR* among the voiceless fricatives on the basis of Manner, as is done traditionally. Of course, on the basis of Place it is a labial (see § 2.1.1). I kept the affricate sade of Hebrew separate from the stops and the fricatives on the basis of Manner. It is a coronal obstruent on the basis of Place (see § 2.1.2).

The status of the jim in *AR* was discussed in § 2.1.1. It is a velar fricative in *CA* and in *AR*, while it is a velar stop in certain Arabic dialects, in Hebrew and in some other Semitic languages. The total number of root patterns which contain the jim is also relatively small and for similar reasons as in the case of the fa' and the sade no conclusions can be drawn as to the status of the jim as a stop or a fricative on the basis of Manner (see for this *Tables 5.3, 5.4 and 6.1*). For the purpose of my study, I ranged it among the voiced fricatives on the basis of Manner. It clearly patterns with the velar stop /k/ in its co-occurrence relationships on the basis of Place.

5.6.3 *The status of the uvular stop /q/*

Tables 5.4 and 6.2 show that as far as its co-occurrence relationships are concerned, the uvular stop /q/ patterns with the velars stops /k/ and /G/ rather than with the uvular fricatives /x/ and /g/. As mentioned in § 4.5, this led me to decide that for the purpose of my study the uvular stop /q/ should be included in the group of velars and not in that of the uvulars. In § 8.3 some of the phonological consequences of this decision are discussed in detail.

5.7 *Co-occurrence restrictions on consonant pairs in the Mediae Geminatae*

Since the Mediae Geminatae (MG's) contain the same consonant in root positions C2 and C3, I studied the co-occurrence relationships in these files only for root positions C1 and C2.

When the consonants are grouped on the basis of Manner no avoided MG's were found. On the basis of Place, however, the following MG's which contain consonants from the same group in root positions C1 and C2 are subject to combinatory constraints (see *Table 5.9*):

1) coronal obstruents as a group in *AR, BH* and *HEB,*
2) coronal sonorants in *AR* and *HEB,*
3) labials in *BH* and *HEB,*
4) coronal stops, coronal fricatives and velars in *HEB.*

On the basis of Place no ordering constraints for consonants from different groups were found.

My findings indicate the following:

Conclusion 2. *The constraints on adjacent positions with respect to root positions C1C2 of the MG's on the basis of Place are rather similar to those in the triliterals. In both cases, consonants from the same group show a clear tendency to combinatory constraints.*

This tendency, however, is less pervasive for the MG's than it is for the triliterals. One reason for this may be that the MG files are relatively small. Their size is only about 10% of that of the triliterals (see *Table 2.3*). This causes both the observed and the expected frequencies for many types of MG's to be rather small. This will affect the statistics and may result in accidental gaps (see § 4.4 and § 5.2).

5.8 *Co-occurrence restrictions on the quadriliterals*

Quadriliterals possess four root positions. Those of the type C1C2C1C2 form a separate file. They are discussed in § 5.9. Root patterns of the type C1C2C3C3 are discussed in § 6.9. There are only five quadriliterals in *BH* and these were not studied (see *Table 2.3*). In *AR* and *HEB* the files of the quadriliterals are considerably larger, but still the numbers of such roots which are not of the types C1C2C1C2 or C1C2C3C3 are far smaller than that of the triliterals (see *Table 2.3*).

For this reason, only stops and fricatives as groups were studied on the basis of Manner and not their voiced and voiceless subsets and neither were the coronal obstruents subdivided into coronal stops and fricatives. On the basis of Place the pharyngeals/laryngeals and the uvular fricatives in *AR* were combined into the group of the gutturals. *Tables 5.10 and 5.11* show my findings.

5.8.1 *Combinatory constraints*

The quadriliterals are subject to a number of combinatory constraints and almost all of these apply to adjacent root positions.

Avoided on the basis of Manner are:

In *AR* and *HEB*:
1) liquids in C1C2, C2C3 and C3C4,
2) stops in C2C3.

In *HEB*:
fricatives in C2C3 and C3C4.
The only combinatory constraint in nonadjacent positions occurs in *AR* and it applies to liquids in C2C4.

Avoided on the basis of Place are:

In *AR* and *HEB*:
1) labials or coronal sonorants in C1C2, C2C3 and C3C4,
2) coronal obstruents in C3C4,
3) gutturals in C1C2.

In *HEB*:
1) coronal obstruents in C1C2 and C2C3,
2) velars in C1C2, C2C3, and C3C4,
3) gutturals in C1C2.

There is only one case of a combinatory constraint which applies to nonadjacent positions. It occurs in *AR* and it applies to labials in C1C3.

5.8.2 *Ordering constraints*

On the basis of Manner, there is one ordering constraint on adjacent root positions and it occurs only in *HEB*:

nasals in C1 followed by liquids in C2.

   Ordering constraints on the basis of Manner which apply to non-adjacent root positions occur either in *AR* or in *HEB*.

   In *AR*:
nasals or glides followed by fricatives in C2C4 and C1C4.

   In *HEB*:
stops in C1 followed by nasals in C4.

   On the basis of Place the following root patterns are subject to ordering constraints:

   In *AR*:
glides in C2 followed by coronal obstruents in C4.

   In *HEB*:
1) velars in C1 followed by gutturals in C2,
2) gutturals in C1 followed by velars in C4.

All these cases of ordering constraints are rather atypical and may well be due to accidental gaps. Still, from the findings in § 5.8.1 and § 5.8.2 the following conclusion can be drawn:

Conclusion 3. *The quadriliterals are similar to the triliterals and the Mediae Geminatae in that they show a tendency for consonants from the same group in adjacent positions to be subject to co-occurrence restrictions.*

5.9 *Co-occurrence restrictions on root patterns of the type C1C2C1C2*

There are 130 roots of the type C1C2C1C2 in *AR*, 3 in *BH* and 174 in *HEB*. Since the number of these roots is very small in *BH*, only the files of *AR* and *HEB* were analyzed. The root patterns of this type contain the same consonant groups in root positions C1 and C3 and also in root positions C2 and C4. As a consequence, the results of the calculations for positions C1C2 and C3C4 are the same and in the reverse order in positions C2C3. For these reasons, only the findings for positions C1C2 are reported. The results are shown in *Tables 5.12 and 5.13*. In general, the frequencies of occurrence of the different root patterns of this type are rather small. For this reason, the consonants were grouped in the same way as in § 5.8.

On the basis of Manner, combinatory constraints exist only in *HEB*. They apply to fricatives as a group and to liquids. One ordering constraint occurs in *AR* and *HEB* and holds with respect to voiceless fricatives in C1 followed by liquids in C2.

On the basis of Place, combinatory constraints were found for the following consonant groups:

1) coronal sonorants in *AR* and *HEB*,
2) coronal obstruents and gutturals in *AR*,
3) velars in *HEB*.

In none of the two languages ordering constraints on the basis of Place were found.

On the basis of Manner and of Place there is a tendency for root patterns of the type C1C2C1C2 with consonants from the same group in adjacent positions to be avoided. What may contribute to this is the fact that such root patterns would contain consonants which belong to the same group in all of their four root positions.

5.10 *Co-occurrence restrictions on triliteral root patterns with three specified root positions*

The co-occurrence relationships of consonant pairs in two of the root positions of the triliterals may well be affected by the consonants which are present in the remaining root position. All three consonant groups which are present in a fully specified triliteral root pattern may determine whether it has an expected frequency or is subject either to co-occurrence restrictions or to co-occurrence preferences. For this reason, I decided to study also the co-occurrence restrictions which apply to triliteral root patterns with three specified root positions. These root patterns form subsets of larger sets with two specified root positions. As a consequence, the number of roots which belong to such a subset is often rather small. Statistial considerations led me to investigate these types of root patterns only in *AR* and *HEB*, because the total number of triliteral roots in *BH* is only about half that in *AR* and *HEB* (see *Table 2.3*).

It will be shown in ch. 6 that many triliteral root patterns with three root positions, all of which contain specific consonant groups, happen to be preferred if there are nasals, liquids, labials or coronal sonorants among them. In the present section the co-occurrence restrictions are described which act on root patterns with three specific consonant groups or with two such groups and an individual labial or coronal sonorant in the remaining position.

5.10.1 *Root patterns with three specific consonant groups*

a) *Avoided root patterns on the basis of Manner*

1. Root patterns which contain nasals in at least one of the three root positions (see *Table 5.14*)

In *AR* and *HEB* are avoided:
nasals in C1 and C2 and stops as a group.

In *AR* are avoided:
nasals in C1 and C2 and fricatives as a group in C3.
When the stops and fricatives are subdivided in their voiced and voiceless subsets there are no avoided root patterns of this type. This is probably due mainly to the low frequencies of such root patterns.

2. Root patterns which contain liquids in at leasr one of the three root positions (see *Table 5.15*)

In *AR* and *HEB* are avoided:
1) liquids in C1 and C2 and voiceless stops or either stops or fricatives (both as a group) in C3,
2) liquids in C2 and C3 and any obstruent in C1 (except voiced fricatives in *HEB*).

In *AR* are avoided:
1 liquids in C1 and C2 and voiced stops or voiceless fricatives in C3.
2) liquids in C1 and C3 and voiced stops or fricatives as a group in C2.

In *HEB* are avoided:
1) liquids in C1 and C3 and voiceless stops in C2,

2) fricatives as a group in C1 and C3 and liquids in C2.

3. *Root patterns which contain both nasals and liquids* (see *Tables 5.14 and 5.15*).

In *HEB* are avoided:
1) nasals in C1 and liquids in C2 and C3,
2) nasals in C1 and C3 and liquids in C2,
3) nasals in C3 and liquids in C1 and C2,
4) nasals in C1, liquids in C2 and stops as a group in C3.

4. *Root patterns which contain two obstruents* (see *Tables 5.16.1 and 5.16.2*)

In *AR* and *HEB* are avoided:
1) stops or fricatives (both as a group) in C1, C2 and C3,
2) fricatives in C2 and C3 and stops in C1 (both as a group).

In *AR* are avoided:
1) stops in C1 and C2 and fricatives in C3 (both as a group),
2) fricatives in C1 and C2 and stops in C3 (both as a group),
3) stops in C2 and C3 and fricatives in C1 (both as a group).

In *HEB* are avoided:
fricatives in C1 and C3 and stops in C2 (both as a group).

b) *Avoided root patterns on the basis of Place*

1. *Root patterns which contain labials in at least one position (see Table 5.17)*

Virtually all root patterns which contain two labials in adjacent positions are subject to very strong co-occurrence restrictions, except for the root pattern in *AR* which also contains coronal fricatives in C3. The other avoided root patterns are listed below.

In *AR* and *HEB* are avoided:
1) coronal stops or coronal obstruents as a group in C2 and C3 and labials in C1,
2) velars in C1 and C3 and labials in C2,
3) gutturals in C1 and C2 and labials in C3.

In *AR* are avoided:
1) labials in C1 and C3 and coronal obstruents as a group in C2,
2) coronal fricatives in C2 and C3 and labials in C1,
3) coronal fricatives in C1 and C3 and labials in C2,
4) coronal fricatives or coronal obstruents as a group in C1 and C2
   and labials in.C3,
5) velars in C1 and C2 and labials in C3,
6) gutturals in C2 and C3 and labials in C1,
7) gutturals in C1 and C3 and labials in C2.

In *HEB* are avoided:
1) labials in C1 and C3 and gutturals in C2,
2) gutturals in C2 and C3 and labials in C1.

2. *Root patterns which contain coronal sonorants in at least one position*
   (see *Table 5.18*)

All root patterns which have two coronal sonorants in adjacent positions are subject to very strong co-occurrence restrictions. The other avoided root patterns are listed below.

In *AR* and *HEB* are avoided:
1) coronal stops, coronal obstruents as a group, velars or gutturals
   in C2 and C3 and coronal sonorants in C1,
2) coronal fricatives, coronal obstruents as a group, velars or gutturals in C1 and C2 and coronal sonorants in C3.

In *AR* are avoided:
1) coronal stops in C1 and C2 and coronal sonorants in C3,
2) coronal fricatives in C2 and C3 and coronal sonorants in C1.

3. *Root patterns which contain both labials and coronal sonorants*
   (see *Tables 5.17 and 5.18*)

In *AR* and *HEB* are avoided:
1) labials in C2 and C3 and coronal sonorants in C1,
2) labials in C1 and C2 and coronal sonorants in C3.

In *AR* are avoided:
1) coronal sonorants in C1 and C3 and labials in C2,
2) labials in C1 and C3 and coronal sonorants in C2.

The findings described in this section up to this point indicate the following:

Conclusion 4. *Most of the avoided root patterns with three specified positions contain consonants from the same group in two positions.*

This finding is not surprising in view of the fact that most of the root patterns with two specified root positions with adjacent or nonadjacent consonants from the same group and arbitrary consonants in the remaining position are subject to very strong combinatory constraints (see § 5.4.2.1). Apparently, this phenomenon is of a more general nature and the consonants in the remaining root position have little influence on this. This phenomenon is important for the evaluation of co-occurrence preferences (see ch. 8).

5.10.2   *Root patterns with two specified consonant groups and a labial or coronal sonorant*

In many cases both the observed and the expected frequencies of these root patterns are very low. However, some conclusions can be drawn from root patterns for which this is not the case. *Table 5.19* shows that avoided root patterns with two consonant groups classified on the basis of Manner almost invariably contain a pair consisting of the liquids as a group and one of the individual liquids /r/ or /l/ or, to some extent, /n/. In addition, the root pattern with nasals in C1, stops in C3 and /m/ in C2 is avoided in *AR* and a similar root pattern with /n/ in C2 is avoided in *HEB*.

On the basis of Place, many root patterns are avoided which contain labials as a group and /m/ or coronal sonorants as a group and /n/, /r/ or /l/ (see *Table 5.20*). A number of root patterns are avoided which contain consonants from the same group in two adjacent positions and one of the sonorants in the remaining position. These results suggest that the following conclusion can be drawn:

Conclusion 5. *As to the co-occurrence restrictions on root patterns with two specified consonant groups and a labial or coronal sonorant /m/ belongs to the identity class of the labials and the consonants /r/ and /l/ belong to that of the liquids. No statement can be made about the status of /m/ and /n/ as nasals.*

CHAPTER SIX

CO-OCCURRENCE PREFERENCES FOR VERBAL ROOTS IN ARABIC AND HEBREW

6.1 *Introductory remarks*

In this chapter my findings for the preferred verbal root patterns in *AR*, *BH* and *HEB* are described. Co-occurrence preferences were investigated for types of root patterns which are similar to those studied for the co-occurrence restrictions which are described in ch. 5. In addition, root patterns of the type C1C2C3C3 were investigated in *HEB*. In the work described in the present chapter, I again subdivided the consonants into phonological groups classified either on the basis of Manner or on that of Place. The statistical methods used were also similar to those employed in ch. 5.

Co-occurrence preferences exist, if the observed frequencies of co-occurrence of combinations of consonants or consonant groups in the verbal roots are significantly larger their expected frequencies. As was discussed in § 5.2, co-occurrence restrictions can be the result of either combinatory or ordering constraints. In some cases, they can be absolute, but they usually are relative (statistical). Some root patterns with three specified positions were shown to exhibit partially absolute co-occurrence preferences (see § 6.7.3). However, most of the cases of co-occurrence preference which I noted in my study were relative (statistical) and not absolute. As in the case of the findings described in ch. 5 statistical calculations were performed in order to arrive at the levels of significance for the differences between the observed and the expected frequencies of the root patterns (see § 4.2).

6.2 *Co-occurrence preferences for triliteral root patterns with two specified consonant groups*

Tables 6.1 and 6.2 show the findings for the preferred root patterns which have members of specific consonant groups in two of their three root positions and arbitrary consonants in the remaining position[1]. There

---

[1] See § 5.6.3 and § 8.3 for the status of the uvular stop /q/ with respect to its co-occurrence restrictions and preferences.

are no preferred consonant pairs which contain consonants from the same group, but many cases of combinatory and ordering preferences exist for consonant pairs from different groups.

6.2.1 *Combinatory preferences for consonant pairs from different groups*

Cases of combinatory co-occurrence preferences are found almost exclusively for consonants in adjacent root positions.

A) *Consonant groups classified on the basis of Manner*

Consonants grouped on the basis of Manner show the following co-occurrence preferences:

a) *In positions C1C2*
   In *AR* and *HEB*:
1) liquids and voiceless stops or stops as a group.

   In *AR*:
1) nasals and fricatives as a group,
2) liquids and voiceless fricatives.

   In *HEB*:
nasals and voiceless stops.

b) *In positions C2C3*
   In *AR, BH* and *HEB*:
liquids and fricatives as a group, voiceless stops or stops as a group.

   In *AR*:
liquids and voiceless fricatives.

   In *HEB*:
1) liquids and voiced stops or voiced fricatives,
2) glides and stops as a group.

c) *In positions C1C3*
   In *AR*:
glides and voiced fricatives.

In *HEB*:
1) voiceless stops and voiceless fricatives,
2) stops and fricatives (both as a group).

B) *Consonant groups classified on the basis of Place*

Consonant groups classified on the basis of Place show the following co-occurrence preferences:

a) *In positions C1C2*
   In *AR*, *BH* and *HEB*:
coronal sonorants and velars.

   In *AR* and *HEB*:
1) labials and coronal obstruents as a group,
2) coronal obstruents as a group and pharyngeals/laryngeals.

   In *AR*:
1) labials and coronal stops or coronal fricatives,
2) coronal fricatives and pharyngeals/laryngeals or glides,
3) coronal obstruents as a group and uvular fricatives.

   In *HEB*:
coronal obstruents as a group and glides.

b) *In positions C2C3*
   In *AR*, *BH* and *HEB*:
1) labials and coronal obstruents as a group,
2) coronal sonorants and velars.

   In *AR*:
1) labials and coronal fricatives,
2) coronal sonorants and coronal fricatives.

   In *BH*:
1) labials and coronal stops,
2) coronal sonorants and pharyngeals/laryngeals.

6.2.2 *Ordering preferences for consonant pairs from different groups*

A) *Consonant groups classified on the basis of Manner*

Such consonants groups show the following co-occurrence preferences:

a) *In positions C1C2*
   In *AR, BH* and *HEB*:
1) nasals followed by voiceless fricatives,
2) voiced stops followed by liquids.

   In *AR* and *HEB*:
glides followed by fricatives as a group.

   In *BH* and *HEB*:
1) nasals followed by fricatives as a group,
2) liquids followed by voiced fricatives.

   In *AR*:
1) voiceless fricatives or fricatives as a group followed by liquids,
2) nasals followed by voiceless stops or voiced fricatives,
3) glides followed by voiceless stops, stops as a group or voiceless fricatives.

   In *BH*:
1) stops as a group followed by liquids,
2) voiceless fricatives followed by voiceless stops.

   In *HEB*:
1) nasals followed by stops as a group,
2) liquids followed by fricatives as a group,
3) glides followed by voiced fricatives.

b) *In positions C2C3*
   In *AR* and *BH*:
voiced fricatives followed by liquids.

   In *AR* and *HEB*:
nasals followed by fricatives as a group.

In *BH* and *HEB*:
1) liquids followed by voiceless fricatives,
2) glides followed by voiced stops.

In *AR*:
1) voiceless stops followed by nasals,
2) liquids followed by voiced stops.

In *BH*:
1) voiced stops followed by liquids,
2) voiced stops followed by voiced fricatives.

In *HEB*:
1) voiceless fricatives followed by voiceless stops,
2) nasals followed by voiceless fricatives.

c) *In positions C1C3*
In *AR* and *BH*:
liquids followed by nasals.

In *BH* and *HEB*:
liquids followed by fricatives as a group.

In *AR*:
1) voiceless stops followed by voiceless fricatives,
2) voiced fricatives followed by liquids or glides.

In *BH*:
1) voiceless fricatives followed by voiceless stops,
2) fricatives as a group followed by stops as a group,
3) glides followed by voiced stops or voiced fricatives.

In *HEB*:
1) voiced fricatives followed by voiced stops,
2) liquids followed by voiced fricatives.

B) *Consonant groups classified on the basis of Place*

Such consonant groups show the following co-occurrence preferences:

a) *In positions C1C2*
  In *AR, BH* and *HEB*:
coronal sonorants followed by pharyngeals/laryngeals.

  In *AR* and *BH*:
labials followed by coronal sonorants.

  In *BH* and *HEB*:
coronal fricatives followed by velars.

  In *AR*:
1) coronal stops followed by coronal sonorants or glides,
2) coronal obstruents as a group followed by coronal sonorants or glides,
3) coronal fricatives followed by uvular fricatives,
4) velars followed by coronal fricatives,
5) uvular fricatives followed by coronal stops,
6) glides followed by coronal obstruents as a group, pharyngeals/laryngeals or velars.

  In *BH*:
1) coronal obstruents as a group followed by labials,
2) coronal sonorants followed by coronal obstruents as a group,
3) pharyngeals/laryngeals followed by labials or coronal obstruents as a group.

  In *HEB*:
1) labials followed by coronal fricatives,
2) coronal stops followed by labials or pharyngeals/laryngeals,
3) coronal sonorants followed by coronal fricatives,
4) velars followed by labials,
5) glides followed by coronal fricatives.

b) *In positions C2C3*
  In *AR, BH* and *HEB*:
1) coronal obstruents as a group followed by coronal sonorants,
2) glides followed by coronal stops or coronal obstruents as a group.

  In *BH* and *HEB*:
labials followed by coronal fricatives.

In *AR* and *HEB*:
coronal sonorants followed by pharyngeals/laryngeals.

In *AR*:
1) labials followed by coronal stops,
2) coronal stops followed by coronal sonorants,
3) velars followed by pharyngeals/laryngeals or coronal fricatives,
4) uvular fricatives followed by coronal obstruents as a group,
5) glides followed by uvular fricatives.

In *BH*:
pharyngeals/laryngeals followed by labials.

In *HEB*:
1) coronal stops followed by labials,
2) coronal fricatives followed by velars,
3) coronal sonorants followed by coronal fricatives,
3) pharyngeals/laryngeals followed by glides.

c) *In positions C1C3*
In *AR*, *BH* and *HEB*:
1) labials followed by velars or pharyngeals/laryngeals,
2) coronal sonorants followed by coronal fricatives.

In *AR*:
1) labials followed by uvular fricatives,
2) coronal stops followed by velars,
3) coronal fricatives followed by uvular fricatives,
4) coronal obstruents as a group followed by velars or uvular fricatives,
5) coronal sonorants followed by coronal obstruents as a group.

In *BH*:
coronal stops followed by glides.

In *HEB*:
1) coronal fricatives followed by coronal stops,
2) velars followed by coronal fricatives.

6.2.3 *Summary of combinatory and ordering preferences for the triliterals*

Many preferred triliteral root patterns with two specified positions contain pairs of consonants which belong to different consonant groups
classified either on the basis of Manner or on that of Place and arbitrary consonants in the remaining position. In the present section these
observations are summarized in a more general and systematic way
in a set of conclusions. To simplify matters an overview is presented
for the three languages as a group, rather than for each of the individual languages.

Conclusion 1. *Combinatory preferences on the basis of Manner are found mainly
in adjacent positions. They apply almost exclusively to pairs of nasals or liquids
with obstruents of different types. On the basis of Place no cases of combinatory
preferences were observed for nonadjacent positions. In adjacent positions, combinatory
preferences mainly involve consonant pairs which consist of labials with coronal
obstruents of different types and also pairs of coronal sonorants with coronal fricatives, velars or pharyngeals / laryngeals.*

Conclusion 2. *Ordering preferences present a more complicated picture. In adjacent positions and on the basis of Manner, the preferred consonant pairs involve
mainly nasals, liquids or glides followed by obstruents of different types. A number of ordering preferences for consonant pairs on the basis of Manner was found
in nonadjacent positions, but it is difficult to provide a more generalized picture
for these. They involve, for instance, obstruents of different types and a variety of
other consonant groups. On the basis of Place, ordering preferences in adjacent positions apply mainly to coronal obstruents of different types followed by labials, coronal
sonorants or glides.*

From conclusions 1 and 2 follows:

Conclusion 3. *In most cases, the preferred consonant pairs of triliterals on
the basis of Manner contain nasals or liquids and on the basis of Place they contain
labials or coronal sonorants.*

It became therefore important to investigate also the preferred root
patterns with two specified positions which contain an individual labial
or coronal sonorant and consonants of one of the other consonant
groups and arbitrary consonants in the remaining position. The findings
for such root patterns are described in § 6.3.

6.3 *Co-occurrence preferences for triliterals with a labial or coronal sonorant and one of the other consonant groups*

A fairly large number of root patterns of these types show combinatory preferences and many exhibit ordering preferences (see *Tables 6.3 and 6.4*).

6.3.1. *Combinatory preferences*

A) *Consonant groups classified on the basis of Manner*

The following cases of combinatory preferences for root patterns with consonant groups on the basis of Manner were noted:

a) *In positions C1C2*
   In *AR* and *BH*:
/r/ and voiceless stops or stops as a group.

   In *AR*:
/n/ and stops as a group.

   In *HEB*:
/n/ and voiceless stops.

b) *In positions C2C3*
   In *AR*, *BH* and *HEB*:
/r/ and stops as a group.

   In *AR* and *BH*:
/l/ and fricatives as a group.

   In *AR* and *HEB*:
/m/ and coronal obstruents as a group.

   In *AR*:
/r/ and voiceless fricatives or fricatives as a group.

   In *BH*:
/r/ and voiceless stops.

In *HEB*:
1) /m/ and voiceless fricatives or fricatives as a group,
2) /r/ and voiced stops.

B) *Consonant groups classified on the basis of Place*

For such consonant groups the following cases of combinatory preferences were found:

a) *In positions C1C2*
   In *AR* and *HEB*:
/n/ and velars.

b) *In positions C2C3*
   In *AR, BH* and *HEB*:
/r/ and coronal fricatives or coronal obstruents as a group.

   In *AR* and *HEB*:
1) /m/ and coronal fricatives or coronal obstruents as a group,
2) /m/ or /r/ and coronal stops.

   In *BH* and *HEB*:
/r/ and velars.

   In *BH*:
/r/ and coronal stops.

   In *HEB*:
/l/ and pharyngeals/laryngeals.

c) *In positions C1C3*
   In *BH*:
/r/ and coronal fricatives or coronal obstruents as a group.

6.3.2. *Ordering preferences*

A) *Consonant groups classified on the basis of Manner*

Ordering preferences for such consonant groups occurred for the following root patterns:

a) *In positions C1C2*
   In *AR* and *BH*:
1) /n/ followed by voiceless stops or voiceless fricatives,
2) stops as a group followed by /l/.

   In *BH* and *HEB*:
1) /n/ followed by stops as a group,
2) /l/ followed by fricatives as a group,
3) /r/ followed by voiced fricatives,
4) voiced stops followed by /l/.

   In *AR*:
1) /m/ followed by voiced fricatives,
2) /n/ followed by fricatives as a group,
3) voiced stops followed by /n/ or /r/.

   In *BH*:
voiced fricatives followed by /n/.

   In *HEB*:
/m/ followed by voiceless fricatives or fricatives as a group.

b) *In positions C2C3*
In *AR*, *BH* and *HEB*:
1) /n/ followed by glides,
2) fricatives as a group followed by /l/.

   In *AR* and *BH*:
1) /r/ followed by voiced stops,
2) voiceless stops followed by /r/.

   In *AR* and *HEB*:
/l/ followed by stops as a group.

   In *AR*:
1) /l/ followed by voiceless stops or voiceless fricatives,
2) /r/ followed by voiceless fricatives,
3) voiced stops or stops as a group followed by /n/,
4) voiced fricatives followed by /r/.

In *BH*:
1) /n/ or /r/ followed by voiceless stops,
2) voiceless fricatives or fricatives as a group followed by /m/.

In *HEB*:
1) /r/ followed by voiced fricatives or fricatives as a group,
2) voiceless stops followed by /r/,
3) fricatives as a group followed by /l/.

c) *In positions C1C3*
In *AR* and *BH*:
/m/ followed by voiceless stops.

In *AR*:
1) /n/ followed by fricatives as a group,
2) /l/ followed by voiced fricatives or nasals.

In *BH*:
liquids followed by /m/.

In *HEB*:
/r/ followed by voiced fricatives or fricatives as a group.

B) *Consonant groups classified on the basis of Place*

The following root patterns exhibit ordering preferences for consonant groups classified on the basis of Place:

a) *In positions C1C2*
   In *AR, BH* and *HEB*:
1) /n/ followed by coronal fricatives or coronal obstruents as a group,
2) /l/ followed by pharyngeals/laryngeals.

In *AR* and *BH*:
/r/ followed by velars.

In *AR* and *HEB*:
/m/ followed by pharyngeals/laryngeals.

In *BH* and *HEB*:
/r/ followed by coronal obstruents as a group.

In *AR*:
1) /n/ followed by uvular fricatives,
2) /l/ followed by labials,
3) coronal stops followed by /r/,
4) coronal obstruents as a group followed by /m/ or /r/.

In *BH*:
1) /n/ followed by coronal stops or velars,
2) /l/ followed by glides,
3) /r/ followed by pharyngeals/laryngeals,
4) labials followed by /l/ or /r/,
5) pharyngeals/laryngeals followed by /m/.

In *HEB*:
velars followed by /m/.

b) *In positions C2C3*
In *AR*, *BH* and *HEB*:
/n/ followed by glides.

In *AR*:
1) /n/, /l/ or /r/ followed by velars,
2) coronal stops followed by /n/,
3) uvular fricatives followed by /m/.

In *BH*:
/l/ followed by pharyngeals/laryngeals.

In *HEB*:
velars followed by /l/.

c) *In positions C1C3*
In *AR*, *BH* and *HEB*:
/m/ followed by velars.

In *AR* and *HEB*:
coronal fricatives followed by /r/.

In *BH* and *HEB*:
/l/ or /r/ followed by labials.

In *AR*:
1) /n/ followed by coronal fricatives,
2) /l/ followed by coronal fricatives or velars,
3) coronal stops followed by /n/,
4) coronal obstruents as a group followed by /r/.

In *BH*:
/r/ followed by coronal fricatives or coronal obstruents as a group.

In *HEB*:
/l/ followed by coronal stops or coronal obstruents as a group.

6.3.3 *Summary of the findings*

In § 6.3.1 and 6.3.2 are described the properties of the triliteral root patterns with two specified positions which contain a labial or a coronal sonorant, one of the consonant groups classified on the basis of Manner or Place and arbitrary consonants in the remaining position. These properties lead to the following conclusions:

Conclusion 4. *Combinatory preferences apply almost exclusively to adjacent consonant pairs. On the basis of Manner, they involve the different types of stops or fricatives and mainly /r/ and, in some cases /m/ or /n/. On the basis of Place, the preferred consonant pairs consist especially of coronal obstruents of different types and /r/ or /m/.*

Conclusion 5. *Ordering preferences apply to both adjacent and nonadjacent root positions. On the basis of Manner, they involve almost exclusively one of the coronal sonorants /n/, /r/ and /l/ followed by different types of stops or fricatives. On the basis of Place, they involve particularly the coronal sonorants /n/, /r/ and /l/ followed by the different types of coronal obstruents. In a number of cases the coronal sonorants can be followed by any of the different consonant groups. In other cases, the coronal sonorants are preceded by labials or by the labial sonorant /m/.*

Conclusions 4 and 5 will be discussed in a greater detail in § 7.3.1.2.3.

6.4 *Co-occurrence preferences for consonant pairs in the Mediae Geminatae*

As in the study of the co-occurrence restrictions on the MG's the co-occurrence preferences were investigated only for root positions C1 and C2 and the grouping of the consonants was similar (see § 5.7).

On the basis of Manner, no preferred MG's occur in *HEB* and there is only one preferred MG in *AR*. It contains voiced fricatives in C1 followed by glides in C2 and C3. In *BH*, however, a series of root patterns shows ordering co-occurrence preferences (see *Table 6.5*):

1) any type of obstruents in C1, followed by liquids in C2,
2) any type of fricatives in C1, followed by nasals in C2,
3) voiceless fricatives in C1, followed by voiced stops in C2,
4) fricatives as a group in C1, followed by stops as a group in C2,
5) voiceless stops or stops as a group in C1, followed by glides in C2,
6) liquids in C1, followed by glides in C2,
7) glides in C1, followed by voiced stops in C2.

On the basis of Place there are no preferred MG's in *HEB* (see *Table 6.6*). A few MG's, however, are preferred in *AR* or *BH*.

In *AR*:
gutturals in C1, followed by glides in C2.

In *BH*:
1) labials in C1, followed by coronal obstruents as a group in C2,
2) coronal fricatives in C1, followed by velars in C2,
3) glides in C2 preceded by coronal sonorants or velars in C1.

6.5. *Co-occurrence preferences for consonant pairs in the quadriliterals*

As in the case of the co-occurrence restrictions on the quadriliterals (see § 5.8) the calculations for co-occurrence preferences were performed only for *AR* and *HEB*. *Table 6.7* shows the findings on the basis of Manner and *Table 6.8* those on that of Place. The tables show that the great majority of the preferred root patterns occur either in *AR* or in *HEB* and not in both languages.

A) *Root patterns classified on the basis of Manner*
a. Combinatory co-occurrence preferences

In *AR*:
pairs of stops as a group, of fricatives as a group, of nasals or of liquids in the nonadjacent positions C1C3.

In *HEB*:
liquids and stops as a group in the adjacent positions C1C2, C2C3 and C3C4.

b. Ordering co-occurrence preferences

1. *In adjacent positions*
In *AR*:
1) stops or fricatives as a group in C2, followed by liquids in C3,
2) liquids in C3, followed by stops as a group in C4.

In *HEB*:
1) stops as a group in C1, followed by nasals in C2,
2) nasals in C1, followed in C2 by fricatives as a group,
3) glides in C3, followed by nasals in C4.

2. *In nonadjacent positions*
In *AR* and *HEB*:
nasals in C2, followed by liquids in C4.

In *AR*:
1) liquids in C1, followed in C3 by fricatives as a group,
2) liquids in C2, followed in C4 by fricatives as a group.

In *HEB*:
fricatives as a group in C1, followed by stops as a group in C3 or C4.

B) *Root patterns classified on the basis of Place*

a. *Combinatory co-occurrence preferences*
In *AR* and *HEB*:
1) coronal obstruents as a group in C1C3,

2) labials in C1 followed by gutturals in C4 and the reverse.

In *HEB*:
1) coronal obstruents as a group in C2C4,
2) labials in C3 followed by coronal obstruents as a group in C4 and the reverse.

b. Ordering co-occurrence preferences

1. *In adjacent positions*

In *AR* and *HEB*:
1) coronal obstruents as a group in C2, followed by coronal sonorants in C3,
2) coronal sonorants in C3, followed by velars in C4.

In *AR*:
1) coronal sonorants in C1, followed by gutturals in C2,
2) coronal sonorants in C2, followed by labials in C3,
3) labials in C2, followed by gutturals in C3,
4) gutturals in C2, followed by coronal sonorants in C3,
5) labials in C3, followed by coronal obstruents as a group in C4,
6) coronal sonorants in C3 followed, by labials in C4,
7) velars in C3, followed by gutturals in C4.

In *HEB*:
1) coronal obstruents as a group in C1, followed by gutturals in C2,
2) velars in C1, followed by coronal sonorants in C2,
3) labials or coronal obstruents as a group in C2, followed by coronal sonorants in C3,
4) coronal obstruents as a group in C2, followed by labials in C3,
5) coronal sonorants in C2, followed by velars or gutturals in C3,
6) gutturals in C3, followed by labials in C4.

2. *In nonadjacent positions*

In *AR*:
coronal sonorants in C2, followed by gutturals in C4.

In *HEB*:
1) velars in C1, followed by coronal obstruents as a group in C3,
2) velars in C2, followed by labials in C4,
3) gutturals in C2, followed by velars in C4,
4) coronal obstruents as a group in C1, followed by velars in C4.

Their is a great variety of preferred quadriliteral root patterns and the great majority of them are found either in *AR* or in *HEB*. Only a few occur in both languages. Nevertheless, the following conclusions can be drawn:

Conclusion 6. *In many cases quadriliteral root patterns which contain nonadjacent consonant pairs from the same group classified either on the basis of Manner or on that of Place, tend to show combinatory co-occurrence preferences.*

Conclusion 7. *On the basis of Manner quadriliteral root patterns with liquids which are followed by stops in adjacent positions tend to show ordering co-occurrence preferences. This is also the case for liquids which are followed by fricatives, but in this case in nonadjacent positions.*

Conclusion 8. *The majority of quadriliteral root patterns classified on the basis of Place which show ordering co-occurrence preferences contain labials and/or coronal sonorants which are adjacent to other consonant groups.*

In § 8.8 my findings with respect to the co-occurrence relationships of consonant groups in the quadriliterals and the triliterals will be compared from a wider perspective.

6.6 *Co-occurrence preferences for consonant pairs in the root patterns of the type C1C2C1C2*

As in § 5.9 only the files of *AR* and *HEB* were analyzed. Due to the relatively small size of these files most observed and expected frequencies are too small for statistical testing (results not shown). Only one preferred root pattern was found in *AR*. It contains coronal sonorants in C1, followed by velars in C2 and it occurs therefore also in positions C3C4 and in the reverse order in positions C2C3.

6.7 *Preferred triliteral root patterns with three specified root positions*

I observed in § 5.10 that it is conceivable that all three consonant groups which are present in a fully specified triliteral root pattern determine its co-occurrence relationships. For this reason, I decided to study also co-occurrence preferences for root patterns with three specified root positions. Since the number of roots of this type is often rather small, I investigated them only in *AR* and *HEB* and the consonants were subdivided in groups as described in § 5.8.

According to Conclusions 1 to 3 in § 6.2.3 most of the preferred triliteral root patterns with two specified root positions classified on the basis of Manner contain pairs of nasals or liquids and different types of obstruents. On the basis of Place, the preferred pairs of such root patterns usually contain labials or coronal sonorants and a variety of other consonant groups. For this reason, I decided to study root patterns with three specified root positions grouped on the basis of Manner with nasals or liquids in one root position and representatives from the different consonant groups in the other two positions. With respect to Place I studied similar root patterns with labials or coronal sonorants.

6.7.1 *Consonant groups classified on the basis of Manner*

Tables 6.9 and 6.10 show that many of the root patterns with three specified positions, which exhibit co-occurrence preferences, contain either nasals or liquids in at least one of the three root positions or both of these.

A. *Root patterns with nasals in at least one of the three root positions (see Table 6.9)*

The following root patterns are preferred:

a) *Nasals in C1*
   In *AR* and *HEB*:
1) voiceless stops in C2 and voiceless fricatives in C3,
2) stops as a group in C2 and fricatives as a group C3,
3) voiceless fricatives in C2 and voiceless stops in C3,
4) fricatives as a group in C2 and stops as a group in C3.

In *AR*:
1) voiceless stops in C2 and voiced fricatives in C3,
2) voiced stops in C2 and voiced fricatives in C3,
3) voiceless fricatives in C2 and voiced stops in C3,
4) voiced fricatives in C2 and voiceless stops in C3.

b) *Nasals in C2*
   In *AR* and *HEB*:
1) voiceless stops in C1 and voiceless fricatives in C3,
2) stops as a group in C1 and fricatives as a group in C3,
3) voiceless fricatives in C1 and voiceless stops in C3,
4) fricatives as a group in C1 and stops as a group in C3.

   In *AR*:
voiced fricatives or fricatives as a group in C1 and glides in C3.

c) *Nasals in C3*
   In *AR* and *HEB*:
voiceless fricatives in C1 and voiceless stops in C2.

   In *AR*:
1) voiced stops in C1 and voiceless stops in C2,
2) voiceless fricatives in C2 and voiceless stops in C3,
3) fricatives as a group in C1 and C2.

   In *HEB*:
glides in C1 and fricatives as a group in C2.

B. *Root patterns with liquids in at least one of the three root positions*
   (see Table 6.10)

The following root patterns are preferred:

a) *Liquids in C1*
   In *AR* and *HEB*:
1) stops as a group in C2 and fricatives as a group C3,
2) voiced fricatives in C2 and voiced stops in C3,
3) fricatives as a group in C2 and stops as a group in C3.

In *AR*:
1) voiceless stops in C2 and voiced stops, voiced fricatives in C3,
2) stops as a group or voiced fricatives in C2 and nasals in C3,
3) glides in C2 and voiced fricatives or fricatives as a group in C3.

In *HEB*:
1) voiceless stops in C2 and voiceless fricatives in C3,
2) voiced stops in C2 and voiced fricatives in C3,
3) voiceless fricatives in C2 and voiceless stops in C3,
4) voiced fricatives in C2 and glides in C3.

b) *Liquids in C2*
In *AR* and *HEB*:
1) voiceless stops in C1 and voiceless fricatives in C3,
2) voiced stops in C1 and C3,
3) voiced stops in C1 and voiceless fricatives in C3,
4) stops as a group in C1 and stops as a group or fricatives as a group in C3,
5) voiceless fricatives in C1 and voiceless or voiced stops in C3,
6) voiced fricatives in C1 and voiced stops in C3,
7) fricatives as a group in C1 and stops as a group in C3.

In *AR*:
1) voiced stops in C1 and voiced fricatives in C3,
2) voiceless fricatives in C1 and C3,
3) fricatives as a group in C1 and C3.

In *HEB*:
1) voiceless stops in C1 and voiced fricatives in C3,
2) voiced fricatives in C1 and C3.

c. *Liquids in C3*
In *AR* and *HEB*:
1) voiceless stops in C1 and voiceless fricatives in C2,
2) stops as a group in C1 and fricatives as a group in C2,
3) voiceles fricatives in C1 and voiceless or voiced stops in C2,
4) fricatives as a group in C1 and stops as a group in C2.

In *AR*:
1) voiceless fricatives in C1 and C2,

2) voiceless fricatives in C1 and voiced fricatives in C2,
3) voiced fricatives in C1 and voiceless fricatives in C2,
4) fricatives as a group in C1 and C2.

In *HEB*:
1) voiced stops in C1 and voiced fricatives in C2,
2) stops as a group in C1 and C2,
3) nasals in C2 and voiced fricatives in C2.

C. *Root patterns with both nasals and liquids*

In *AR* and *HEB*:
1) nasals in C1, liquids in C3 and fricatives as a group in C2,
2) nasals in C3, liquids in C1 and fricatives as a group in C2.

In *AR*:
nasals in C1, liquids in C3, and voiceless fricatives in C2.

In *HEB*:
nasals in C3, liquids in C1 and voiceless fricatives in C2.

6.7.2 *Consonant groups classified on the basis of Place*

Tables 6.11 and 6.12 show that many of the root patterns with three specified positions which contain either labials or coronal sonorants or both of these are subject to co-occurrence preferences:

A. *Root patterns with labials in at least one of the three root positions*
   (see *Table 6.11*)

a) *Labials in C1*
   In *AR* and *HEB*:
1) coronal fricatives in C2 and velars or gutturals in C3,
2) coronal obstruents as a group in C2 and velars or gutturals in C3,
3) gutturals in C2 and coronal stops, coronal obstruents as a group in C3.

In *AR*:
coronal stops in C2 and gutturals or glides in C3.

In *HEB*:
coronal stops in C2 and velars in C3.

b) *Labials in C2*
   In *AR* and *HEB*:
1) coronal stops or coronal obstruents as a group in C1 and or gutturals in C3,
2) velars in C1 and coronal fricatives, coronal obstruents as a group or gutturals in C3,
3) gutturals in C1 and coronal fricatives or coronal obstruents as a group in C3.

   In *AR*:
1) coronal fricatives in C1 and coronal stops, coronal fricatives or gutturals in C3,
2) coronal obstruents as a group in C1 velars in C3,
3) gutturals in C1 and coronal stops in C3.

   In *HEB*:
coronal stops in C1 and coronal fricatives in C3.

c) *Labials in C3*
   In *AR* and *HEB*:
1) coronal fricatives in C1 and gutturals in C2,
2) coronal obstruents as a group in C1 and gutturals in C2,
3) velars in C1 and coronal stops or coronal obstruents as a group in C2,
4) gutturals in C1 and coronal stops, coronal fricatives coronal obstruents as a group in C2.

   In *AR*:
1) velars in C1 and coronal fricatives in C2,
2) glides in C1 and velars in C2.

   In *HEB*:
1) coronal fricatives in C1 and velars in C2,
2) glides in C1 and coronal obstruents as a group in C2.

B. *Root patterns with coronal sonorants in at least one of the three root positions* (see *Table 6.12*)

a) *Coronal sonorants in C1*
   In *AR* and *HEB*:
1) coronal stops in C2 and gutturals in C3,
2) coronal fricatives in C2 and velars in C3,
3) coronal obstruents as a group in C2 and velars or gutturals in C3,
4) velars in C2 and coronal fricatives, coronal obstruents as a group or gutturals in C3,
5) gutturals in C2 and coronal obstruents as a group in C3.

   In *AR*:
1) coronal fricatives in C2 and gutturals in C3,
2) velars in C2 and coronal stops in C3,
3) gutturals in C2 and coronal fricatives or glides in C3.

b) *Coronal sonorants in C2*
   In *AR* and *HEB*:
1) coronal stops in C1 and gutturals in C3,
2) coronal fricatives in C1 and velars in C3,
3) coronal obstruents as a group in C1 and velars or gutturals in C3,
4) velars in C1 and coronal fricatives, coronal obstruents as a group or gutturals in C3,
5) gutturals in C1 and coronal obstruents as a group or velars in C3.

   In *AR*:
1) coronal stops in C1 and and velars in C3,
2) coronal fricatives in C1 and gutturals in C3,
3) gutturals in C1 and coronal fricatives in C3.

c) *Coronal sonorants in C3*
   In *AR* and *HEB*:
1) coronal fricatives in C1 and velars in C2,
2) coronal obstruents as a group in C1 and gutturals in C2,
3) gutturals in C1 and coronal fricatives or coronal obstruents as a group in C2.

In *AR*:
gutturals in C1 and coronal stops in C2.

In *HEB*:
coronal obstruents as a group or gutturals in C1 and velars in C2.

C. *Root patterns with both labials and coronal sonorants*

a) *Labials in C1 and coronal sonorants in C2 or C3*
   In *AR* and *HEB*:
1) labials in C1, coronal sonorants in C2 and coronal obstruents as a group velars or gutturals in C3,
2) labials in C1, coronal sonorants in C3 and coronal stops, coronal obstruents as a.group or gutturals in C2.

   In *AR*:
1) labials in C1, coronal sonorants in C2 and coronal stops in C3,
2) labials in C1, coronal sonorants in C3 and coronal fricatives or velars in C2.

   In *HEB*:
labials in C1, coronal sonorants in C2 and coronal fricatives in C3

b) *Labials in C2 and coronal sonorants in C1 or C3*
   In *AR* and *HEB*:
1) labials in C2, coronal sonorants in C1 and coronal fricatives or coronal obstruents as a group in C3,
2) labials in C2, coronal sonorants in C3 and coronal stops coronal obstruents as a group or velars in C1.

c) *Labials in C3 and coronal sonorants in C1 or C2*
   In *AR* and *HEB*:
1) labials in C3, coronal sonorants in C1 and coronal obstruents as a group, velars or gutturals in C2,
2) labials in C3, coronal sonorants in C2 and coronal obstruents as a group, velars or gutturals in C1.
   In *AR*:
1) labials in C3, coronal sonorants in C1 and coronal fricatives in C2,
2) labials in C3, coronal sonorants in C2 and coronal fricatives in C1.

In *HEB*:
labials in C3, coronal sonorants in C1 and coronal stops in C2.

6.7.3 *Summary of the findings for the preferred root patterns with three specified consonant groups*

A root pattern with three specified root positions exhibits true combinatory co-occurrence preferences if it remains preferred for all of the theoretically possible permutations of its consonant groups. Such root patterns do not occur. However, preferred root patterns with three specified root positions exist in which only two consonant groups classified on the basis of Manner or on that of Place can be permuted. These root patterns exhibit what could be termed partial combinatory preferences. All other preferred root patterns with three specified root positions are subject to ordering co-occurrence preference.

A) *Partial combinatory co-occurrence preferences on the basis of Manner*

In *AR* and *HEB*:
1) nasals in positions C1 or C2, when combined with voiceless stops and voiceless fricatives or with stops as a group and fricatives as a group,
2) liquids in any of the three positions, when combined with stops as a group and fricatives as a group,
3) fricatives as a group in C2, when combined with nasals and liquids.

In *HEB*:
liquids in any of the three positions, when combined with voiceless stops and voiceless fricatives.

B) *Partial combinatory co-occurrence preferences on the basis of Place*

In *AR* and *HEB*:
1) labials in one of the three positions and combined with either coronal obstruents as a group and coronal sonorants or with coronal obstruents as a group and gutturals,
2) coronal sonorants in C1 or C2, when combined with coronal stops and gutturals.

In *AR*:
1) labials in C1 or C2, when combined with coronal obstruents as a group and gutturals,

2) coronal sonorants in C1 or C2, when combined with coronal fricatives and gutturals.

In *HEB*:
coronal sonorants in C1 or C2, when combined with coronal fricatives as a group and velars.

There is no doubt that root patterns which contain three specified positions which exhibit co-occurrence preferences are very frequent in both *AR* and *HEB*. However, it is difficult to decide from *Tables 6.9 to 6.12* and from the description of the results in § 6.7.1 and § 6.7.2 whether phonological or statistical factors are involved in the co-occurrence preferences. In § 7.5 and ch. 8 these findings will be rearranged in a specific fashion in an attempt to find a phonological explanation for this phenomenon or to provide suggestions for further work along these lines.

6.8 *Triliteral root patterns with three specified positions which contain an individual labial or coronal sonorant*

In view of the findings described in § 6.7, it became of interest to determine to what degree the individual sonorants contribute to the co-occurrence preferences for the root patterns with three specified root positions. For this purpose, root patterns were studied which contain the labial sonorant /m/ or one of the coronal sonorants /n/, /l/ or /r/ in one position and any of the consonant groups classified on the basis of Manner or Place in the other two positions. Again, only *AR* and *HEB* were studied. These types of root patterns constitute smaller subsets of the larger sets with three specified root positions which contain the groups of the nasals, liquids, labials or coronal sonorants. The frequencies of many of these subsets are rather small. For this reason the consonants were subdivided again into groups as in § 5.8. *Tables 6.13 and 6.14* show the findings.

6.8.1 *Consonant groups classified on the basis of Manner*

Table 6.13 shows the preferred root patterns classified on the basis of Manner. They contain a labial or a coronal sonorant in one position and all of them exhibit ordering preferences. In the description below the sequences of the pairs of consonant groups figure in the order in which they occur in these root patterns in addition to the sonorant. The following preferred root patterns were found:

In *AR* and *HEB*:

The sequence of stops followed by fricatives and:

1) /m/ in C2,
2) /n/ or /r/ in C1 or C2,
3) /l/ in C2.

The sequence of fricatives followed by stops and:

4) /m/ in C1,
5) /n/ in C2,
6) /l/ in C1, C2 or C3,
7) /r/ in C2 or C3.
8) /l/ in C3 with nasals and fricatives.

In *AR*:

/m/ in:

1) C2 with liquids followed by fricatives,
2) C3 with liquids followed by stops.

/n/ in:

1) C1 with fricatives followed by stops, fricatives or liquids,
2) C2 with stops or fricatives followed by glides,
3) C3 with liquids followed by stops.

/l/ in:

C1 with stops followed by nasals.

/r/ in:

1) C2 with stops in two positions,
2) C3 with fricatives in two positions,
3) C3 with stops followed by fricatives,
4) C3 with nasals followed by fricatives.

In *HEB*:

/m/ in:

1) C1 with fricatives followed by liquids,
2) C3 with liquids or glides followed by fricatives.

/n/ in:

C3 with liquids followed by fricatives.

/l/ in:
1) C1 with fricatives followed by nasals,
2) C3 with stops followed by fricatives.

/r/ in:
C1 with fricatives followed by nasals.

6.8.2 *Consonant groups classified on the basis of Place*

Table 6.14 shows the preferred triliteral root patterns with three specified positions on the basis of Place. They contain a labial or a coronal sonorant in one position and all of them exhibit ordering preferences. In the description below the position of the sonorant is given
and the sequence of the two consonant groups in the two remaining
positions.

In *AR* and *HEB*:
/m/ in:
1) C1 with coronal obstruents followed by velars,
2) C1 with gutturals followed by coronal obstruents,
3) C2 with coronal obstruents followed by coronal sonorants or
   gutturals,
4) C2 or C3 with velars or gutturals followed by coronal obstruents,
5) C2 with velars followed by gutturals,
6) C3 with coronal sonorants followed by gutturals.

/n/ in:
1) C1 with coronal obstruents followed by velars or gutturals,
2) C1 or C2 with velars followed by coronal obstruents,
3) C2 with gutturals followed by velars,
4) C3 with coronal obstruents followed by labials.

/l/ in:
1) C1 or C3 with labials followed by coronal obstruents,
2) C1 with gutturals followed by labials, coronal obstruents or velars,
3) C2 with labials followed by velars or gutturals,
4) C2 with coronal obstruents followed by gutturals,
5) C2 with velars or gutturals followed by labials,
6) C3 with coronal obstruents followed by labials,
7) C3 velars followed by labials.

/r/ in:
1) C1, C2 and C3 with labials followed by and coronal obstruents,
2) C1 with coronal obstruents, velars or gutturals followed by labials,
3) C2 or C3 with labials followed by velars,
4) C2 with coronal obstruents followed by velars,
5) C2 with velars followed by coronal obstruents,
6) C2 with gutturals followed by coronal obstruents or velars,
7) C3 with coronal obstruents followed by gutturals and in the reverse order

In *AR*:
/m/ in:
1) C1 with coronal obstruents followed by gutturals,
2) C1 with gutturals followed by coronal sonorants or velars,
3) C3 with coronal obstruents followed by coronal sonorants or gutturals,
4) C3 with coronal sonorants followed by velars.

/n/ in:
1) C1 with coronal obstruents followed by coronal sonorants,
2) C1 with velars followed by gutturals,
3) C1 with gutturals followed by coronal obstruents,
4) C2 with gutturals followed by glides,
5) C3 with coronal obstruents followed by gutturals and in the reverse order.

/l/ in:
1) C1 with labials followed by velars,
2) C1 with velars followed by labials or gutturals,
3) C2 with coronal obstruents followed by velars and in the reverse order,
4) C2 with gutturals followed by velars,
5) C3 with coronal obstruents followed by coronal sonorants or gutturals
6) C3 with gutturals followed by coronal obstruents.

/r/ in:
1) C1, C2 or C3 with velars followed by coronal obstruents or gutturals,
2) C1 with velars followed by gutturals,

3) C1 with gutturals and glides,
4) C2 with labials followed by gutturals and the reverse,
5) C2 or C3 with coronal obstruents followed by labials or gutturals,
6) C3 with velars followed by coronal obstruents.

In *HEB*:
/m/ in:
C3 with glides followed by coronal obstruents.

/n/ in:
1) C2 with coronal obstruents followed by gutturals,
2) C2 with velars followed by labials.

/l/ in:
1) C1 with gutturals followed by glides,
2) C2 with labials followed by coronal obstruents,
3) C2 with velars followed by gutturals,
4) C3 with coronal obstruents followed by velars,
5) C3 with gutturals followed by velars.

/r/ in:
1) C1 with coronal obstruents followed by gutturals,
2) C3 with coronal obstruents followed by velars,
3) C3 with gutturals followed by velars.

6.8.3 *Summary of the findings for the triliterals with three specified positions and a labial or a coronal sonorant*

The findings indicate that with respect to co-occurrence preferences on the basis of either Manner or Place there is only a limited degree of patterning of the nasals /m/ and /n/ or of the coronal sonorants /n/, /l/ and /r/. I shall return to these observations in § 8.6.

6.9 *Co-occurrence preferences among the quadriliterals of the type C1C2C3C3*

The root patterns of this type form an interesting group. Their file in *AR* contains only four roots (see *Tables 4.7.1 and 4.8.1*), which is too small for a meaningful study. In *HEB*, however, it contains 131 roots and only this file was studied. Many of these roots arose in *MIH*. The distribution of the consonant groups over the four root positions in this relatively small file is rather skewed. Because of the small size of this file a statistical analysis was not useful and only the observed frequencies of the different types of root patterns are discussed. *Tables 6.15 and 6.16* show my findings for this file in *HEB*.

The root patterns were grouped both on the basis of Manner and on that of Place. Over one third of the file consists of roots with liquids in root positions C3 and C4 (51) and over one half are roots with coronal sonorants in this position (68). For the individual coronal sonorants in positions C3 the values are 17 for /n/, 21 for /l/ and 30 for /r/. Apparently, a reduplication of the consonant which is present in position C3 to position C4 has taken place in these types of quadriliterals and it occurred preferably for the coronal sonorants.

In general, the distribution of the different consonant groups in positions C1 and C2 is rather even. For the root patterns with /r/ in root positions C3 and C4, however, the number of voiceless stops and fricatives and of coronal fricatives in position C1 is relatively large and that is also the case for voiceless stops and fricatives and for labials in position C2.

Many roots of the type C1C2C3C3 are new verbs which arose in *MIH* and they often have roughly the same meaning as the corresponding triliteral root from which they originated. Still others seem to add a causative meaning to the triliteral root. A more detailed phonological study of the properties of these roots may be worthwile, but it would fall outside the scope of the present investigation.

CHAPTER SEVEN

CO-OCCURRENCE RESTRICTIONS AND CO-OCCURRENCE PREFERENCES IN ARABIC AND HEBREW. REFINEMENT AND SUMMARY OF THE FINDINGS

7.1 *Introductory remarks*

This chapter is intended to refine and summarize my findings which I described in chs. 5 and 6. In ch. 8 I shall make an attempt to provide phonological explanations for these findings, taking into account some of the most recent theoretical developments concerning verbal root structure in Arabic and Hebrew.

When studying the co-occurrence relationships of root patterns in Arabic and Hebrew, one should bear in mind that there is a relationship between co-occurrence restrictions and co-occurrence preferences. Avoidance and preference are two sides of the same coin. This implies that if certain root patterns are avoided, other root patterns should be preferred, and vice versa. If there are indications that phonological factors are involved, one should therefore determine whether either the avoidance or the preference, or even both of them, can be explained phonologically or should be due to chance. This will be a major consideration in § 7.5 of the present chapter and in ch. 8.

For the purpose of the present chapter it is necessary to give a more detailed description of the properties of the different root patterns. This requires that in this chapter the tables show the observed (No) and expected frequencies (Ne) of occurrence and also the levels of significance for the difference between these two frequencies (P). Avoidance and preference are marked by '-' and '+' signs, respectively (Si). Blanks in the P-column's indicate expected frequencies. For lack of room the Z-values are not shown.

7.2 *Co-occurrence restrictions on triliterals with two specified root positions*

7.2.1 *Restrictions on pairs of consonant groups*

Some consonant groups and some individual consonants are subject to positional constraints or to positional preferences (see § 5.3.1. and

§ 5.3.2). This has led to Conclusion 1 in § 5.3.2. The co-occurrence restrictions on pairs of consonants in the triliteral verbal roots of *AR*, *BH* and *HEB* were characterized in ch. 5 by the following two types of Morpheme Structure Constraints (MSC's): combinatory and ordering constraints. Although cases of absolute combinatory constraints do exist (see § 5.4.1), the large majority of both combinatory and ordering constraints are relative (statistical). This implies that there always are exceptions to such constraints.

7.2.1.1 *Co-occurrence restrictions on the basis of Manner*

7.2.1.1.1 *Pairs of consonant groups classified on the basis of Manner*

The findings on the basis of Manner described in § 5.4.2 (see also *Table 5.3*) lead to the following conclusions:

Conclusion 1. *Pairs of stops, fricatives, or liquids in the triliteral root patterns of AR, BH and HEB are subject to very strong combinatory constraints. This is also the case for two nasals or two glides in adjacent positions*[1].

Conclusion 2. *Pairs of obstruents in the triliteral root patterns of AR, BH and HEB that differ in the feature [α cont] are not avoided.*

However, the situation with respect to the role of the feature [α cont] in root patterns classified on the basis of Manner is more complicated, as will become clear in § 7.5.1 from the discussion of the root patterns with three specified root positions.

When voicing differences are taken into account, there are the following constraints on pairs of consonant groups:

1) in *AR* and *HEB*: voiced stops in C1, followed by voiceless stops in C2 (ordering constraint),
2) in *AR* and *BH*: voiceless fricatives in C1 followed by voiced fricatives in C2 (ordering constraint).
3) in *HEB*: voiceless and voiced fricatives (almost complete combinatory constraint).

---

[1] Not avoided are stops in nonadjacent positions in *AR*, nasals in the adjacent positions C2C3 in *BH* and glides in nonadjacent positions in all three languages. The number of roots with two glides is very small indeed, and so are their expected frequencies.

These findings lead to the following conclusion:

Conclusion 3. *Voice does not play a role in the co-occurrence restrictions on pairs of stops or fricatives in the triliterals.*

A consonant pair consisting of nasals followed by liquids in root positions C1C2 is subject to an ordering constraint. I shall return to this finding in the discussion of the relationship between the labial and coronal sonorants in § 8.6.

7.2.1.1.2 *Pairs of individual labial or coronal sonorants and consonant groups classified on the basis of Manner*

Table 5.7 (see § 5.6.1.2) showed that very strong combinatory constraints hold with regard to the following consonant pairs:

1) /l/ or /r/ with liquids.
2) /n/ and liquids or nasals in adjacent positions.
    An ordering constraint was found for nasals followed by the labial /m/ in adjacent positions. Nasals as a group are also subject to co-occurrence restrictions, as are the coronal sonorants (see § 7.2.1.1.1). These findigs suggest that the following conclusion can be drawn:

Conclusion 4. *In the co-occurrence restrictions on root patterns which contain a pair consisting of an individual labial or coronal sonorant and a consonant group classified on the basis of Manner two identity classes appear to exist:*
a) nasals: /m/ and /n/.
b) coronal sonorants: /n/, /l/ and /r/.

I shall return to this conclusion in more detail in § 8.6.

7.2.1.2 *Co-occurrence restrictions on the basis of Place*

7.2.1.2.1 *Pairs of consonant groups classified on the basis of Place*

The findings described in § 5.4.2.1 (see *Table 5.4*) show that pairs of consonants which belong to the same group on the basis of Place are subject to very strong co-occurrence restrictions in all three languages. This leads to the following conclusion:

Conclusion 5. *Very strong combinatory constraints apply to consonant pairs in the root patterns of AR, BH and HEB which consist of adjacent or nonadjacent labials, coronal stops, coronal fricatives, coronal obstruents as a group, coronal sonorants, velars or pharyngeals/laryngeals[2].*

In addition, certain root patterns which contain pairs of consonants which belong to different consonant groups on the basis of Place also are subject to co-occurrence restrictions. This leads to the following conclusions:

Conclusion 6. *Adjacent pairs consisting of uvular fricatives and either velars or pharyngeals/laryngeals are subject to combinatory constraints in AR and this is also the case for pairs of uvular fricatives and pharyngeals/laryngeals in nonadjacent positions.*

Conclusion 7. *In AR adjacent pairs of coronal stops and coronal fricatives are subject to combinatory constraints. In BH and HEB ordering constraints exist on pairs of coronal stops followed by coronal fricatives in the adjacent positions C1C2.*

Conclusion 7 suggests that the following conclusion can be drawn:

Conclusion 8. *The feature [cont] does not seem to play a role in the co-occurrence restrictions on pairs of coronal obstruents grouped on the basis of Place.*

As will be shown in § 8.4, the feature [cont] is involved, however, in the co-occurrence relationships in root patterns with three specified positions which contain coronal obstruents.

7.2.1.2.2 *Pairs of individual labial or coronal sonorants and consonant groups classified on the basis of Place*

Very strong combinatory constraints were found for the following root patterns (see *Table 5.8*):

1) Labials as a group with /m/.
2) The coronal sonorants as a group with the individual coronal sonorants /n/, /l/ and /r/.

---

[2] A pair of uvular fricatives is avoided in *AR* only in positions C1C2.

From this the following conclusion can be drawn:

Conclusion 9. *In the co-occurrence restrictions on root patterns with two specified positions with an individual labial or coronal sonorant and consonant groups classified on the basis of Place, /m/ patterns with the labials and /n/ with the other coronal sonorants /l/ and /r/.*

Interestingly, root patterns which contain /l/ followed by a coronal stop or a coronal fricative are subject to co-occurrence restrictions in *BH*. This could be due to the coronality of /l/. These and other properties of the labial and coronal sonorants are discussed in § 8.6.

7.2.1.2.3. *Pairs consisting of individual labial and coronal sonorants*

Tables 7.1 and 7.2.1 to 7.2.3 show the properties of root patterns with individual labials and coronal sonorants[3]. The root patterns with the same labial or the same coronal sonorant in positions C2 and C3 are omitted, because they are Mediae Geminatae, which were studied as a separate file.

The findings shown in these tables should be interpreted with care, because in many cases both No and Ne are so low that when avoidance is found for a root pattern this may be due to an accidental gap (see § 4.4). This is particularly the case for *BH* with its relatively small file of triliterals. However, the following general picture clearly emerges:

1) Root patterns with two individual labials in adjacent positions are subject to very strong co-occurrence restrictions. However, root patterns with nonadjacent labials often have expected frequencies.
2) The same applies to root patterns with a pair of individual coronal sonorants and particularly, with a pair consisting of the liquids /l/ and /r/. To a lesser extent, this is also the case for pairs of /n/ and one of the liquids /l/ and /r/.
3) Almost all pairs of the labial /m/ and any of the coronal sonorants (including /n/) have expected frequencies.

This leads to the following conclusion:

Conclusion 10. *In the co-occurrence restrictions which hold with respect to*

---

[3] See also § 5.6.1.1 and *Tables 5.5 and 5.6* for these types of root patterns.

the root patterns with two adjacent sonorants, /m/ strictly behaves as a labial and /n/ as a coronal sonorant.

I shall return to this in § 8.6.

7.3. Co-occurrence preferences for triliterals

7.3.1. Root patterns with two specified positions

The cases of co-occurrence preferences for root patterns of these types are described in § 6.2 and *Tables 6.1 and 6.2*. Root patterns which contain consonant pairs from the same group classified on the basis of Manner or Place are subject to combinatory constraints (Conclusions 1 and 5 in § 7.2.1.1). This is also the case for a number of root patterns that contain consonant pairs from two different groups classified on the basis of Place (Conclusion 6). However, most of the preferred root patterns with consonant pairs from different groups classified on either basis exhibit ordering preferences. In the large majority of these root patterns these consonant groups are in adjacent positions and the discussion in the present section will be limited to these root patterns.

7.3.1.1. Preferences on the basis of Manner

The findings shown in *Table 6.1* led to Conclusions 1 and 2 in § 6.2.3. The following generalizations can be made:

Conclusion 11. *Consonant pairs on the basis of Manner which exhibit combinatory or ordering preferences in adjacent positions almost exclusively contain nasals or liquids and, in addition, stops or fricatives.*

Conclusion 12. *Such consonant pairs with nasals or liquids and, in addition, voiceless or voiced obstruents exhibit combinatory preferences, but they tend to be scattered between AR and HEB and only few occur in BH.*

From Conclusion 12 follows:

Conclusion 13. *There is no indication that Voice plays a role in combinatory or ordering preferences for root patterns with two specified positions on the basis of Manner.*

In § 7.5.1.1 my findings are discussed for the preferred root patterns classified on the basis of Manner, with three specified positions and which contain nasals or liquids. These findings will provide a clearer picture of the role of nasals and liquids may play in co-occurrence preferences on the basis of Manner.

7.3.1.2. *Preferences on the basis of Place*

7.3.1.2.1. *Comparison of root patterns with coronal stops or coronal fricatives*

Table 7.3 shows the root patterns in *AR*, *BH* and *HEB* with two specified positions which contain adjacent pairs consisting of coronal stops, coronal fricatives or coronal obstruents as a group and members from one of the other consonant groups. Arbitrary consonants are present in the remaining position[3]. Root patterns with glides were excluded from these tables for reasons discussed in § 2.2.

The preferred root patterns with either coronal stops or coronal fricatives are rather scattered and they occur mainly in *AR* and *HEB* and often only in one of these two languages. This makes it difficult to decide whether the feature [cont] plays a role. However, the root patterns with three specified positions which are discussed in § 7.5.2.1.1 indicate that this feature may play some role.

7.3.1.2.2 *Root patterns with coronal obstruents as a group and other consonant groups*

Consonant pairs on the basis of Place which exhibit combinatory preferences occur only in adjacent positions and, as was shown in *Table 6.2*, they are in part scattered among the three languages. Still the following conclusion can be drawn:

Conclusion 14. *Most root patterns with two specified positions on the basis of Place which show combinatory preferences contain the following pairs:*
a) labials and coronal obstruents.
b) coronal sonorants and coronal obstruents, velars, pharyngeals / laryngeals or uvular fricatives.
c) coronal obstruents and pharyngeals / laryngeals or uvular fricatives.

---

[3] The root patterns shown in *Table 7.3* can also be found in *Table 6.2*.

Ordering preferences of consonant pairs on the basis of Place occur in both adjacent and nonadjacent positions. They are rather varied and exhibit considerable scattering among the three languages. In spite of this, the following more general conclusion can be drawn from Conclusions 11, 12 and 14 (see for the former two also Conclusion 3 in ch. 6):

Conclusion 15. *In most cases, the preferred consonant pairs of triliterals on the basis of Manner contain nasals or liquids and on the basis of Place they contain labials or coronal sonorants.*

In view of Conclusion 15 it became of interest to obtain information on root patterns with pairs consisting of one of the consonant groups and an individual labial or coronal sonorant. These root patterns are discussed in § 7.3.1.2.3.

7.3.1.2.3 *Triliteral root patterns with an individual labial or coronal sonorant and one of the consonant groups*

These preferred root patterns were described in § 6.3 and in *Tables 6.3 and 6.4*. I have rearranged this material according to the individual labial or coronal sonorant which is present in the consonant pair. This rearranged material on the basis of Manner is shown in *Table 7.4* for pairs in the adjacent positions C1C2 and C2C3 on the basis of Manner and in *Table 7.5* for similar pairs on the basis of Place. In these tables the stops and the fricatives are not subdivided with respect to voice and the coronal obstruents are not subdivided into coronal stops and fricatives.

On the basis of Manner, preferred root patterns with /m/ only contain fricatives, while those with /n/ also contain stops. On the basis of Place, /m/ and coronal obstruents exhibit combinatory preferences in positions C2C3 in *AR* and *HEB*. Preferred root patterns with /n/ occur with coronal obstruents, velars and uvular fricatives and in these root patterns /n/ usually precedes the consonant group. This leads to the following conclusion:

Conclusion 16. *In preferred root patterns with two specified positions /m/ and /n/ do not behave as an identity class, neither on the basis of Manner nor on that of Place.*

On the basis of Manner, stops and /r/ in the adjacent positions C1C2 and C2C3 show combinatory preferences[4]. Fricatives and /l/ exhibit combinatory preferences in C2C3 in *AR*, while in *HEB* the only preferred root pattern is that with /r/ in C1 and fricatives in C2. As a rule, in at least two of the three languages more root patterns on the basis of Place, which contain /r/ adjacent to coronal obstruents or velars are preferred than similar root patterns which contain /l/. There are other differences between these liquids with respect to the preferred root patterns. In general, however, in cases where a root pattern with one of the liquids is preferred, its observed frequency with the other liquid is usually higher than its expected one, although not significantly so. The properties of the root patterns with /n/ differ considerably with respect to preference from those with /r/ and /l/. From these facts the following conclusion can be drawn:

Conclusion 17. *The properties of the liquids /l/ and /r/ in preferred root patterns with two specified positions classified on the basis of either Manner or Place differ to some extent, but they still tend to pattern as an identity class. On the other hand, /n/ in these root patterns does not pattern with the liquids and only in part with /m/.*

7.4 *Co-occurrence relationships of the quadriliterals with two specified root positions*

In this section I shall discuss the cases of co-occurrence restrictions and preferences which hold with respect to the quadriliteral root patterns. In § 6.9 I already discussed the root patterns of the type C1C2C3C3.

7.4.1 *Quadriliterals different from C1C2C1C2 or C1C2C3C3*

As shown in § 5.8 and *Tables 5.10 and 5.11*, a number of quadriliterals which contain two specified root positions and which are not of the types C1C2C1C2 or C1C2C3C3 were found to exhibit combinatory or ordering constraints on adjacent positions. In addition, cases of combinatory and ordering preferences were found to exist for nonadjacent positions (see § 6.5 and *Tables 6.7 and 6.8*). *Tables 7.6 and*

---

[4] However, not in C1C2 in *BH.*

7.7 summarize the findings which are important for a more detailed discussion in this section.

a) *Co-occurrence restrictions*

Pairs of consonants from the same group on the basis of Manner in the adjacent positions C1C2, C2C3 and C3C4 were found to be subject to combinatory constraints. These constraints apply to a pair of liquids in *AR* and *HEB*, to stops or fricatives mainly in positions C2C3, but not to fricatives in *AR*. In *HEB* they apply also to nasals, but only in positions C1C2 and C2C3. On the basis of Place, the combinatory constraints on pairs of consonants from the same group in adjacent positions are more universal, in particular, for labials or coronal sonorants. In addition, such constraints exist in *HEB* for adjacent pairs of coronal obstruents[5] and also of velars. Gutturals show these constraints in both *AR* and *HEB*, but only in positions C1C2.

The most likely explanation for these findings may be as follows:

Conclusion 18. *The combinatory constraints on consonant groups from the same groups classified on the basis of Manner or Place in the adjacent positions of the quadriliterals are due to an effect similar to that which acts on the triliterals.*

Ordering constraints on the basis of either Manner or Place are rather atypical: they occur either in *AR* or in *HEB*. The files of the quadriliterals are relatively small (336 in *AR* and 765 in *HEB*). As a consequence, the observed and expected frequencies for many of the different root patterns are also small. Therefore, some these of ordering constraints may well be due to accidental gaps.

b) *Co-occurrence preferences*

Combinatory preferences on the basis of Manner are found in *AR* for pairs of stops, fricatives, nasals or liquids in the nonadjacent positions C1C3. Combinatory preferences for pairs of consonants belonging to different groups are found in *HEB* for adjacent pairs of stops and liquids in positions C1C2, C2C3 and C3C4.

---

[5] But in *AR* only in positions C3C4.

Ordering preferences on the basis of Manner occur in *AR* for quadriliterals with stops in C2 and liquids in C3 and in the reverse order in positions C3C4. A root pattern with nasals in C2 and liquids in C4 exhibits an ordering preference in *AR* and *HEB*.

On the basis of Place, a pair of coronal obstruents in positions C1C3 is subject to combinatory preference in *AR* and *HEB* and, only in *HEB*, also in positions C2C4. Cases of ordering preferences do not occur on this basis. This leads to the following conclusion:

Conclusion 19. *Consonant groups from the same groups classified on the basis of Manner or of Place in the quadriliterals tend to be subject to combinatory preferences in nonadjacent positions.*

In § 8.8 a comparison will be made between the cases of co-occurrence constraints and co-occurrence preferences of the triliterals and the quadriliterals.

7.4.2. *Quadriliterals of the type C1C2C1C2*

Root positions C1 and C3 contain the same consonant in the quadriliterals of this type and so do positions C2 and C4. Because of this, the co-occurrence relationships in these root patterns turn out to be the same for the adjacent positions C1C2 and C2C3. Therefore, I described these relationships in § 5.9 and §6.6 only for positions C1C2. The number of quadriliteral roots of this type is small: only 130 occur in *AR* and 174 in *HEB* (see *Table 2.3*). This results in low observed and expected frequencies of the different groups of root patterns. Still it is of interest to discuss some of the findings. In *Table 7.8* the root patterns are shown which contain consonant pairs from the same group classified on the basis of Manner or Place in adjacent positions. It is clear that there is a tendency for such pairs of consonants to exhibit combinatory constraints in these positions, particularly in the case of consonant groups classified on the basis of Place. This constraint parallels that found in the triliterals. This is not surprising, since, as has been said already in § 5.9, such quadriliterals would contain consonants from the same group in all of their four root positions.

7.5. *Co-occurrence preferences for triliterals with three specified root positions*

In this section I shall discuss the subsets of root patterns which contain consonant groups classified on the basis of Manner or Place in their three root positions. They are subsets of larger sets of root patterns with specific consonant groups in two positions and with arbitrary consonants in the remaining position. These larger sets will also be discussed.

The observed and expected frequencies of root patterns with three specified positions are often relatively small. In such cases, statistical calculations may yield unreliable results (see § 4.4). For this reason the stops and the fricatives were not subdivided into voiced and voiceless consonants. For the same reason, the coronal obstruents were not subdivided into coronal stops and fricatives, except in the case of the findings which are discussed in § 7.5.2.1.1. In addition, the uvular fricatives and the pharyngeals/laryngeals in *AR* were combined into the group of the gutturals.

In the present section, the findings which were described in § 6.7 and § 6.8 and in *Tables 6.9 to 6.14* are rearranged in another series of tables. This was done to bring out the salient points more clearly and to facilitate the discussion.

7.5.1. *Preferences on the basis of Manner*

7.5.1.1. *Root patterns with three specified consonants groups*

The tables of this section show the root patterns which contain the following consonant groups in two of their three positions:

1) stops (*Table 7.9.1*),
2) fricatives (*Table 7.9.2*),
3) a pair of stops and fricatives (*Tables 7.10.1 and 7.10.2*),
4) either nasals or liquids adjacent to stops or fricatives (*Tables 7.11.1 to 7.11.4*),
5) nasals as well as liquids (*Tables 7.12*).

7.5.1.1.1. *Root patterns with either stops or fricatives in two positions*

Tables 7.9.1 and 7.9.2 show that the larger sets of root patterns with either two stops or two fricatives and arbitray consonants in the re-

maining position are subject to combinatory constraints[6] (see also
§ 5.4.2.1). As can be seen, this is largely due to the root patterns which
contain either three stops or three fricatives. The root patterns which
contain two stops and one fricative or the reverse also contribute to
the combinatory constraints, especially in *AR*, but they do so to a lesser
extent. They either are significantly avoided or their observed frequencies are smaller than their expected ones, but not significantly so.

None of the root patterns which contain nasals and either two stops
or two fricatives are preferred. They have expected frequencies and
some of them even tend to be avoided, but not significantly so. The
root patterns of this type which are preferred contain liquids: (st)(li)(st)
in *AR* and *HEB*, (fr)(li)(fr) and (fr)(fr)(li) in *AR* and (st)(st)(li) in *HEB*.
But they do not outweigh the avoided subsets of the larger sets to which
they belong and which in most cases are avoided. That a number of
these root patterns with liquids are preferred may therefore be due
to chance rather than to phonological factors.

It is clear that there is a tendency to avoid root patterns with three
obstruents, in particular, if they all share the feature [+cont] or [-cont].
I shall return to this point in § 8.4.

7.5.1.1.2. *Root patterns with both stops and fricatives*

Tables 7.10.1 and 7.10.2 show root patterns with three specified positions and with both stops and fricatives. The following subsets of this
type are preferred:

1) Nasals or liquids in C1 or C2[7],
2) Liquids in C3[8].

These root patterns are subsets of the larger sets with arbitrary consonants in one of their root positions. The only significantly preferred
larger sets are found in *HEB*: (st)(X)(fr) and (fr)(X)(st). Therefore, in
this language the avoided subsets are outweighed by the preferred
subsets (st)(na)((fr), (st)(li)(fr), (fr)(na)(st) and (fr)(li)(st). The other larger
sets are preferred, but not significantly so. This leads to the following
conclusion:

---

[6] The observed frequency of (st)(X)(st) in *AR* is smaller than its expected one,
but not significantly so.
[7] The root pattern (li)(st)(fr) in *AR* is not preferred, but its observed frequency
exceeds its expected one, but not significantly so.
[8] With nasals in C3 in *AR* and *HEB* the observed frequencies are larger that
the expected ones, but not significantly so.

Conclusion 20. *The root patterns with both stops and fricatives and with nasals or liquids in C2 in HEB may be preferred for phonological reasons. Most of the other preferred root patterns may be preferred rather by chance.*

7.5.1.1.3. Root patterns with nasals or liquids adjacent to stops or fricatives

Tables 7.11.1 to 7.11.4 show the preferred root patterns with both stops and fricatives and with nasals or liquids[9]. These root patterns are subsets of the larger sets which contain both stops and fricatives and have arbitrary consonants in the remaining position. The following of these larger sets are significantly preferred:

(na)(st)(X) in *HEB*,   (na)(fr)(X) in *AR* and *HEB*,
(li)(st)(X) in *AR* and *HEB*,   (li)(fr)(X) in *HEB*,

                                                          (fr)(na)(X) in *AR*,
(st)(li)(X) in *AR* and *HEB*,   (fr)(li)(X) in *AR*,

(X)(na)(fr) in *AR* and *HEB*,
(X)(li)(st) in *AR* and *HEB*,   (X)(li)(fr) in *AR* and *HEB*,

(X)(st)(li) in *AR* and *HEB*,   (X)(fr)(li) in *AR* and *HEB*.

The observed frequencies of the other larger sets are larger than their expected ones, but not significantly so[10]. The avoided subsets which belong to the larger sets (li)(st)(X), (st)(li)(X), (fr)(li)(st), (X)(li)(st), (X)(li)(fr) and (X)(st)(li) in *AR* and *HEB* and to (li)(fr)(X) and to (X)(fr)(li) in *AR* are neutralized by the preferred subsets. These facts together suggest that the following conclusion can be drawn:

Conclusion 21. *Most of root patterns with nasals or liquids adjacent to stops or fricatives are preferred. Phonological factors may cause the preference for such root patterns with nasals or liquids in C1 or C2 or for those with liquids in C3.*

---

[9] The root patterns with nasals in C3 in *AR* and *HEB* and (li)(st)(fr) in *AR* are not preferred, but their observed frequencies exceed their expected ones, but not significantly so.

[10] But for (X)(na)(st) its oberved frequency hardly differs from its expected one in both *AR* and *HEB*.

Apparently, there is a contradiction between Conclusions 20 and 21.
I shall discuss this in § 8.6.

7.5.1.1.4. *Root patterns with both nasals and liquids*

The root patterns which contain both nasals and liquids and, in addition, stops or fricatives are shown in *Table 7.12*. Among the four root
patterns with nonadjacent nasals and liquids the only preferred ones
are (li)(fr)(na) and (na)(fr)(li) in *AR* and *HEB* and (li)(st)(na) in *AR*. The
other root patterns in which the nasals and liquids are adjacent have
expected frequencies[11].

In § 8.6, I shall discuss some of the phonological consequences of
my findings with respect to the preferred root patterns which are
described in § 7.5.1.1.

7.5.1.2 *Root patterns with an individual labial or coronal sonorant and stops and/or fricatives*

I presented in *Table 6.13* the findings for the root patterns of these
types on the basis of Manner. I have rearranged them in *Tables 7.13
and 7.14* in order to facilitate the interpretation.

As shown in *Tables 7.10.1 and 7.10.2* the root patterns which have
nasals in C1 or C2 and also contain stops and fricatives are preferred.
Table 7.13 shows that this is also the case for the root patterns which
contain /m/ or /n/ in C1 or C2 instead of nasals, although their
observed and expected frequencies do not always differ significantly.
Root patterns with individual nasals in C1 and, in addition, either two
stops and two fricatives have expected frequencies (see *Table 7.14*). But
(n)(fr)(fr) is preferred, although only in *AR*. All other root patterns of
this type with /n/ or /m/ in C2 or C3 have expected frequencies.
These findings suggest that the following conclusion can be drawn:

Conclusion 22. *Root patterns with three specified positions, which contain
/m/ or /n/ and, in addition, stops and/or fricatives are rather similar with respect
to co-occurrence preference, but it is not unequivocally clear whether in these root
patterns these consonants form an identity class of nasals.*

---

[11] The root pattern (li)(na)(st) is even avoided in *HEB*.

Table 7.13 shows that root patterns which contain /r/ and both stops and fricatives are preferred in *AR* and *HEB*, except for (r)(fr)(st) in *AR* and *HEB* and (st)(fr)(r) in *HEB*, which have expected frequencies. Similar root patterns with /l/ instead of /r/ are also preferred in *AR* and *HEB*, except for (l)(st)(fr) in *AR* and *HEB* and (st)(fr)(l) in *AR.* In all cases, the root patterns with /r/ or /l/ which are not preferred have observed frequencies which are higher than the expected ones, but not significantly so. Thus, the properties of these types of root patterns with /r/ or /l/ are rather similar. However, the following root patterns with either two stops or two fricatives are preferred only in *AR* (see *Table 7.14*):

1) /r/ in C1 and two stops,
2) /r/ in C2 and two stops or two fricatives,
3) /r/ in C3 and two fricatives.

None of the corresponding root patterns with /l/ are preferred in either *AR* or *HEB*. They either have expected frequencies or their observed frequencies are somewhat larger than their expected ones, but not significantly so. That implies that the properties of such root patterns with /l/ and /r/ are similar but differ in some respects.

As is shown in *Tables 7.13 and 7.14* /n/ does not pattern clearly with /r/ and /l/ in the co-occurrence preferences. The following conclusion can be drawn:

Conclusion 23. *The root patterns with /r/ or /l/ and with both stops and fricatives have rather similar properties with respect to their co-occurrence preference and they tend to behave as an identity class of liquids. Certain root patterns with either two stops or two fricatives and /r/ are preferred, while those with /l/ are not. In these root patterns /r/ and /l/ do not behave as an identity class and /n/ does not pattern with either /r/ or /l/.*

These findings are discussed in § 8.6 from a wider perspective.

7.5.2 Preferences on the basis of Place

7.5.2.1 Root patterns with three specified consonants groups

For reasons mentioned above at the beginning of § 7.5 I shall discuss mainly root patterns which contain coronal obstruents as a group and in which the uvular fricatives and pharyngeals/laryngeals in *AR* are combined into the group of the gutturals. The only exception are those discussed in § 7.5.2.1.1.

The number of consonant groups with three positions specified on the basis of Place is larger than on that of Manner. As a consequence, the number of root patterns classified on the basis of Place is considerably larger than on that of Manner. This causes the mutual relationships of the preferred root patterns classified on the basis of Place to be more complicated than on that of Manner.

7.5.2.1.1 *Root patterns with coronal stops, coronal fricatives or coronal obstruents as a group*

I shall first pay attention to the root patterns classified on the basis of Place which contain in one position either coronal stops, coronal fricatives or coronal obstruents as a group and in the other two positions any of the consonant groups, except coronal obstruents (see *Tables 7.15.1 to 7.15.3*)[12]. The comparison of these root patterns leads to the following conclusions:

Conclusion 24. *There are no striking differences with respect to preferences between the root patterns which contain either coronal stops or coronal fricatives in C1 or in C2 and other specific consonant groups in the other two positions.*

Conclusion 25. *Significantly more of such root patterns are preferred with coronal fricatives in C3 than with coronal stops in this position and the former consonants are the main cause for the preference for root patterns with coronal obstruents as a group in C3. This suggests that the feature [continuant] may play a role in the co-occurrence preferences of obstruents.*

I shall return to these points in § 8.4.2.

7.5.2.1.2. *Root patterns with various consonant groups*

The total number of root patterns with three specified root positions (including those with coronal obstruents as a group) is 60, disregard-

---

[12] Because of the rather intractable behavior of the glides the root patterns which contain these consonants have been excluded from these tables and from the subsequent ones (see § 2.2).

ing those with glides or those which contain consonants from the same group in two or three positions. Out of this total, 18 are not preferred in either *AR* or *HEB*. In addition, there is 1 root pattern which is preferred only in *HEB* and 4 root patterns which are preferred only in *AR*. The root patterns which are not preferred have the following properties:

1) *Table 7.16* shows that 12 of the 18 root patterns which are not preferred contain both velars and gutturals and, in addition, either labials or coronal sonorants. Only 2 out of the 8 root patterns with adjacent velars and gutturals are preferred: (so)(ve)(gu) in *AR* and *HEB* and (gu)(ve)(so) only in *HEB*. However, among the 4 root patterns of this type in which the velars and gutturals are nonadjacent the following 3 are preferred in both *AR* and *HEB*: (ve)(la)(gu), (ve)(so)(gu) and (gu)(so)(ve). Only few of the 12 root patterns which are not preferred have observed frequencies slightly larger than the expected ones.

2) *Table 7.16* also shows that among the 6 root patterns which contain coronal obstruents, velars and gutturals only 2 are preferred: (co)(gu)(ve) with adjacent velars and gutturals only in *AR* and (gu)(co)(ve) with nonadjacent velars and gutturals only in *HEB*. The root patterns which are not preferred often have observed frequencies which are even slightly smaller than their expected ones. Out of the total of 60 root patterns with three specified positions these 6 root patterns are the only ones which contain neither glides nor labials, coronal sonorants or consonants from the same group in two or three of their positions.

The facts mentioned in these points 1 and 2 lead to the following conclusion:

Conclusion 26. *Preferred root patterns which contain both velars and gutturals are relatively rare, in particular if these consonants are adjacent. Most of these root patterns have expected frequencies.*

All root patterns with three specified root positions which contain ve and/or gu and which have expected frequencies are arranged in *Table 7.17* according to the consonant groups present in root positions C1 and C2 (*type 1*) or in positions C2 and C3 (*type 2*). The following *type 1* root patterns have a tendency to have expected frequencies[13]:

(la)(ve)(X)[14], (co)(ve)(X)[15], (ve)(gu)(X) and (gu)(ve)(X)[16].

The situation is less clear for the *type 2* root patterns. The following of these show a tendency to have expected frequencies:

(X)(ve)(so)[17] and (X)(la)(ve)[18].

These findings lead to the following tentative conclusion:

Conclusion 27. The *root patterns with three specified positions which are neither avoided nor preferred tend to contain the following consonant groups:*
1) adjacent velars and gutturals.
2) coronal obstruents, velars and gutturals.
3) velars in C2.

As it turns out, the great majority of the preferred root patterns on the basis of Place contain labials, coronal sonorants or both. There are 31 such root patterns in both *AR* and *HEB*, 4 only in *AR* and 1 only in *HEB* (see *Tables 7.18 and 7.19*). An important question which remains to be answered is whether the preference for these root patterns is due to phonological factors or to chance. Before making an attempt to answer this question, it is necessary to make a small digression by examining the root patterns with three specified positions which contain the same consonant groups in two or three of their positions. They are listed in *Tables 7.20.1 to 7.20.3*. As it turns out, virtually all root patterns with the same consonant groups in adjacent positions are avoided, as are most of those with such consonant groups in nonadjacent positions. Almost all of the root patterns of the latter type, if they are not not significantly avoided, have observed frequencies which are smaller than the expected ones, but not significantly

---

[13] X can be any of the consonant groups, except those which are present in any of the other two positions. The latter root patterns are strongly avoided (see the discussion later in this section).

[14] But (la)(ve)(so) is preferred in *AR*.

[15] But (co)(ve)(so) is preferred in *HEB*.

[16] For these two types see points 1 and 2 above.

[17] But (la)(ve)(so) is preferred in *AR* and (co)(ve)(so) and (gu)(ve)(so) in *HEB*).

[18] But (co)(la)(ve) is preferred in *HEB*.

so. It is to be expected that these avoided root patterns are compensated by other root patterns which are preferred. In § 7.5.1.1 I argued that the preference for certain root patterns with three specified positions on the basis of Manner may be due to phonological factors (see Conclusions 20 and 21). This involved the arrangement of the root patterns as subsets of larger sets. The situation is more complicated, however, in the case of the preferred root patterns which have three specified positions on the basis of Place, because the number of consonant groups classified on this basis is larger than on that of Manner. Nevertheless, I followed a similar procedure for the preferred root patterns classified on the basis of Place as in § 7.5.1.1 for those grouped on the basis of Manner.

In order to obtain some information on this point, these preferred root patterns were subjected to the following test. Each of the preferred root patterns which contain labials, coronal sonorants or both and other consonant groups in the remaining position(s) are placed on the top of a small list and they serve as 'source root patterns' for these lists. These lists consist of the root patterns which share the same consonant groups in two of their three root positions with the 'source root pattern', but differ in the consonant group in the remaining position. The members of such a list of root patterns also include the 'source root pattern'. They constitute subsets of the larger set of root patterns which contains the same two specified root positions and arbitrary consonants in the remaining position. These larger sets are also listed. As an example *Table 7.21* shows this procedure for three different preferred 'source root patterns': which contain in one position either labials or coronal sonorants or with two positions filled with labials and coronal sonorants. Five of the larger sets in this table are preferred in both *AR* and *HEB*: (co)(la)(X), (X)(co)(so), (gu)(co)(X), (X)(so)(ve), and (la)(X)(ve). Two larger sets are preferred only in *AR*: (co)(X)(ve) and (la)(so)(X). Two larger sets have expected frequencies and occur in both *AR* and *HEB*: (X)(la)(ve) and (gu)(X)(so).

In this way, I have investigated all possible subsets and larger sets. The results are summarized in *Table 7.22*. For each of the 'source root patterns' this table indicates whether the three larger sets to which it belongs have an expected frequency, are preferred or (in some cases) are avoided. For 'source root patterns', which contain either labials or coronal sonorants or both of these, about one half of the larger sets is preferred if the consonant group in C1 or in C3 is varied. This is the case for only one third or less of the larger sets which are related to preferred 'source root patterns' which either contain both velars and gutturals (*Table 7.23*) or coronal obstruents, velars as well as gutturals (*Table 7.24*). The proportion of preferred larger sets for which the consonant group in C2 in the source root patterns is varied is considerably lower. This suggests that position C2 may play a relatively unimportant role in the phonology of preference.

When one tries to determine whether the preference for root patterns on the basis of Place is due to phonological factors the following facts have to be taken into account:

1) There are preferred 'source root patterns' with three specified positions which give rise to larger sets with expected frequencies (see *Tables 7.22 and 7.23*). It seems probable that the preference for most or even all of these 'source root patterns' is not due to phonological factors, but is caused rather by chance. They would then serve to compensate the avoided root subsets in order to yield the larger sets which have expected frequences.

2) There are also subsets of root patterns with three specified positions which have expected frequencies but which still give rise to preferred larger sets: 3 in *AR* and *HEB* , 1 in *AR* and 2 in *HEB* (see *Tables 7.24 and 7.25*). Some larger sets are even avoided although they contain a preferred 'source root pattern'. This is the case for (ve)(gu)(la) and (ve)(gu)(co) in *AR* and for (ve)(gu)(so) in *HEB*.

In order to obtain information on the question whether phonological factors are involved in the preference for the root patterns classified on the basis of Place, I reasoned as follows. It seems likely that root patterns in *AR* and/or *HEB* which are preferred for phonological reasons will be found among the group of the preferred 'source root patterns' which belong to two or even three preferred larger sets. This group of 24 preferred root patterns is listed in *Table 7.26* according to the two root positions which they have in common. When this group (*group 1*) is compared to the 36 preferred root patterns which in both *AR* and *HEB* are members of fewer than two preferred larger sets (*group 2*) the following facts emerge:

1) *Group 1* root patterns have no velars in C1, while *group 2* contains 10 root patterns with velars in this position.

2) The 5 root patterns of *group 1* with labials in C1 have no velars or gutturals in C2. Among 5 such root patterns of *group 2* there are 2 with velars and 2 with gutturals in C2.

These facts suggest that the following tentative conclusion can be drawn:

Conclusion 28. *Root patterns with three specified positions classified on the basis of Place which are preferred for phonological reasons may have the following properties:*
1) Velars are absent in C1.
2) Labials in C1 are preferably followed in C2 by coronal obstruents and not by velars or gutturals.

7.5.2.2 *Root patterns with an individual labial or a coronal sonorant and two specific consonant groups*

Table 7.27 shows these types of root patterns classified on the basis of Manner. The properties of the root patterns which contain the liquids /l/ or /r/ are rather similar, although there are differences. The properties of root patterns with the nasals /m/ or /n/ differ more, but they also show some similarities and the same is the case if the root patterns with /n/ are compared to those with /l/ and /r/. Many of the differences between the root patterns with these consonants may be due to their low observed and expected frequencies. For this reason, the calculated levels of significance may not be very reliable (see § 4.4).

Tables 7.28.1 to 7.28.3 show these types of root patterns classified on the basis of Place. Listed in these tables are only the root patterns which are preferred in both *AR* and *HEB* or in only one of these two languages. In most cases both the observed and expected frequencies of these types of root patterns are also rather small. Yet, an overall picture does emerge. The properties of the root patterns with /l/ or /r/ are rather similar also on the basis of Place, but it is difficult to determine whether the properties of root patterns with /n/ resemble those with /l/ or /r/ or are rather more like those with the labial nasal /m/. These facts lead to the following conclusion:

Conclusion 29. *The coronal sonorants /r/ and /l/ in preferred root patterns with three specified positions classified on the basis of Manner or Place tend* *to behave as an identity class, but it is unclear whether /n/ patterns as a nasal or as a coronal sonorant.*

I shall discuss these findings and other evidence on nasals and liquids in § 8.6.

7.6 *Comparison of the Mediae Geminatae and the triliterals with three specified positions*

I made the observation in § 5.7 that the MG's with a pair of consonants from the same group on the basis of Manner in root positions C1C2 are not subject to co-occurrence restrictions. On the basis of Place, on the other hand, a variety of such restrictions were found in one or more of the three languages. Apparently, the MG's with consonant groups on the basis of Place are similar to the triliterals with respect to the co-occurrence restrictions on root positions C1C2[19]. In *Table 7.29.1* the root patterns are listed which have consonants from the same group on the basis of Manner in C2 and C3 from which the MG's are excluded. Similar root patterns classified on the basis of Place are listed in *Table 7.29.2*. In these tables a comparison is made between, on the one hand, the observed frequencies of the triliteral root patterns from which the MG's have been excluded and, on the other hand, the sum of these frequencies with those of the MG's which have the same consonant groups in C1 and C2 as in the triliterals. It can be seen that in most cases these sum values approach or even surpass the values of the expected frequencies for the root patterns from which the MG's have been excluded. It is clear that the following conclusion can be drawn:

Conclusion 30. *The constraints on consonants from the same group in root positions C2 and C3 of the triliterals are neutralized in the MG's.*

This is a natural consequence of the representation for the MG's as proposed by McCarthy (1979 and 1981). In his proposal there is only one consonant in these positions which is associated with two root nodes (see § 2.3.2).

---

[19] However, there are a number of MG's in *AR* and *BH* with different consonant groups in C1 and C2 which are preferred (see § 6.4).

CHAPTER EIGHT

THEORETICAL IMPLICATIONS

8.1 *Introduction*

The purpose of my study was to investigate the phonological basis of
the co-occurrence relationships of the consonants in the verbal roots
of *AR, BH* and *HEB*. Chs. 5 and 6 contain a detailed description of
my findings concerning the triliteral and quadriliteral root patterns and
the Mediae Geminatae. These findings were further refined and summarized in ch. 7. In the present and final chapter the theoretical
implications of my results will be discussed.

I shall start this discussion in § 8.2 by evaluating the potential of
the OCP (or the NBC) as an explanatory tool for my findings. The
co-occurrence relationships of the uvular stop /q/ with the velars and
the gutturals is important for the interpretation of my results. My work
has led me to propose a phonological representation for this consonant which differs in several respects from McCarthy's proposal. In
§ 8.3 I shall discuss the co-occurrence relationships of this consonant
with other consonants and my proposed representations for it and for
the velars and the gutturals. This will be followed in § 8.4 by a discussion of my findings concerning the role of the feature [continuant]
in the co-occurrence relationships of the consonant groups classified
on the basis of Manner or Place in root patterns with three specified
positions. My results indicate that the co-occurrence restrictions on
this feature cannot be explained by the OCP. In § 8.5 follows an analysis of a number of proposals to capture Sonority and Manner in
feature geometry, which leads in § 8.6 to an analysis of the co-occurrence relationships of the nasals, the liquids and the coronal sonorants.
In § 8.7 the properties of root patterns with three positions specified
on the basis of Place are discussed. In § 8.8 the properties of the triliterals and quadriliterals are compared. In § 8.9 explanations which have
been proposed for the co-occurrence restrictions which differ from the
OCP (NBC) are discussed. Some of the possible reasons for the fact
that most of the co-occurrence restrictions are statistical (relative) are
outlined in § 8.10. Finally, the results for *AR, BH* and *HEB* are compared in § 8.11 and some of the possible reasons for the differences

between the co-occurrence relationships of the consonants in these languages are enumerated in § 8.12.

8.2 *Co-occurrence restrictions, the OCP and the NBC*

In § 3.4 earlier studies by other authors were summarized which dealt with the co-occurrence restrictions on pairs of consonants in the verbal roots of Semitic. In general, my findings concerning this phenomenon confirm previous work on Arabic which was carried out by Cantineau, Greenberg and particularly the work by Yip and McCarthy.

Yip and McCarthy (see § 3.3.1 and § 3.3.2) showed that in *AR* pairs of consonants which possess the same Place Node, tend to be subject to combinatory constraints. These constraints also hold within the group of gutturals, which comprise the laryngeals, the pharyngeals and the uvular fricatives. They ascribe these co-occurrence restrictions to the Obligatory Contour Principle (OCP) or the No-branching Condition (NBC), which is supposed to act on individual Place features. In this approach, the verbal roots in the Semitic languages are considered to be nonconcatenous morphemes. The vowels form a separate morpheme which is specific for each binyan of the verb. The affixes constitute morphemes which are separate from both the root and the vowel morpheme. These different morphemes are located on separate tiers which are conflated into one tier at a later stage of the derivation. Ascribing the co-occurrence restrictions to an effect of the OCP or of the NBC on root consonants with common features requires that spreading of the features of the consonants and of whole consonant phonemes occurs only to the right. Indeed, in the Semitic languages many Mediae Geminatae exist which have identical consonants in root positions C2 and C3. McCarthy assumes that such roots arise by a phonological process of spreading of the consonant in root position C2 to C3, i.e. to the right. He based this concept of spreading to the right on the fact that in *AR* only one root of the type C1C1X exists: 'ddy', while many MG's are found. I will show in § 8.10.1 that the situation with respect to roots of the type C1C1C2 in *BH*, and particularly in *HEB*, is more complicated.

Like Yip and McCarthy, I will base the interpretation of my findings concerning the co-occurrence restrictions on the consonant groups in Arabic and Hebrew which are classified on the basis of Place on the OCP. I will show in § 8.4 that the situation with respect to the consonant groups on the basis of Manner is more complicated.

8.3 *The co-occurrence relationships of the uvular stop /q/*

In a recent paper McCarthy (1994) gives a series of phonological arguments in support of his proposal for the existence of an identity class of gutturals, comprising uvular fricatives, pharyngeals and laryngeals which does not include the velar stops. He characterized these gutturals as a group of consonants which all have the feature [pharyngeal]. His case for proposing this identity class of gutturals is very strong. The most important reasons for this proposal can be summarized as follows:

1) The co-occurrence restrictions act on the gutturals as a group in the verbal roots of Arabic.
2) Guttural Vowel Lowering in the basic derivational class of the Arabic verb.
3) Lowering of /i/ to /a/ after a guttural consonant in certain Bedouin dialects.
4) Epenthesis of /a/ to avoid syllable-final gutturals in other Bedouin dialects.
5) Vowel reduction to shwa in the initial syllable of a word in Tiberian Hebrew which leads to a vowel-colored shewa if this vowel is preceded by a guttural.
6) Insertion of an /a/ to follow a guttural or in front of a word final guttural in Tiberian Hebrew.
7) Guttural degemination occurs in Tiberian Hebrew and in Tigre, while gemination of other consonants is allowed.

A problem exists, however, with respect to the uvular stop /q/. In conformity with its place of articulation, it should be a uvular and also a guttural. But according to the information which was provided by McCarthy, the uvular stop /q/ behaves as a velar rather than as a uvular in its co-occurrence restrictions. He tried to explain this contradictory behavior of the uvular stop /q/ by proposing that the velar stops possess the feature [dorsal] and the gutturals the feature [pharyngeal] and that the uvular fricatives and the uvular stop posess both of these features. As is shown by his representations, reproduced in (1), he further assumed that true gutturals are approximants[1].

---

[1] The glottal stop probably excepted.

(1) *Low Gutturals* (ʔ,h,H,9)   *Uvular Gutturals* (x,g)

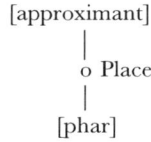

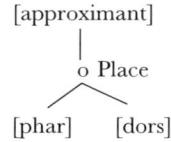

        [approximant]   [approximant]
            | |
          o Place   o Place
            | ╱‾‾‾╲
          [phar]   [phar]   [dors]

    Coronal Emphatics (T,D,S,V)   *Uvular Stop* (q)

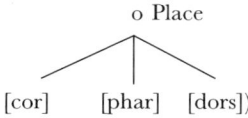

          o Place   o Place
        ╱‾‾‾|‾‾‾╲   ╱‾‾‾╲
  [cor]   [phar]   [dors])   [phar]   [dors]

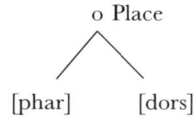

In view of the contradictory behavior of the uvular stop /q/ in Mc-
Carthy's approach I decided at an early stage of my study that it was
necessary to investigate this problem in more detail. For this purpose,
I studied the co-occurrence relationships (i.e., both avoidance and
preference) of the uvular stop /q/ with the two velar stops /k/ and
/G/ in *AR*, *BH* and *HEB* and with the uvular fricatives /x/ and /g/
in *AR*. I presented my findings on this subject in *Tables 5.4 and 6.2*.
These tables show that the co-occurrence relationships of the uvular
stop /q/ in these three languages and of the uvular fricatives /x/ and
/g/ in *AR* differ in the following respects:

1) They both pattern in their co-occurrence restrictions with the velar
stops in *AR*, *BH* and *HEB*. As was noted already by McCarthy, the
uvular fricatives in *AR* pattern in their co-occurrence restrictions also
with the pharyngeals/laryngeals, but the uvular stop does not do so.
In *HEB* there is only one avoided root pattern of this type. As is shown
in *Table 5.4* , it has pharyngeals/laryngeals in C2 and the uvular stop
in C1.

2) *Table 6.2* shows that there are also differences with respect to co-
occurrence preference between the root patterns which contain the
uvular stop or the uvular fricatives. Root patterns in *AR*, *BH* and *HEB*
which contain coronal sonorants followed in the adjacent positions
C1C2 and C2C3 either by the uvular stop or by velar stops are pre-

ferred[2]. The reverse sequence of velar stops in C1, followed by coronal sonorants in C2 is preferred only in *HEB*. Root patterns with the velar stops in C2 and the coronal sonorants in C3 are preferred in *AR*, *BH* and *HEB*. The sequence of the uvular stop in C1 followed by coronal sonorants in C2 is preferred only in *HEB*. In *AR* there is only one similar preferred root pattern with uvular fricatives. It contains coronal sonorants in C1 followed by uvular fricatives in C2. From these facts I draw the following conclusion:

Conclusion 1. *The co-occurrence relationships of the uvular stop show that it does not belong to the identity class of the gutturals, as defined by McCarthy, but rather to that of the velar stops, but the uvular fricatives do belong to the former class.*

As is shown in the representations in (1), McCarthy assigns the features [phar] and [cor] to the group of velarized or emphatic coronals in Arabic, which comprises the Sad, Dad, Ta' and Za'. He considers [dorsal] to be a redundant feature for these emphatics. In his representation of the low gutturals and the uvular gutturals the feature [approximant] is present in their Root Nodes. McCarthy assigns the feature [phar] to the uvular stop /q/ as well as to the emphatic coronals. Thus, it is to be expected that in its co-occurrence relationships the uvular stop /q/ will pattern with the emphatic coronals and the latter will also do so with the gutturals. I decided to study this, but only in Arabic, because there are four emphatics in this language, while Hebrew has only one: the Tet (see § 2.1). My findings are shown in *Table 8.1*. They demonstrate that pairs of emphatic coronals have a strongly tendency to be avoided[3]. Root patterns which contain emphatic coronals followed by /q/ in adjacent or nonadjacent positions have expected frequencies. Such pairs, if present in the reverse order, even tend to be favored. The findings for pairs consisting of the emphatics and gutturals have similar properties. On the basis of these findings the following statement can be made:

---

[2] Except for the root pattern in *HEB* which has coronal sonorants in C2 and the uvular stop in C3.

[3] Its is immaterial for these results whether these consonants originally had a feature for glottalization or for lateral in the case of D (see § 2.1).

Conclusion 2. *The uvular stop and the emphatics do not pattern as an identity class with respect to either their co-occurrence restrictions or their co-occurrence preferences and neither do the emphatics with the gutturals.*

Cantineau (1946) already mentioned in his paper on Classical Arabic that the emphatics are mutually incompatible. This is probably due to the fact that they are coronal obstruents and because of this fact alone they are already expected to be subject to co-occurrence restrictions. My evidence shows that it is unlikely that an alleged common feature [phar] would be the cause of this constraint. It therefore appears to me that their emphatic character will have to be represented in a way which is different from that proposed by McCarthy. Perhaps, a possible role for a Tongue Root Node, such as Retracted Tongue Root (RTR) should be explored for this purpose, because the root of the tongue is moved towards the pharynx when these consonants are pronounced. This may merit further research.

McCarthy gave the same representation for the uvular stop and the uvular fricatives, but he surmises that the latter, and the other gutturals are approximants[4]. However, the uvular stop and the uvular fricatives differ in that the uvular stop does not possess any of the seven different phonological characteristics of the gutturals which led McCarthy to assign the feature [phar] to the identity class of the gutturals (see above). On the other hand, the uvular fricatives possess all of these characteristics and thus properly belong to the identity class of the gutturals. The representations for the velar stops, the uvular stop and the uvular fricatives, as proposed by McCarthy, fail to provide an adequate explanation for the co-occurrence relationships of the uvular stop in Arabic and Hebrew. A possible key to a solution of this problem can be found in the fact that the velar stops and the uvular stop are [-cont], while the uvular fricatives are [+cont]. This situation is taken into account in the representations which I should like to propose for these consonants in (2). My representations for the low gutturals are similar to those proposed by McCarthy, but I have dropped the feature [approximant] for these consonants. I am adding the feature [-cont] to the representations for the velar stops and the uvular stop /q/, and [+cont] to those for the uvular fricatives and the low gutturals[5]. In addition, I omit the feature [phar] for the uvu-

---

[4] The glottal stop cannot be an approximant and it is also unclear how fricatives can be approximants.

[5] Among the four low gutturals only the glottal stop is [-cont].

lar stop, at least in Arabic, while in Hebrew it may bear this feature. With this proposal I can explain, on the basis of the OCP, why the low gutturals pattern in their co-occurrence restrictions with the uvular fricatives, because they have in common the feature [phar]. Likewise the uvular fricatives will pattern with both the uvular stop and the velar stops because of their common feature [dorsal]. That only in Hebrew there is partial patterning of the uvular stop /q/ with the pharyngeals/laryngeals could be due to the fact that it would possess the feature [phar] in Hebrew but not in Arabic. The patterning of the uvular stop and the velar stops in their co-occurrence preferences may be due to the fact that these consonants have the features [dorsal] and [-cont] in common. The incomplete patterning in co-occurrence preferences of the uvular fricatives with the velar stops can then be accounted for by the fact that these consonants differ in the feature $[\alpha \text{ cont}]$. This explanation implies that if consonants have in common one or two features this may result in co-occurrence restrictions, irrespective of the other features in which they differ. This raises the possiblity that features may not be equally strong in causing such restrictions. This possibility should also be taken into account in the evaluation of the gradient model of OCP-Place as proposed by Frisch, Broe and Pierehumbert (1997). I discussed this model in § 3.3.3 and in § 8.10 some of its implications will be mentioned.

(2) a. *Low Gutturals* (?,h H,9)

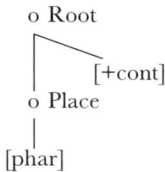

```
        o Root
         ⌐‾‾⌐
      |     [+cont]
     o Place
      |
    [phar]
```

b. *Uvular Fricatives* (x,g)

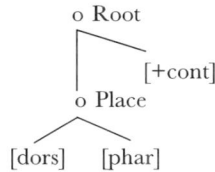

```
        o Root
         ⌐‾‾⌐
      |     [+cont]
     o Place
      ⌒
   [dors]  [phar]
```

c. *Uvular Stop* (q)

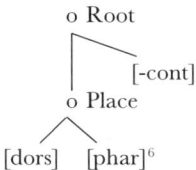

```
        o Root
         ⌐‾‾⌐
      |     [-cont]
     o Place
      ⌒
   [dors]  [phar]⁶
```

d. *Velar stops* (k,G)

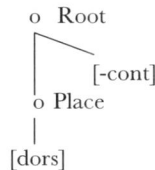

```
        o Root
         ⌐‾‾⌐
      |     [-cont]
     o Place
      |
    [dors]
```

---

[6] [phar] only in Hebrew? (see text).

My proposal shows some similarity to that of Yip (1989), who also stated that the feature [α cont] may play a role in the way the uvular stop and the uvular fricatives differ in their co-occurrence restrictions. However, in her proposal, she did not use McCarthy's feature [phar], but she assigned the feature [dors] to all of the back consonants. I think that it is preferable to maintain the feature [phar] for the gutturals.

In a recent paper van der Hulst and Mous (1992) discussed the transparency of consonants to vowel copying in Iraqw, a Cushitic language spoken in Tanzania. In this language the laryngeals, pharyngeals, uvular fricatives, uvular stop and velars all are transparent to this phenomenon. The implication is that in Iraqw the velars, the uvular stop and the gutturals form an identity class for this transparency phenomenon. In Arabic and Hebrew the situation is different. In these languages the gutturals form a group, which in many phonological phenomena is separate from both the velar stops and the uvular stop /q/. As is shown above, the uvular stop in Arabic and Hebrew patterns with the velar stops in both its co-occurrence restrictions and co-occurrence preferences. In Hebrew the only remaining uvular is the uvular stop, because in this language the uvular fricatives have merged with the low gutturals. Only in this language does the uvular stop pattern to some extent with the gutturals in the co-occurrence restrictions, but it patterns in most cases with the velar stops in a number of preferred root patterns in both Arabic and Hebrew. The uvular stop in Arabic does not pattern with the pharyngeals/laryngeals in its co-occurrence restrictions, but it does so with the uvular fricatives. These facts show that in Arabic and Hebrew a separation exists between the low gutturals and the velar and uvular stops with respect to their co-occurrence relationships, while the uvular fricatives in Arabic take an intermediate position. In addition, the uvular stop tends to pattern with the velar stops in both Arabic and Hebrew.

It would be of interest to see whether the feature [phar] also plays a role in the phonology of Iraqw, of other Cushitic languages and of Berber. If it does it would be intriguing if its properties in these languages would differ from those in Arabic and Hebrew.

My findings show that the uvular stop /q/ is rather similar in its co-occurrence relationships to those of the velar stops in both Arabic and Hebrew, while in Arabic it differs in this from the uvular fricatives. In addition, it is the only uvular in Hebrew. These properties of the uvular stop /q/ became clear already in the early phases of my study. For this reason I decided to group the uvular stop /q/ with the velar stops in all further work. This group is abbreviated as (ve) in the Tables and in the text[7].

8.4 *The role of [continuant] in the co-occurrence relationships*

In my proposal for the representation of the uvular stop /q/ the feature $[\alpha\ \text{cont}]$ is important to differentiate it from the uvular fricatives. It will become clear in § 8.4.1 that this feature plays a crucial role in the co-occurrence relationships of consonant groups classified on the basis of Manner. Its role in such relationships on the basis of Place is less obvious. This is discussed in § 8.4.2.

8.4.1 *Root patterns classified on the basis of Manner*

In § 7.2.1.1.1 and 7.5.1.1 I described my findings for the root patterns with two and three specified consonant groups classified on the basis of Manner. In the present section I will show that the contradiction between Conclusions 20 and 21 in ch. 7 is only apparent, if the root patterns with observed frequencies, although larger than the expected ones but not significantly so, are also taken into account. The facts relevant for the discussion of the phonological implications in the present section are shown in *Tables 8.2.1 and 8.2.2*. In (3) are shown

	in *AR* and *HEB*			only in *AR*			only in *HEB*		
(3)	C1	C2	C3	C1	C2	C3	C1	C2	C3
	[-cont]	/liquid/	[-cont]	[+cont]	/liquid/	[+cont]	[-cont]	[-cont]	/liquid/
				[+cont]	[+cont]	/liquid/			

	in *AR* and *HEB*			in *AR* and *HEB*					
(4)	C1	C2	C3	C1	C2	C3			
	/nasal/	[-cont]	[+cont]	/nasal/	[+cont]	[-cont]			
	/liquid/	[-cont]	[+cont]	/liquid/	[+cont]	[-cont]			
	[-cont]	/nasal/	[+cont]	[+cont]	/nasal/	[-cont]			
	[-cont]	/liquid/	[+cont]	[+cont]	/liquid/	[-cont]			
	[-cont]	[+cont]	/liquid/	[+cont]	[-cont]	/liquid/			

---

[7] See also § 4.5 and § 5.6.3.

the preferred root patterns with three specified positions classified on the basis of Manner which contain liquids and obstruents with the same feature [α cont]. Preferred root patterns with nasals or liquids and obstruents which differ in the feature [α cont] are shown in (4).

The root patterns shown in (3) are subsets of larger sets with two stops or two fricatives in adjacent or nonadjacent positions and arbitrary consonants in the remaining position. Virtually all of these larger sets are avoided. Most of the subsets with nasals in C1, C2 or C3 tend to be avoided. Those with liquids in C1 tend to be preferred, while most of those with liquids in C2 or C3 are preferred or tend to be so in both *AR* and *HEB* or in only one of these two languages. Since these root patterns with liquids are subsets of avoided larger sets which contain arbitrary consonants in stead of nasals or liquids, the preferred subsets with liquids do not neutralize the co-occurrence restrictions on the avoided subsets. This suggests that the following conclusion can be drawn:

Conclusion 3. *Root patterns which contain two obstruents both of which have the feature [-cont] or [+cont] and with liquids in the remaining position C2 or C3 are probably not preferred for phonological reasons but are so rather by chance (see also § 7.1).*

Strong co-occurrence restrictions exist with respect to root patterns which contain two consonants which agree in the feature [α cont] and with arbitrary consonants in the remaining position. If the remaining position contains another consonant which is either [+cont] or [-cont] the root pattern is either significantly avoided or tends to be so. However, if the consonant in the remaining position is a liquid, it is often preferred. This leads to the following two conclusions:

Conclusion 4. *The OCP does not hold for the co-occurrence restrictions on root patterns with a pair of obstruents which have the same feature [α cont]. The co-occurrence restrictions on such root patterns should be explained in a different way.*

Conclusion 5. *For a proper phonological analysis of the verbal root patterns classified on the basis of Manner it is not adequate to study only root patterns with two specified positions. It is essential to take into consideration root patterns which contain specific consonant groups in their three root positions.*

The root patterns shown in (4) are subsets of larger sets of root patterns with adjacent or nonadjacent stops and fricatives and which contain arbitrary consonants in the remaining position. Usually, these larger sets have observed frequencies which are larger than the expected ones, but not significantly so. Only in *HEB* the two larger sets with the arbitrary consonants in C2 are preferred. All subsets of the larger sets with liquids in position C2 or C3 or nasals in C1 or C2 are preferred in both *AR* and *HEB*[8]. The preferred subsets more than outweigh the subsets which only have obstruents in these positions. These latter root patterns either are significantly avoided or tend to be so. Therefore, the conclusion can be drawn that the preference of the subsets with liquids in position C1, C2 or C3 or nasals in C1 or C2 may be due to phonological factors. This is even more likely to be the case for the subsets with nasals or liquids in C2 in *HEB*, because the larger sets to which they belong are significantly preferred. This leads to the following conclusion:

Conclusion 6. *Preferred root patterns with two obstruents which differ in the feature [α cont] and, in addition, contain nasals in C1 or C2 or liquids in C1, C2 or C3 may be preferred for phonological reasons.*

In this way the contradiction which apparently existed between Conclusions 20 and 21 in § 7.5.1.1 is solved. At the present time, it is difficult do define the phonological factors which determine the preference of the root patterns with nasals and liquids which are mentioned in Conclusion 6. This may well be due to the fact that the current models of feature geometry are not adequate to explain the phonology of preference on the basis of Manner. In § 8.5 and § 8.6 I shall discuss this in more detail.

8.4.2 *Root patterns classified on the basis of Place*

The following findings are relevant for a discussion of a possible role for the feature [cont] in the preferred root patterns with two or three specified positions and classified on this basis:

---

[8] The observed frequencies of the root patterns /liquid/[-cont][+cont] in *HEB* and [-cont][+cont]/nasal/ and [+cont][-cont]/nasal/ in *AR* and *HEB* are larger than their expected frequencies, but not significantly so.

1) There is an ordering constraint in *BH* and *HEB* on root patterns with coronal stops and coronal fricatives in the two adjacent positions C1C2 and arbitrary consonants in the remaining position[9].

2) According to Conclusion 25 in § 7.5.2.1 the coronal obstruent in position C3 of preferred root patterns with three specified positions is usually a coronal fricative rather than a coronal stop.

3) It was shown in § 8.3 that in its co-occurrence relationships the uvular stop /q/ in Arabic and Hebrew patterns with the velar stops rather than with the gutturals in *AR, BH* and *HEB* (which are fricatives, except for the glottal stop) or with the uvular fricatives in *AR* .

The facts mentioned under 1 above show that root patterns which contain an adjacent pair consisting of coronal stops and coronal fricatives and arbitrary consonants in the remaining position are subject to ordering or even combinatory constraints. This would suggest that the feature [α cont] does not play a role in the co-occurrence restrictions on the coronals in these root patterns. However, the facts mentioned under 2 indicate that root patterns with three specified positions and coronal obstruents in C3 are preferred rather with coronal fricatives than with coronal stops in that position. This suggests that the feature [α cont] does play a role in these root patterns. The facts mentioned under 3 and the discussion in § 8.2 of the properties of the uvular stop /q/ show that the feature [α cont] is of crucial importance in differentiating it from the gutturals in its co-occurrence relationships. Apparently, the feature [-cont] suffices to keep the uvular stop separate from the uvular fricatives which are [+cont]. This causes this stop to pattern with the velar stops which also are [-cont].

My findings do not give further information on the status of the feature [α cont] in root patterns classified on the basis of Place. The coronals are the only consonant group on the basis of Place for which a separation of the consonants on the basis of the feature [α cont] is meaningful in the study of co-occurrence relationships. The relatively small group of the gutturals in both *AR* and *HEB* and the equally small group of the labials in *AR* contain consonants which are [+cont] and others which are [-cont]. For this reason, it is not clear whether

---

[9] In *AR* this constraint is combinatory for positions C1C2 and C2C3 (see Conclusion 7 in § 7.2.1.2.1).

the feature [α cont] also has an effect on the co-occurrence relationships of these consonant groups.

8.5 *Sonority and Manner features*

My findings concerning co-occurrence preferences for the verbal roots of Arabic and Hebrew were described in ch. 6 and 7. As was shown in § 8.4.1, these findings strongly suggest that Manner and Sonority play an important role in the co-occurrence phenomena with respect to Manner. The co-occurrence restrictions on pairs of consonants which have the same feature [α cont] are often abolished, if the root patterns also contain liquids or nasals. For this reason, I shall review in the present section some of the attempts which were made in the phonological literature to capture the notions of Manner and Sonority within the framework of feature geometry. A great variety of such proposed models has been published, but at the present time none of these models is generally accepted. My description of these models in this section will serve as a preliminary to a discussion of the co-occurrence relationships of the nasals, the liquids and the coronal sonorants in § 8.6.

8.5.1 *Can Sonority be defined phonologically?*

Already in the second half of the 19th century it became clear that the Sonority of phonological segments is of great importance for the structure of syllables. The notion of Sonority has also played a role in structuralist phonology (see e.g. Hankamer and Aissen 1974 and Clements 1990 for references). In the early days of generative phonology several attempts were made to characterize Sonority phonologically. In their groundbreaking book Chomsky and Halle (1968, p.302) gives the following definition of sonorants:

> *"Sonorants are sounds produced with a vocal tract cavity configuration in which spontaneous voicing is possible; obstruents are produced with a cavity configuration that makes spontaneous voicing impossible."*

Ladefoged (1971, p.58) characterizes sonorants as follows:

> *"A particular group of sounds with an auditory property which arises from their having a comparatively large amount of acoustic energy within a clearly defined formant structure."*

However, the phonetic definitions of neither Chomsky and Halle nor

Ladefoged did lead to a satisfactory phonological characterization of Sonority.

Selkirk (1984) makes an attempt to quantify Sonority by assigning Sonority indices to the different vowels and consonants, ranging from 0.5 to 10. This resulted in a Sonority Scale. She then reformulated a principle that had already been stated in various ways by previous investigators (p. 116):

Sonority Sequencing Generalization

"In any syllable, there is a segment constituting a sonority peak that is preceded and/ or followed by a sequence of segments with progressively decreasing sonority values."

She applies this principle and her Sonority Scale to the structure of syllable rimes in English and Spanish. However, her effort to quantify Sonority on the basis of this Sonority Scale seems rather ad hoc and has little explanatory potential.

Clements (1990, p. 283) makes the following statement:

"Phoneticians have generally elected to focus their attention on the search for physical or perceptual definitions of Sonority, while phonologists have looked for formal explanations, sometimes claiming that Sonority has little if any basis in physical reality."

In order to be able to provide a phonological explanation of syllable structure he divides the consonants into Sonority groups by characterizing them on the basis of a set of features. He distinguished the following Sonority groups:

O= obstruents, N = nasals, L = liquids, G = glides, and V = vowels.

He arrives at a Sonority Scale for these groups by determining the sum of their positive features (5). The next step was the introduction of Sonority and Manner features into feature geometry. This will be discussed in the next section.

(5)

O	< N	< L	<	G < V	
−	−	−	−	+	syllabic
−	−	−	+	+	vocoid
−	−	+	+	+	approximant
−	+	+	+	+	sonorant
0	1	2	3	4	(sonority rank)

8.5.2 *Sonority and Manner features in feature geometry*

In the early days of generative phonology the phonemes, as defined in the structuralist approach, are represented by flat bundles of features (Chomsky and Halle 1968). However, it soon became clear that in many phonological phenomena the features show dependency or hierarchical relationships and that they operate in recurrent groups (see den Dikken and van der Hulst 1988 and Kenstowicz 1994 for references to the older literature). This has led to a number of approaches, such as feature geometry (Clements 1985, Sagey 1986 and 1988 and others), Government and Charm Phonology (Kaye, Lowenstamm, and Vergnaud 1985 and Harris 1990), Dependency Phonology (Anderson and Ewen 1987 and Durand 1990), and Radical Phonology (van der Hulst 1989 and 1993).

Since I am of the opinion that feature geometry is the most convenient way to explain my findings, I decided to base the discussion of the representation of Sonority and Manner features in the present section on this concept. A variety of hierarchical models for feature geometry have been proposed in the literature which represent these features in different ways. Below I discuss some of the models which are most relevant for my study. For brevity details of the feature trees proposed in these models are given here only to the extent that they are required for showing the location of the Sonority and Manner features in these trees.

The model proposed by Clements (1985) consists of a set of feature tiers which show a hierarchical dependence (6). In this model Laryngeal (Lar) and Supralaryngeal (SL) tiers are connected to the Root Node. The Place (PL) and the Manner tiers are dependents of the SL tier and the Manner features are dependents of the Manner tier.

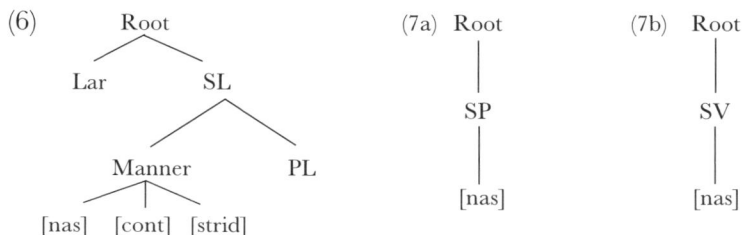

The model proposed by Sagey (1986) contains a Soft Palate Node (SP). This Node and the Place Node (PL) are dependents of the Supralaryngeal Node (SL). In this model the SP Node has [nas] as its only dependent and [cont] is connected directly to the Root Node. In 1988 she modified this model, attaching all Manner features directly to the Root Node.

In Pulleyblank's (1988) model [cont] is a direct dependent of the Root Node and [son], [nas] and the PL Node are dependents of the SL Node. His model did not show the position of lateral.

In his study of the phenomenon of nasal harmony in a number of languages, Piggott (1992) makes the suggestion that the appropriate representation of [nasal] depends on the language. He proposes that in languages where the spreading of [nas] is always arrested by a consonant, it is a dependent of the Soft Palate (SP) Node (7a). In languages where opaque segments are absent, nasality will spread freely. According to Piggott [nas] in these languages is a dependent of the Spontaneous Voicing (SV) Node (7b).

Davis (1989) argues for the location of [cont] as a dependent of the SL Node.

In the model proposed by Rice and Avery (1991), both [lat] and [nas] are dependents of a Spontaneous Voice (SV) Node. In two later papers, Rice (1992 and 1993) termed this Node the Sonorant Voice Node. This Node was meant to replace the feature [son]. In addition, an Air Flow (AF) Node was introduced in this model which is a dependent from the Root Node. It has [cont] as its dependent (8a). The coronal obstruents were taken to be underlyingly underspecified for Place, unless the features which are dependents of coronal are mentioned in phonological processes. According to Rice, stops bear an empty AF Node, while the marked fricatives have the feature [cont] on their AF Node (8b and 8c). Obstruents do not possess the SV Node. Nasals are unmarked and they are represented by an unspecified SV Node. This Node is specified for lateral if it represents laterals, which Rice considers to be marked consonants (8d and 8e).

Another view on the feature [nas] was expressed by Trigo (1993). She places both [nas] and [cont] under the SL Node. According to her, [nas] can be either equipollent or privative. In languages where this feature crucially distinguishes among two or more elements (phonemes) in the underlying inventory, it is equipollent. In her view, it is privative in the vast majority of languages.

(8a)

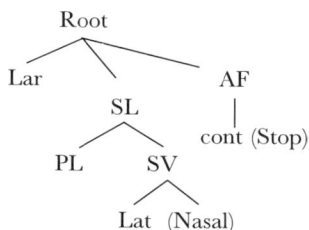

(8b)   (8c)   (8d)   (8e)

Coronal stop   *Coronal fricative*   *Coronal nasal*   *Coronal lateral*

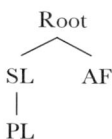   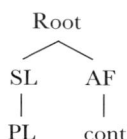   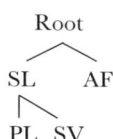   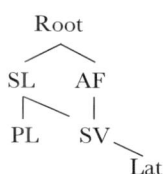

As to the feature [lat] Spencer (1984) suggests that it should be eliminated altogether and that the variety of rhotics and laterals should be distinguished by combinations of the features [voc], [cons], [son], [cont], [distr], [cor], [ant], and [back]. He further made the suggestion that one should appeal to the feature [grooved] for the rhotics and to [high] for the laterals.

According to Lindau (1985) the rhotics, like many other phonological classes, do not have a single underlying phonetic correlate. She proposes that these consonants should be characterized by their types of closure, the formants of the approximant part of their open phase and their pattern of rapid pulses.

Brown (1995) notes that in many previous models [lat] was posited as a dependent of the Root, the Sonorant Voice or the Coronal Node or of both of the latter two Nodes. She drew attention to the fact that both the lateral approximants and the lateral fricatives require an adequate representation. She observes that sonorant laterals sometimes behave as sonorants in rules affecting sonorancy. Non-sonorant laterals, however, behave as coronals in rules which affect place of articulation and according to her, laterality in that case should be considered to be a Place rather than a Manner feature. Her proposals for the representation of laterality in these two types of consonants are given in (9) and (10).

(9)   *Lateral approximant*   (10)   *Lateral fricative*
         (*sonorant*)   (*non-sonorant*)

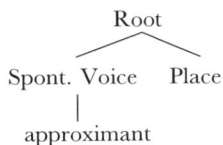

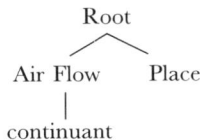

              Root   Root
         ╱‾‾‾‾‾╲   ╱‾‾‾‾‾╲
Spont. Voice   Place   Air Flow   Place
     | |
 approximant   continuant

The foregoing discussion of a variety of attempts which were made
to incorporate Manner and Sonority in the feature tree of geometric
models clearly shows that there still is a wide divergence of opinion
on the way Manner and Sonority features should be represented in
geometric models and that general agreement on this is woefully lacking. This may be due in part to the wide variety of languages in which
Manner and Sonority have been studied and in which these entities
can be expected to function in rather different ways. However, this
cannot be a valid argument in generative grammer, since it would
contradict the principles on which the concepts of UG (Universal
Grammar) are founded. The models which incorporate Nodes such
as Soft Palate (Piggott 1992) and Spontaneous Voicing (Rice and Avery
1991, Rice 1993 and Brown (1995) have added important aspects to
the system. In the next section I will make use of a model for the nasals
and liquids which bears some similarity to those of these authors. In
any case, I have the impression that even these proposals still lack essential features, because the current geometric models are based mainly
on articulators. In my opinion, it may be necessary to take into account accoustic and perceptual features in order to arrive at a satisfactory representation of Manner and Sonority in geometric models.
In § 8.10.3.1 I shall return to this point. However, it is clear that linguists who subscribe to feature geometry as a fruiful tool for describing phonological structure and processes generally agree that the Place
Node should have at least the following dependents:

[labial], [coronal] and [velar].

As was discussed already in § 8.3, McCarthy (1994) has argued con-
vincingly in recent years for the existence of an additional feature [phar]
as a dependent of the Place Node.

8.6 *The co-occurrence relationships of nasals, liquids and coronal sonorants*

After having discussed in § 8.5 a series of geometric feature models which include features for Sonority and Manner, I now turn to the co-occurrence relationships of the nasals, the liquids and the coronal sonorants as groups and as individual consonants. My findings with respect to the co-occurrence relationships of these consonants were decribed in chs. 5 to 7. Later in this section, I will propose representations for the nasals and the liquids which may explain some of the properties of these consonants. One of the aims of the present section is to establish to what extent these three consonant groups represent identity classes, as far as their co-occurrence relationships are concerned.

The facts described in Conclusions 4, 9, 10, 16 and 17 of ch. 7 lead to the following more general conclusions:

Conclusion 7. *The nasals /m/ and /n/ form an identity class of nasals only for the co-occurrence restrictions on root patterns classified on the basis of Manner with two specified positions and which contain nasals as a group and (in addition) /m/ or /n/. In other root patterns this is not the case and /n/, in its co-occurrence relationships, tends to pattern with the coronal sonorants /l/ and /r/. In root patterns classified on the basis of Place /m/ patterns with the labials and /n/ with the coronal sonorants.*

Conclusion 8. *In most root patterns classified on the basis of Manner or Place /l/ and /r/ pattern together in their co-occurrence relationships as an identity class of liquids or of coronal sonorants.*

This leads to the following conclusion:

Conclusion 9. *In root patterns classified on the basis of Place, the Place features [labial] of /m/ and of [coronal] of /n/ override their common feature [nasal].*

The root patterns (l)(cs)(X), (l)(cf)(X) and (l)(co)(X) in *BH* are subject to an ordering constraint (see *Table 5.8*). This suggests that in this case the Place feature [cor] overrides the feature [lat]. This may be due to the fact that both /l/ and the coronal obstruents have the common Place feature [cor].

Table 8.3 shows that *AR*, *BH* and *HEB* among the root pattern with both nasals and liquids only those with nasals in C1, liquids in C2 and arbitrary consonants in C3 are avoided. All other root patterns with adjacent nasals and liquids have observed frequencies which are lower than their expected frequencies, but not significantly so. In § 7.5.1.1.4 I discussed the root patterns which contain both nasals and liquids and, in addition, stops or fricatives (see also *Table 7.12*). I noted there that the root patterns in which the nasals and liquids are adjacent have expected frequencies and that (li)(na)(st) is even avoided in *HEB*. These facts suggest that the representations for the nasals and the liquids should take into account the phonological properties which they have in common. I decided to base the representations for these consonants on the models which were proposed by Rice and Avery (1991) and Rice (1993) and which I discussed in § 8.5.2. These authors made the suggestion that both the nasals and the laterals are dominated by an SV Node. They suggested that this Node represents nasals if unspecified and laterals if it is specified for the feature [lat]. In order to distinguish the sonorant laterals from the non-sonorant or fricative laterals Brown (1995) decided to insert an additional feature [approximant] as a dependent of the SV Node. She suggested that this feature [approximant] should also be present in the representation for the rhotics. In order to explain the co-occurrence relationships of the nasals and the liquids I should like to propose an extension of these models by attaching the features [lat] and [rhotic] either to [approximant] or directly to the SV Node. In my proposed extension of the models of Rice and Avery and of Brown the nasals and the liquids have an SV Node in common. This Node is bare for the nasals and bears the feature [lat] for /l/ and [rhotic] for /r/. My model is shown in (11). The facts which I discussed above and the models in (11) support the following conclusion:

Conclusion 10. *Root patterns with adjacent nasals and liquids contain adjacent SV Nodes and such root patterns tend to be avoided. Only for (li)(na)(st) are the co-occurrence restrictions strong enough to cause avoidance to a significant degree.*

While the properties of /n/ with respect to its co-occurrence relationships vary, /l/ and /r/ almost always form an identity class of liquids or of coronal sonorants. My model nicely depicts the close relationship between /l/ and /r/. I am aware of the fact that it fails to clarify the properties of /n/, unless one would accept that the fact that

/n/ fails to pattern consistently with /l/ and /r/ is to be ascribed to the absence of a dependent on its SV Node.

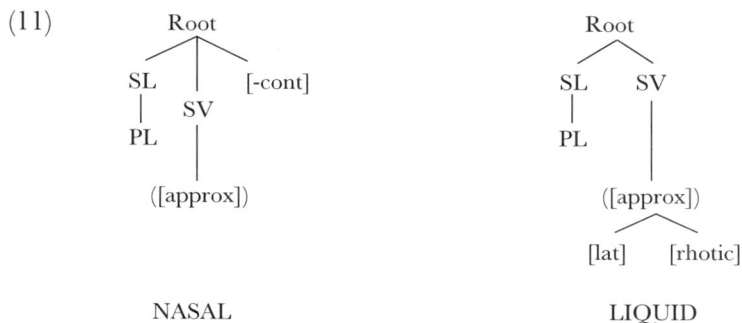

(11)

```
        Root                                    Root
       ╱ ┆                                     ╱  ╲
   SL   ┆  [-cont]                         SL     SV
   ┆   SV                                  ┆      ┆
   PL    ┆                                 PL     ┆
         ┆                                        ┆
     ([approx])                            ([approx])
                                            ╱    ╲
                                         [lat]   [rhotic]

        NASAL                               LIQUID
```

In § 8.5.2 several models which were proposed in the literature for the representation of Manner and Sonority in feature geometry were discussed. In these models the feature [cont] is taken to be a direct dependent of the Root Node, of a Manner Node or of an Air Flow Node, which themselves are direct dependents of the Root Node. My evidence on the role of the feature [cont] in the co-occurrence relationships of root patterns classified on the basis Manner or Place does not make it possible to decide at what position in the feature tree this feature should be placed. For this reason, [cont] figures as a direct dependent of the Root Node, e.g. in my proposed representation for the uvular stop /q/ in § 8.3. This is commonly the case in most of the current geometrical models.

8.7 *Root patterns with three specified positions classified on the basis of Place*[10]

8.7.1 *Root patterns with expected frequencies*

Most of the root patterns with an adjacent pair of velars and gutturals and with arbitrary consonants (see *Table 5.4*) or other consonant groups in the remaining position are neither avoided nor preferred (see § 7.5.2.1.2, Conclusions 26 and 27). The properties of these root patterns lead to the following conclusion:

---

[10] For such root patterns on the basis of Manner see § 8.4.

Conclusion 11. *There may be co-occurrence restrictions on the root patterns with three specified positions classified on the basis of Place which contain both velars and gutturals in adjacent positions. But they are not strong enough to cause avoidance to a significant degree.*

At the present time, I am not able to provide a phonological for this phenomenon (see also § 8.7.2).

8.7.2 *Preferred root patterns*

When studying the co-occurrence relationships of root patterns in Arabic and Hebrew one should bear in mind that a relationship should exist between co-occurrence restrictions and co-occurrence preferences. Avoidance and preference are two sides of the same coin. This implies that if certain root patterns are avoided, other root patterns should be preferred for statistical reasons, and vice versa. It follows that, if there are indications that phonological factors may be involved, one should be able to provide a phonological explanation of either the avoidance or the preference. This will be a major consideration for the discussion of the root patterns with three specified positions classified on the basis of Place. Direct evidence was found for the existence of phonologically based preference for a similar type of root patterns classified on the basis of Manner (see § 8.4). However, it has turned out to be difficult to determine in a direct way whether the preferred root patterns classified on the basis of Place are preferred for phonological reasons or are so rather by chance. The following solution for this problem was chosen (see also § 7.5.2.1.2). Preferred subsets which have three specified positions are members of three different larger sets with two specified positions and arbitrary consonants in the remaining position. I assumed that root patterns which are preferred for phonological reasons are most likely to be found among the group of preferred subsets which belong to two or even three preferred larger sets. These root patterns lack velars in root position C1 and, when present in C2, velars tend not to be preceded by coronal obstruents and not to be followed by coronal sonorants. Interestingly, as mentioned in § 7.5.2.1.2, many root patterns with velars in root position C2, in stead of in C1, tend to have expected frequencies rather than to be preferred.

I am not able to give a phonological explanation for the special position of the velars in the co-occurrence relationships of root patterns with three specified positions and classified on the basis of Place. Also unexplained is the fact that most root patterns with three specified positions which contain velars adjacent to gutturals have expected frequencies, even if in addition, they also contain labials or coronal sonorants (see § 8.7.1). Apparently, velars and gutturals have properties which are not expressed by the current proposals for geometrical models of feature hierarchy, including the models which I presented in (2) of § 8.3. These phenomena should be an area for further research.

8.8 *Quadriliterals and triliterals. Similarities and differences in their co-occurrence relationships*

In § 7.4.1 (see Conclusion 18) I showed that quadriliteral root patterns which are not of the types C1C2C1C2 or C1C2C3C3 tend to show co-occurrence restrictions on adjacent consonants from the same group, classified either on the basis of Manner or on that of Place. This was also found to be the case for quadriliterals of the type C1C2C1C2. As in the case of the triliterals one could try to explain this phenomenon by the OCP or the NBC. On the other hand, interestingly, a number of quadriliteral root patterns not of the types C1C2C1C2 or C1C2C3C3 tend to be preferred, if they contain the same consonant group classified either on the basis of Manner or on that of Place in nonadjacent rather than in adjacent positions (see § 7.4.1, Conclusion 19). This makes it doubtful whether the above co-occurrence restrictions should be ascribed to the OCP. No simple phonological explanation is available for this phenomenon. Perhaps, a more morphological approach might be pursued here. Such root patterns happen to show structural similarities to the quadriliterals of the type C1C2C1C2. These latter root patterns contain consonants in nonadjacent positions which are not only from the same group, but which even are completely the same. This leads to the following conclusion:

Conclusion 12. *In preferred quadriliterals which are not of the types C1C2C1C2 or C1C2C3C3 and which contain consonants from the same group in nonadjacent positions reduplication of features has occurred rather than of whole consonants.*

Of interest is also that the root pattern with nasals in C2 and liquids in C4 is preferred in *AR* and *HEB* (see *Table 6.7*). One could speculate that in this case there has been a reduplication of the SV Node. It is known that many quadriliterals are denominals or are based on loanwords. This may be one of the reasons why differences exist between the triliterals and the quadriliterals with respect to their co-occurrence restrictions and preferences.

In *HEB* and particularly in *MIH*, certain triliterals show a tendency to reduplicate the consonant which is present in root position C3. This process yields quadriliterals of the type C1C2C3C3. In over one half of these root patterns the consonants in C3 are coronal sonorants (see § 6.9). This striking phenomenon merits further research.

8.9 *Other explanations for the co-occurrence restrictions*

In § 8.9.1 to § 8.9.3 I shall discuss work of authors who do not use the OCP to explain the co-occurrence restrictions on the consonants in the verbal roots. I shall discuss the work of Bohas (1997) in § 8.9.4. While adopting the OCP, this author does this in a way that differs from McCarthy's approach.

8.9.1 *Intersyllabic consonant clusters*

In the earlier literature, before the OCP and the NBC had been formulated, some investigators speculated that the co-occurrence restrictions may be due to intersyllabic clusters. When reviewing this earlier work in § 3.2 I mentioned the study by Reiner (1966) of Akkadian. In her book, she ascribed the co-occurrence restrictions to the fact that in some of the inflectional forms of the Akkadian verb the first and second or the second and third consonants of a verbal root will appear as a consonant cluster, which lacks an intervening vowel. Similarly, Kurylowicz (1972) stated that the mutual incompatibility of two consonants in root positions C1 and C2 in Classical Arabic and in Biblical Hebrew could be due to their immediate contiguity in the imperfect and the imperative, where there is no intervening vowel. Weitzman (1987) also drew attention to this fact. In many of the declined forms of a verb stem in Arabic and Hebrew a vowel between two root consonants is absent, indeed. This implies that these consonants are separated by a syllable border. Thus, it is of interest to see whether the existence of such intersyllabic consonant clusters could serve to explain the co-occurrence restrictions on consonant pairs. In a recent paper, Murray and Vennemann (1983) studied the role of syllable borders in Germanic phonology. They ranged the consonants according to a property which they termed their consonantal strength:

glides	liquids	nasals	voiced fricatives	voiceless fricatives voiced stops	voiceless stops
1	2	3	4	5	6

On the basis of this scale they formulated the following law which was supposed to act on syllable borders (p. 530):

The Syllable Contact Law

"The preference for a syllabic structure A^SB, where A and B are marginal segments and a and b are the Consonantal Strength, values of A and B respectively, increases with the value of b minus a."

This law then would have as a corollary:

"The tendency for a syllabic structure A^SB to change, where A and B are marginal segments and a and b are the Consonantal Strength values of A and B respectively increases with the value of a minus b."

This, of course, is the reverse of what is observed in cases of co-occurrence restrictions, because the closer a consonant pair is on the sonority scale the stronger will be the co-occurrence restriction on its appearance in the roots. Still, it seemed of interest to see in what situations vowelless syllable contact in the declined forms of the verbal stems in Arabic and Hebrew occurs. In *Table 8.4* the incidence of such adjacent consonant clusters in positions C1C2 or C2C3 is given for the perfect and the imperfect in Arabic and Hebrew. This table shows that, in principle, adjacent consonants at the syllable borders could be a factor in the co-occurrence restrictions in Hebrew, because intersyllabic consonant clusters can occur in positions C1C2 as well as in positions C2C3. In Arabic, however, this is the case only in positions C1C2 and this precludes the possibility that clusters of adjacent consonants in positions C2C3 can be a factor in this language. By inference, this makes it also unlikely that it plays a role in Hebrew. In principle, the Syllable Contact Law could still be postulated to have a bearing not on co-occurrence restrictions, but rather on co-occurrence preference. Again however, the cases of co-occurrence preference for positions C2C3 in Arabic would remain unexplained.

8.9.2 *Verbal roots are an abstraction and the OCP is not needed*

In two recent papers, Bat-El (1994 and 1995) expresses the opinion that the concept of triliteral verbal roots is an abstraction. She also dismisses the OCP as a possible explanation for the co-occurrence restrictions. In these papers she adduces convincing evidence to support her proposal that in *MIH* the consonantal verbal roots have no function in the grammar of denominal verb stems with four or more consonants or of denominal triliterals derived from monosyllabic nouns or adjectives. She derives these stems by processes of Melody-to-Template Association and Stem Modification. The stem is bisyllabic and the process of stem formation is governed by a number of principles, conditions and rules which are subject to an order of priority. In this way Bat-El is able to explain why consonant clusters which are present in nominal bases which originate from loan words with four or five consonants are preserved in the verbs derived from them. She proposes that the association of the segments to a template is subject to the following set of constraints, principles and rules:

Prosodic Structure
a. Template: $[\sigma\sigma]_F$ <rigid>
b. Onset Principles: $*_s[V$ <absolute>
c. Closed Syllable Condition: $*V]$verb

Prosodic Principles
d. Template satisfaction
e. Maximization of Association: <absolute>
f. Prosodic Licensing

Prosodic rules
g. reduplication
h. stray erasure

Segmental rules
i. Melodic Overwriting

Principle *a* requires that the stem is a foot consisting of two syllables. The process of syllabification is edge-in. According to Principle *b* and Condition *c* the stem should begin and end with a consonant. In order to satisfy an empty slot in the template, a default high glide is introduced (according to Principle *d*), or a stem consonant is reduplicated (according to Rule *g*). Principle *e* requires that all consonants of the stem be associated with the template. Stray vowels are deleted according to rule *h*. Finally, the rule of Melodic Overwriting (*i*) adjusts the vowel pattern to that of the binyan. In order to be able to arrive at the proper derivation, Bat-El then applies one of the tenets of Optimality Theory (see her papers for references) by stating that in *MIH* a part of the constraints, principles and rules exhibit an order of priority. This is shown in the list above. She further makes the suggestion that the order of these priorities is parametrized in UG and that the parameters may differ in their settings for different languages.

Bat-El has shown in her work that the phonology of the majority of the verbal denominatives in *MIH* can be explained by the solicitous use of the above constraints, principles and rules and of the order of priority which she assigns to them. This approach also enables her to explain the preservation of consonant clusters in the verbs, which are present in the nominal bases which originate from loan words which contain four or five consonants. The author considers her proposal to be attractive because the principles, constraints, and rules which are required for the processes of Melody-to-Template Association and Stem Modification are also available within general prosodic theory. Bat-El's work on denominal verbs in *MIH* is quite impressive, but her ideas concerning the triliteral roots of the Hebrew verb are controversial. She dismisses altogether the existence of such roots in the grammar of Hebrew and even in the older stages of that language. She also denies that they exist in the intuition of the native speakers of *MIH*. She notes that the abstract concept of the triliterality of the verbal roots arose in the Middle Ages and makes the following statement about this concept (Bat-El 1994, p. 594):

"I have proposed in this paper an analysis of Modern Hebrew verb structure that does not rely on the principles of Root-to-Template Association. In particular, it

does not admit the morphological and phonological segregation between consonantal roots and vocalic patterns, nor that the prosodic template is specific to each binyan. It is argued that there is no consonantal root in the morphology, that the vocalic pattern is part of a morphological process, and that the template is common to all verbs, regardless of their binyan".

To support this statement Bat-El claims that the semantic relationships between the binyanim of a root are unclear and that this is another reason to dismiss the existence of consonantal roots. However, she fails to present adequate evidence in support of this far-reaching statement. There is a very practical reason to be doubtful of the usefulness of this generalization. If her idea were to be accepted, the different binyanim of each root would have to be entered into the dictionary as separate entries. This would make life very difficult for the learners of the language, whether *BH* or *MIH*. They would then have to leaf continuously through the dictionary in order to find other binyanim with the same root consonants. Moreover, in many cases, the semantics of the different binyanim of a particular root is factually and intuitively related, although not always, of course. Everyone who has only a beginner's knowledge of Hebrew is familiar with this phenomenon and uses it with eagerness. It would therefore be very nice to find the binyanim closely together on the same page of the dictionary, as is done in all older and current dictionaries. Yet, Bat-El apparently dismisses this semantic relationship as being of no great importance, although it exists also in Arabic and in other Semitic languages.

In addition to this mainly practical objection, a more fundamental reason can be given for not dismissing the reality of the triliteral root. Bat-El's arguments are very strong for the new denominals with 4, 5 or even 6 consonants in *MIH* and they also seem to be valid for the denominal triliterals which are derived in *MIH* from monosyllabic nouns or adjectives or, as I presume, even from disyllabic ones. In fact, her proposal may serve to explain why a relatively large number of denominal roots are found in *MIH* which have the same consonant in C1 and C2 (for a discussion of this phenomenon see § 8.10.1). However, *MIH* contains many triliteral verbs which not only are not denominal but which have given rise to deverbal nouns instead. Many of these verbs were inherited from older phases of Hebrew or from other Semitic languages (see § 2.2 and § 4.5). How should one describe the phonology of these verbs which, in principle, can have the same and, very often, even have more binyanim than the modern denominal verbs (e.g., see the examples given by Bat-El). In what way should these be entered into the lexicon? By each of the separate binyanim in which they happen to occur in the language or just by their triconsonantal root? The latter seems far simpler and more consistent.

An interesting question which should be studied is whether the inherited, older triliteral roots, which are not denominative, constitute part of the intuitive linguistic machinery used by the current native speakers of *MIH* by asking them to produce nouns from these triliteral roots or from their binyanim and not only verbs from nouns, as was done by Bat-El and others. In my opinion, such a study should confirm the existence of triliteral roots also in the intuition of the native speakers of the language. Even if the results of such a study were negative, this still would not have an effect on the reasonable supposition that triliterality must have functioned in the older phases of Hebrew and, for that matter, in the Semitic languages in general, even if this concept was not part of the conscious formal knowledge of the speakers.

I should also like to take issue with Bat-El's generalized proposal on another important point. In her 1994 paper (p.594) she makes the following remark:

"the co-occurrence restrictions on the consonants could be explained within the theory of feature geometry, which allows vowels and consonants to appear on separate phonologically motivated tiers".

Unfortunately, Bat-El does not make an attempt to formulate such an explanation. In any case, this would require that the concept that common features exist for consonants and vowels be dropped. However, a more serious objection is that it would become difficult to decide at what level in lexical or in post-lexical phonology the co-occurrence restrictions will act on the consonants of the verb. It seems unlikely that this would be at a surface level of the paradigm of a particular binyan, because the surface forms of this paradigm already bear the affixes which serve to express the specifications for person, gender and number. These affixes are known not to participate in the co-occurrence restrictions, neither in Arabic nor in Hebrew (see § 2.3.2, § 2.3.3 and § 3.2.4), and that fact would remain unexplained.

This problem could not even be solved if it were decided, that for example, in Arabic or in Hebrew the co-occurrence restrictions would apply to the form for the singular of the third person masculine perfect of a particular binyan. This is because in the conjugations of many of the binyanim these forms bear affixes already inherently, even in the singular of the third person masculine perfect. In addition, many verbs do not occur in all binyanim. And, most importantly, the co-occurrence restrictions happen not to act on the nouns from which Bat-El choses to derive all verbs and thus, they should also give rise most liberally to many "forbidden" verbal roots (see § 8.10.2). For all these reasons, it seems to be justified and also far simpler to consider the majority of the consonantal roots to be the lexical entry for the verbs, at least for the triconsonantal verbs which were inherited from the older stages of the languages. It seems justified to suppose that in these older stages the co-occurrence restrictions on these consonants were active at the level of the roots or of their biconsonantal precursors (see § 8.93 and § 8.9.4). A more detailed discussion of my views on this matter will follow in § 8.10.

8.9.3 *Unknown morphological processes in unwritten precursor languages*

In a recent paper Paradis and Prunet (1993) call into question the existence of Morpheme Structure Constraints[11]. In their opinion the dictionary (DICT) constitutes the first input list for the morphological and phonological processes. They view DICT as the storage place for the stems and assume that in this compartment no morphological or phonological changes of the stems can take place. They suppose that such changes occur only at the lexical and the post-lexical levels. These authors make the following claim in their paper (p. 236):

"MSC's are unnecessary, because their role, that of capturing morpheme regularties, can be fulfilled by post-morphemic constraints, be they diachronic or synchronic".

In their view, lexical derivations are bidirectional and the speakers 'deconstruct' surface forms to arrive at their common stems and then store these in the DICT.

Paradis and Prunet apply these ideas to the co-occurrence restric-

---

[11] See also Paradis (1993) and Lacharité and Paradis (1993).

tions on homorganic consonants in Semitic. Their line of thought is as follows:

1)   The homorganicity restrictions are not absolute but rather are tendencies.
2)   The distributional gaps which are now observed show that constraints existed, but that does not prove that they are still active, or that they ever applied to the DICT entries.
3)   The constraints in pre-Proto-Semitic operated across morpheme boundaries and they were post-morphemic constraints acting at lexical or post-lexical levels.

According to their proposal the restrictions are not caused by MSC's but they should be ascribed to historical vestiges of post-morphemic constraints which were last active in pre-Proto-Semitic times. The restrictions never acted in the DICT at any historical stage. The authors claim further that the speakers of Semitic languages lack intuitions on the well-formedness of DICT entries.

Unfortunately, it is difficult, if not impossible to reconstruct unproven post-morphemic processes which occurred in hypothetical and unwritten constructs, such as Proto-Semitic. To reconstruct such processes for still more hypothetical constructs such as pre-Proto-Semitic would be an even more complicated task. Therefore, it does not come as a surprise that Paradis and Prunet did not really try to do so. However, they did make an attempt to do something like this by citing and interpreting work by Ehret (1989) on the possible semantic functions of the final root consonant in the triconsonantal roots of Arabic.

There have been discussions in the literature already for a considerable time on the rather obvious semantic similarities which are known to exist in the Semitic languages between triliteral verbal roots which correspond to each other with respect to the consonants in two of their root positions and differ with respect to the consonant in the remaining position. The literature on this subject deals mainly with roots which have in common the consonants in C1 and C2 and which differ in the consonant in C3. Many references to the older work on this subject can be found in Botterweck (1952) and Bohas (1997). Larger and smaller groups of such verbs exist in Arabic, Hebrew and also in the other Afroasiatic languages (see among others Diakonoff 1988, ch. 2 and Elmedlaoui 1995). Obvious semantic relationships often exist

between the members of such a group of verbs. The study of this phenomenon has led to a whole series of hypotheses, involving the lexical-
ization of various consonantal prefixes and suffixes. But so far, none
of these hypotheses have merited general acceptance (see among others Moscati et. al. 1969, § 11.5).

Let us now return to the paper by Ehret (1989). This author surmised that in Arabic the third root consonant of a triliteral root serves
as a suffix which differentiates a more general semantic field of an
originally biconsonantal nucleus. He distinguished 37 different mono-
consonantal suffixes of this kind. Part of these suffixes are supposed
to be overlapping, because they differentiate the semantic field of the
biconsonantal stems in a similar way. If these overlaps are taken into
account, there would be 23 different morphosemantic categories left.
One is often at a loss when trying to understand the semantic differences between these proposed 23 categories and one wonders whether the speakers of pre-Proto-Semitic could have had an easier task in
this respect. Ehret makes the suggestion that if the co-occurrence
restrictions in old Afroasiatic would block the use of a particular suffix, one of its overlapping companions was used. This suggestion was
taken up by Paradis and Prunet. I shall leave aside the large number
of suffixes and categories which were proposed by Ehret and shall limit
myself to the categories which Paradis and Prunet mention in their
paper. Basing themselves on the work of Ehret, they specifically single out the overlapping morphosemantic suffixes which were supposed
to attribute the following meanings to the biconsonantal roots: diffusive
v, r; finitive k, l; finite formative b, g; durative g, k, d, t; fortative s,
m[12]. Following Ehret, they assume that these suffixes became lexical-
ized already in pre-Proto-Semitic. The semantic categories as used by
Paradis and Prunet are conceptually somewhat simpler to understand
than those proposed by Ehret. However, they follow Ehret in assuming that the choice of a particular member consonant from a particular set of morphosemantic suffixes was determined by the require-
ment to evade a co-occurrence restriction. Among Ehret's 37 semantic
categories 11 contain a single consonant and 12 contain two or more
consonants. Now, to prove this statement it would be necessary to
investigate at the very least the following three questions:

---

[12] I have replaced the symbols for the consonants used by Paradis and Prunet
by those which I use in this book.

1) There are consonants which are affixed in position C3 that originate from a semantic category in which it is the only member.
If it were subject to co-occurrence restrictions with the consonant in position C2 would such a root then occur rarely or even
never?
2) Can it be proved that the selection for position C3 of a consonant from a set of a particular semantic category with two or
more consonants is really determined by the co-occurrence restrictions involving positions C2 and C3?
3) How can the co-occurrence restrictions be explained which act
on pairs of consonants in root positions C1 and C2 or C1 and
C3?

Paradis and Prunet do not provide answers to these questions. In the
absence of appropriate answers, their and Ehret's suggestions regarding the selection of consonants in C3 will remain purely hypothetical,
as hypothetical as are attempts to reconstruct post-morphemic processes in hypothetical constructs of Pro- or pre-Proto-languages.

8.9.4 *The OCP acts on biconsonantal precursors of the roots*

Quite recently, a rather intriguing book was published by Bohas
(1997). He proposes a theory on the original biconsonality of the
triliteral verbs in Arabic, which deviates a great deal from the ideas
on this subject which have been current in the literature up to the
present time. The following concepts are basic to his theory:

1) *The matrix* (μ): This is an ordered or a non-ordered (reversible)
pair of two different articulation sites which covers a semantic
field. These articulation sites are labial, coronal, velar, uvular,
pharyngeal and glottal.
2) *The etymon* (ε): This is an ordered or a non-ordered (reversible)
pair of two phonemes which possess the articulation sites of the
matrix. It covers the same semantic field as the matrix.
3) *The root*: This is an etymon enlarged by spreading of the second
consonant to C3 (Mediae Geminatae) or by the free affixation
to C1, C2 or C3 of either (a) a sonorant, the glides /w/, /y/ or
the sonorants /l/, /r/, /m/, /n/ (which carry the vowel that is
assigned to it in the lexicon) or (b) another type of consonant.

These roots are semantically related to the etymon from which they are derived.

Bohas gives only one example of such a matrix which is said to carry the specific semantic load of "cutting":

$$\mu\{[\text{uvular}],[\text{coronal}]\} \text{ or } \{[\text{dorsal}],[\text{coronal}]\}$$
$$[\text{-high}]$$

An etymon can consist of:

1) two obstruents (including f),
2) one obstruent and a sonorant,
3) two sonorants,
4) two gutturals (9, H, ', h)
5) a guttural and a sonorant.

The association of the features with the matrix and of the consonants with an etymon is supposed to be from left to right and, in both both cases, this association is subject to the OCP. This precludes the existence of roots with the same consonant in C1 and C2. While Ehret (1989) and Paradis and Prunet (1993) assign general semantic functions to the consonants which were supposed to be affixed to the etymons to form the roots, Bohas very carefully does not do so. He merely states that /m/ was a functional prefix which was lexicalised and that perhaps the same may be the case for /t/. According to him, the basic (primitive) nouns are not derived from etymons. Quadriliterals of the type C1C2C1C2 are considered to be reduplicated etymons and many examples of these are shown in his list of etymons and roots.

The theoretically possible number of etymons (excluding those with w or y and those which contain the same consonants) is: $(26\text{X}(26\text{-}1))/2 = 325$. This number includes the etymons which would be prohibited by the OCP. Bohas lists 135 non-ordered (reversible) etymons in his book which he and his group analyzed and which show many of the characteristics mentioned above. He claims that etymons which are prohibited by the OCP do not occur and that the third consonants which were affixed to the etymons are not subject to the OCP with respect to the consonants of the etymons.

Bohas also mentions a number of cases of what he terms "croisements", the equivalent of "blends" in English. Two examples are:

batta + takka → bataka
jadda + daffa → jadafa

These cover the semantic fields of 'cutting' and 'to haste, to be in a hurry', respectively.

Although Bohas' theory is of great interest, a number of critical remarks seem to be in order:

1) In many cases Bohas uses deverbal nouns as additional evidence to reinforce his claim or even to prove the reality of a particular etymon.
2) Of course, in his list of 325 theoretical etymons there are many which are ruled out by the OCP. However, he does not state whether all or the majority of these are really absent.
3) One wonders which of the etymons present in his list and which are not ruled out by the OCP, are not attested.
4) No non-reversible etymons are mentioned which are allowed by the OCP.
5) In his list with the 135 reversible etymons and the roots derived from them the reversible etymons (', h), (s,T) and (C,T) occur. Although these etymons conform to the stipulations by Bohas, they contradict the version of the OCP of McCarthy. The first etymon contains two gutturals and the latter two etymons contain two coronals.
6) More serious seems the fact that none of the 135 listed etymons show violations of the OCP between the consonants of the etymons and the consonantal affixes. This does not support Bohas' claim that the OCP only acts on the etymon and that this is supposed to solve the problem which is due to the fact that the effect of McCarthy's OCP is statistical and not absolute.

The approach by Bohas and his group is of great interest for a better understanding of the diachronic history of the verbal root in the Semitic languages. In spite of the above mentioned shortcomings of this work, further investigations along this line may yield interesting information on the properties of these verbal roots. I am of the opinion, however, that if at a certain stage third consonants were added to biconsonantal precursors, such consonants should have been subject to the co-occurrence restrictions and preferences, just like these precursors (see § 2.2).

8.10 *Co-occurrence restrictions and co-occurrence preferences. Rules and exceptions.*

To my knowledge my work is the first systematic study of the co-occurrence restrictions which act on consonant groups classified on the basis of Manner in the verbal roots of Arabic and Hebrew and similarly of the co-occurrence preferences for such consonant groups classified on the basis of either Manner or Place.

In § 8.9.1 to § 8.9.4 I discussed several proposals which were advanced in the literature to explain the co-occurrence restrictions in ways which differ from the OCP approach advocated by McCarthy:

1) They are due to intersyllabic clusters.
2) The verbal roots are not a reality but an abstraction and the OCP is not needed for an explanation (Bat-El).
3) They can be explained by morphological processes in unwritten precursor languages (Paradis and Prunet),
4) The OCP is involved, but it acts exclusively on biconsonantal etymons and not on the affixed consonants (Bohas).

I have made clear in the discussion of these proposals, that in my opinion, the first three of these cannot serve as an adequate explanation. I consider the fourth proposal an important contribution to the diachronic history of the verbal roots in the Semitic languages. But the evidence which has been provided up to now does not support the claims made by Bohas, although his ideas may eventually provide one of the reasons why the majority of the co-occurrence restrictions are not absolute but rather are relative (statistical).

In § 3.3.3 and 3.4.2.2 I discussed the work of Frisch, Broe and Pierehumbert (1997), who proposed a gradient model of OCP-Place. Although I noted that there are a number of unclear aspects to this proposal and to the way in which it was shaped, the ideas behind such a model are of interest. It apparently constitutes the first serious attempt to provide a quantitative account of the co-occurrence restrictions on consonant pairs in Arabic by grading the constraints due to the OCP.

In § 8.3 I discussed my proposed models for the gutturals, the velars and the uvular stop /q/. In order to be able to explain their co-occurrence relationships it is necessary to assume that in order for the OCP to hold that for these relationships the feature [dors] is be able to outweigh the feature [+cont] of the uvular fricatives

and [-cont] of the velar stops in order for these consonants to pattern in the co-occurrence restrictions as they do. In addition, I have
shown that [nas], [lab] and [cor] are not of equal strength and that
the latter two Place feature outweigh the Manner feature for the nasals
/m/ and /n/ (see Conclusion 9, § 8.6). This implies that the OCP
should not be defined only by the number of different features but
also by their strength.

After having read this book up to this point, it will have become
clear to the reader that basically I am subscribing to McCarthy's
concepts of the OCP and of the spreading of features and consonants
from left to right. I am of the opinion, that at the present time, these
concepts are the best tools available to explain the co-occurrence restrictions on consonant groups which are classified on the basis of Place
in the triliteral verbal roots of Arabic and Hebrew. As is shown in ch.
5, the OCP is about equally strong for consonants from the same group
in adjacent and nonadjacent positions. But the OCP does not hold
for the feature [α cont] in root patterns classified on the basis of Manner
(see § 8.4.1) and the co-occurrence restrictions on it would require
another explanation, which does not seem to be available at the present
time.

In the next section I shall try to give an explanation for the fairly
large number of roots of the type C1C2X in *MIH*. After this, I shall
discuss one of the possible reasons why the overwhelming cases of the
co-occurrence restrictions are relative (statistical) and not absolute.
Finally, I shall turn to the question whether preference for certain root
patterns is due to phonological factors.

8.10.1 *Explaining the fairly large number of roots of the type C1C1X in MIH*

In § 8.9.2 I discussed in detail Bat-El's work and I expressed the opinion
that her concepts seem to work quite well, but only for the new-formations of denominal verbs in *MIH*. Below I shall apply her ideas to
the roots of the type C1C1X in Hebrew. I mentioned in § 8.2 that
McCarthy explained the Mediae Geminatae by assuming that spreading of features and consonants occurs from left to right. He based this
assumption on the fact that in *AR* 'ddy' is the only root of the type
C1C1X and that it is the only exception to the spreading rule. In
§ 8.2 I also mentioned that the situation is more complicated in *BH*
and *HEB*, because they contain more roots of this type and the same
holds true for Ethiopian Semitic (see Bohas 1997 among others for

references). In *BH* three exceptions to McCarthy's spreading rule occur: the roots 'ddh' (which is equivalent to 'ddy' in *AR*), '99r' and 'cc?' (see *Table 8.5*). In *HEB* (mainly in *MIH*), an additional 12 roots of this type are found. This means that in *MIH* a total of 15 exceptions to this rule exist. The existence of these roots would suggests that the constraint on spreading from right to left is very strong in *AR*. In *BH* it would be not so strict and even less so for phases of Hebrew more recent than *BH* and this then would imply that some degree of speading from right to left should have been allowed here. However, I think that another and more acceptable explanation of this phenomenon can be given, which is based on the ideas of Bat-El. At least half of the roots in *MIH* which apparently violate the rule of spreading from left to right are denominal triliterals which are not part of the old heritage of triliterals. These and other denominal triliteral roots in which C1 and C2 bear the same Place feature can easily be explained by the processes of Melody-to-Template Association and Stem Modification as proposed by Bat-El. To give an example,:in this way the adjective 'ma:ma: ' (real) has yielded 'mime: ' (to realize). This way of producing denominal verbs is not forbidden, because the OCP acts only on original verbal roots and not on nouns and denominal verbs (see § 8.10.2 for a discussion of this point).

8.10.2 *Reasons why the co-occurrence restrictions are relative (statistical) and not absolute*

Bat-El's ideas on the formation of denominal verbs may also be helpful in finding an explanation for the fact that the co-occurrence restrictions are almost always relative (statistical) and not absolute. In *MIH* a prolific formation of mainly quadriliteral, but also of triliteral denominal verbs has taken place which still continues up to the present day. In its earlier period of rapid expansion *MIH* had to incorporate many loanwords from Aramaic, Arabic and Indoeuropean languages and this required new methods of verb formation. In the older stages of Hebrew (*BH*), quadriliteral denominal verbs hardly existed. However, this does not necessarily mean that in those stages triliteral roots were not formed from nouns. In any case, it seems that in *MIH* the principle of the triliterality of the original older roots, which implies the operationality of the OCP, and the newer mechanism of denominal verb formation exist side by side. In this way, *MIH* has become a mixture of both older and newer principles, both of which are still active in this form of the language and both determine its verbal phonology and morphology. This is not a revolutionary thought, because the same happens to be the case for many other aspects of the syntax, the phonology and the lexicon of *MIH*, which also is a mixture of older and newer principles (see Weinberg 1966, Bolozky 1978, Kutscher 1971 and 1982, Dor 1995 and many other authors). The moot question now is if one could show whether the verb also had such a mixed character in the older phases of Arabic and Hebrew. It is not easy to determine whether in these older phases a verb is denominal or a noun is deverbal, because it will often be difficult to judge which arose first: the verb or the noun. This is problematic for *BH* and *CA*, but perhaps not for *AR* and the Arab dialects, which like *MIH*, also absorbed many loan words at a relatively late stage of their development. In order to find information on this problem, I decided to investigate the possible existence of denominal verbs which violate the OCP in *HEB* and in *AR*. For Hebrew this is relatively easy, because information on the period of Hebrew in which a noun or a related verb was first attested is given in the dictionary of Even-Shoshan (1968-1970). When scrutinizing my file of *HEB* I found a total of 349 triliteral verbal roots which violate the OCP. Among these roots there are 64 for which a noun was definitely attested before the related verbal root and there are 115 for which this may be so, although both the noun and the verbal root occur at the same stage of the language. Unfortunately, no historical dictionary for Arabic exists. This makes it impossible to make an unequivocal statement about the situation in this language. Nevertheless, out of a total of 372 violations of the OCP there are 122 verbal roots which may have originated from nouns.

An important corollary of the existence in Arabic and Hebrew of a sizable number of denominal verbs which violate the OCP would be the following. The mixed character of the verb in Arabic and Hebrew which results from this may well be one of the reasons why the co-occurrence restrictions are predominantly relative in both Arabic and Hebrew. On the one hand, for most original triliteral verbs which are not denominal the appropriate consonants would have been selected by the OCP or the NBC. These verbs then often gave rise to verbal nouns. On the other hand, denominal verbs which arose in the earlier phases of the language and which are still formed at the present time, are not subject to co-occurrence restrictions. This would be the case, because primary nouns have been found not to be subject to the OCP. This may be so because vowels are part of their lexical structure (see Diakonoff 1988, ch.2). As a consequence, the denominal verbs which are derived from these nouns are also not subject to the OCP. Since already in *BH* the restrictions are relative, this would imply that the competition between the original and the denominal triliterals should already have been in full swing at the time of *BH*. Of course, this competition may also have occurred already in the precursor languages of Hebrew and Arabic or even in early Afroasiatic, but at this stage of our knowledge on this subject, I do not think that it could be very useful to speculate about this possibility. In any case, it would be of considerable interest to study the phonology of denominal verb formation in *AR* and in the Arabic dialects. These forms of Arabic deviate from *CA*, just like *MIH* does from the older forms of Hebrew, although *AR* does so to a smaller degree (Blau 1981).

Another point which should be made here is the following. There are many investigators who share the notion that coronals are under-specified (see Paradis and Prunet 1991 among others for references). The autosegmental model of the verbal roots in the Semitic languages and the OCP have as a consequence that the coronals should already be specified for this feature at the level of the lexicon, because underspecified coronals cannot be subject to co-occurrence restrictions. To my knowledge, no systematic study of coronal underspecification in Arabic or Hebrew has as yet been made. It would be interesting, if other phonological reasons could be found which would require the coronals to be specified for Place already in the lexicon.

8.10.3 *Preference by chance or by phonological factors*

8.10.3.1 *Root patterns classified on the basis of Manner*

Root patterns which contain pairs of consonants from the same group classified on the basis of Manner (stops, fricatives, nasals and liquids) and with arbitrary consonants in the remaining position are almost always strongly avoided in *AR*, *BH* and *HEB*. As is shown in § 8.4.1, root patterns which contain consonants which contain the same feature [α cont] in three positions also are strongly avoided. Root patterns with contain consonants with the same feature [α cont] in two positions and consonants with the feature [-α cont] in the remaining position are also avoided or tend to be so. This would suggest that the features [+cont] for the stops and [-cont] for the fricatives are subject to the OCP. However, I showed that the picture is more complicated. If the remaining position contains liquids, or in certain cases nasals, these root patterns are preferred or tend to be so. I concluded (see Conclusion 4), therefore, that the OCP does not hold for the co-occurrence restrictions on root patterns with a pair of obstruents withe the same feature [α cont]. I am not able to give a phonological inter-pretation of this fact at the present time.

None of the root patterns which contain both stops and fricatives and arbitrary consonants in the remaining position are subject to co-occurrence restrictions. Most of them show a weak tendency to be preferred. The root patterns of this type which contain nonadjacent stops and fricatives and arbitrary consonants in C2 even are signifi-cantly preferred in *HEB* (see *Tables 7.10.1 and 7.10.2*). I concluded that the root patterns which contain both stops and fricatives and nasals in positions C1 or C2 or liquids in C1, C2 or C3, are significantly preferred for phonological reasons. Thus, such a root pattern is pre-ferred if a consonant with an SV Node is present in C1 or C2. This SV Node can either be bare (representing [nas]) or be specified for [lat] or [rhot]. Such root patterns are also preferred in case that they contain liquids in C3. But this is not the case with nasals in that po-sition. That would imply that for these latter root patterns to be pre-ferred an SV node specified for [lat] or [rhot] is required.

All root patterns with adjacent nasals and liquids have expected frequencies[13]. The adjacent consonants in these root patterns both contain an SV Node. One of these is bare and the other one is spec-ified for [lat] or [rhot]. Apparently, two adjacent SV Nodes of differ-ent types are at most marginally subject to the OCP, but two adja-cent SV Nodes of the same type, i.e. two adjacent nasals or liquids, are subject to strong co-occurrence restrictions. This is also in accord-ance with the fact that /l/ and /r/ clearly form an identity class of liquids or coronal sonorants, while the relationship of /n/ with the nasal /m/ on one hand and with the liquids (or coronal sonorants) /l/ and /r/ on the other hand is less obvious (see § 8.6 for more de-tails).

8.10.3.2 *Root patterns classified on the basis of Place*

As was discussed in § 7.5.2.1 and in § 8.7.2, it turned out to be more difficult to decide which of the root patterns with three specified positions classified on the basis of Place are preferred for phonolog-ical reasons than for those classified on the basis of Manner. In fact,

---

[13] The root pattern (na)(li)(X) is even avoided.

I have not been able to gather direct evidence on this. Still, preference is not random. Whatever may be the phonological interpretation, the great majority of preferred root patterns with three specified positions contain either labials or sonorants or both of these. The root patterns with three specified positions which have expected frequencies are also not random. According to Conclusion 28 in § 7.5.2.1.2, they often contain adjacent velars and gutturals or coronal obstruents as well as velars and gutturals. They also tend to have velars in C2. I do not have a ready phonological interpretation for these facts, nor for the lack of velars in position C1 in the group of preferred root patterns with three specified positions which most likely harbor those which are preferred for phonological reasons.

8.10.3.3 *The lack of proper accoustic and perceptual features*

My analysis of the preferred root patterns with three specified positions which contain consonant groups classified on the basis of Manner or of Place, as given in § 8.10.3.1 and § 8.10.3.2, respectively, is more a factual description of my findings than a rigorous phonological interpretation. This may well be due to the fact that in current geometric models a proper representation of acoustic and perceptual features is lacking. In § 8.5 I discussed the multifarious proposals which have been made in the literature for the representation of Manner and Sonority in feature geometry. I noted that none of these current models is really adequate. I ascribed this to the fact that the features in these models are mainly articulator-based. In my opinion, this should be due to the inadequate representation of the phonology of acoustic and perceptual factors in these models. I have the impression that this results in the loss of essential information and that this may well be a reason why the currently proposed feature systems are inadequate in capturing Manner and Sonority. This fallacy is very obvious in the case of the geometric model, but I am of the opinion that the investigators who subscribe to other models of representation should also pay attention to this problem. In spite of the lack of success in the past to provide an adequate phonetic and phonological definition of Manner and Sonority, one should continue to make efforts to do so. With the advances in phonetics during recent years such investigations should become feasible. It seems to me that this situation may also be one of the reasons why at this stage, the description of my findings on co-occurrence restrictions and co-occurrence preferences on the basis of Manner or of Place has to remain largely descriptive rather than explanatory.

8.11 *Comparison of the co-occurrence relationships of the consonants in the verbal roots of AR, BH and HEB*

One of the purposes of my study was to compare the co-occurrence relationships of the consonants in the verbal roots of *AR*, *BH* and *HEB*, in order to determine whether these three languages are similar or differ in this respect. In the final section of this chapter I shall compare the co-occurrence restrictions and the co-occurrence preferences on the basis of Manner and on that of Place for the following groups of roots:

Group 1: Triliterals with a pair consisting of the same consonant group or of two different consonant groups and arbitrary consonants in the remaining position.
Group 2: Triliterals with an individual labial or coronal sonorant in one root position, a specific consonant group in another position and arbitrary consonants in the remaining position.
Group 3: Quadriliterals not of the types C1C2C1C2 or C1C2C3C3 with specific consonant groups in two root positions and with arbitrary consonants in the two remaining positions.
Group 4: Quadriliterals of the type C1C2C1C2 with specific consonant groups in all their four root positions.
Group 5: Triliterals with specific consonant groups in all their three root positions.
Group 6: Triliterals with specific consonant groups in two root positions and an individual labial or coronal sonorant in the remaining position.
Group 7: Triliterals with individual labial or coronal sonorants in two root positions and arbitrary consonants in the remaining position.
Group 8: Mediae Geminatae.

For statistical reasons, the properties of the relatively small file of verbs in *BH* will not be compared in all respects to those of the files of *AR* and *HEB*. The co-occurrence relationships of *Groups 1 and 2* were compared for all three languages. *Groups 3-6* were compared only for

AR and *HEB* and *Groups 7 and 8* in part for all three languages and in part only for *AR* and *HEB*.

Below the cases of co-occurrence restrictions and co-occurrence preferences on the basis of Manner and of Place are compared.

A) *Root patterns classified on the basis of Manner*

a) *Triliterals with two specified root positions*
The co-occurrence restrictions on the large majority of *Group 1* root patterns are rather similar in the three languages (see *Table 5.3*). This is also the case for the *Group 2* root patterns (see *Table 5.7*).

As to the co-occurrence preferences for the root patterns of *Groups 1 and 2*, these are rather similar in *AR* and *HEB* (see *Table 6.1*). With respect to the preferred root patterns of *Group 2* there are no systematic differences between *AR* and *HEB* (see *Tables 6.3, and 7.4*). However, a number of these types of root patterns have expected frequencies in *BH*.

b) *Quadriliterals with two specified root positions*
For *Group 3* root patterns co-occurrence restrictions on pairs of adjacent stops or liquids are found in both *AR* and *HEB*. For adjacent fricatives they occur only in *AR* and for adjacent nasals only in *HEB* (see *Tables 5.10 and 7,6*).

Co-occurrence preferences on pairs of consonants from the same group in nonadjacent positions of *Group 3* root patterns are found only in *AR*. They occur for pairs of stops, fricatives, nasals or liquids (see *Tables 6.7, and 7.6*). Combinatory preferences for adjacent pairs of stops and liquids are found only in *HEB* (*Tables 6.7 and 7.6*). However, if such a root pattern is not preferred in *AR* its observed frequency in this language it is larger than expected, but not significantly so. Combinatory preference for a pair of adjacent coronals is found in both *AR* and *HEB*.

Group 4 root patterns with an adjacent pair of fricatives or liquids are avoided only in *HEB* (see *Table 5.12 and 7.8*). No preferred root pattern of this type were found.

c) *Triliterals with three specified root positions*
The co-occurrence restrictions on *Group 5 and 6* root patterns were studied only in *AR* and *HEB*. They are rather similar in these languages for *Group 5* (see *Tables 5.14,, 5.16.1 and 5.16.2*) and so are the

co-occurrence preferences (see *Tables 6.9, 6.10, and 7.9.1 to 7.12*). Many root patterns of *Group 6* are subject to co-occurrence restrictions or to co-occurrence preferences in both *AR* and *HEB* (see *Tables 5.7, 6.3 7.13 and 7.14*). If a root pattern of these types is avoided (or preferred) in one of the two languages but not in the other language, its observed frequency is usually lower (or higher) than its expected frequency, but not significantly so.

d) *Triliterals with individual labial or coronal sonorants in two root positions*
The co-occurrence restrictions on root patterns of *Group 7* with two labials (see *Table 5.5*) or with two coronal sonorants (see *Table 5.6*) are rather similar for *AR*, *BH* and *HEB*, but in *BH* they virtually always have expected frequencies. This is likely to be due to the very low frequencies of these root patterns in this language, which in any case has a relatively small file of roots. There are only few avoided root patterns with two nasals.

e) *Mediae Geminatae*
Only positions C1 and C2 of root patterns of *Group 8* were studied. Consonant groups classified on the basis of Manner are not subject to co-occurrence restrictions. A number of root patterns are preferred (see *Table 6.5*). They occur almost exclusively in *BH* and contain liquids or nasals in C2. In all three languages the presence of the same consonant in positions C2 and C3 of the root patterns of the Mediae Geminatae neutralizes the effect of the OCP on the presence of the same consonant group in positions C2 and C3 (see *Table 7.29.1*).

B) *Root patterns classified on the basis of Place*

a) *Triliterals with two specified root positions*
The co-occurrence restrictions on *Group 1* and *Group 2* root patterns are very similar for the three languages with a only a few exceptions. However, co-occurrence restrictions on root patterns with /l/ in position C1 and coronal obstruents in position C2 are found only in *BH* (see *Tables 5.4 and 5.8*).

In general, the co-occurrence preferences for *Group 1* and *Group 2* root patterns are also very similar for the three languages, although there are more exceptions in this case. *AR* shows more preferred root patterns than *BH* and *HEB*. However, this phenomenon is not systematic (see *Tables 6.2, 6.4 and 7.5*).

For both co-occurrence restrictions and preferences many of the deviations are found mainly in *BH*.

b) *Quadriliterals with two specified root positions*
The co-occurrence restrictions in *AR* and *HEB* on root patterns of *Group 3* (see *Tables 5.11 and 7.7*) and *Group 4* (see *Tables 5.13 and 7.8*) are found mainly for those which contain the same consonant group in adjacent positions. The differences between the two languages are not systematic.

There is a clear tendency in *AR* and *HEB* for root patterns of *Group 3* with the same consonant group in nonadjacent positions to be preferred (see *Tables 6.8 and 7.7*). However, there are more differences between these two languages than in the case of the co-occurrence restrictions. There is only one preferred root pattern of *Group 4* which occurs in *AR*.

The differences between the *Group 3* and *Group 4* root patterns in *AR* and *HEB* are probably due in part to chance, because the files of these root patterns are relatively small. On the other hand, a reason for these differences may also be the fact that relatively many denominal quadriliterals occur in *MIH*.

c) *Triliterals with three specified root positions*
Root patterns of *Group 5* which are subject to co-occurrence restrictions almost exclusively contain pairs of the same consonant group (see *Tables 5.17 and 5.18*). There are no significant differences in this respect between *AR* and *HEB*.

Co-occurrence preferences for *Group 5* root patterns are also very similar in *AR* and *HEB* (see *Tables 6.11 and 6.12*). They almost exclusively contain labials or coronal sonorants or both of these. Root patterns which are preferred in only one of the two languages often have observed frequencies in the other language which are higher than their expected frequencies, but not significantly so (see *Tables 7.15.1 to 7.15.3, 7.18 and 7.19*).

Many *Group 6* root patterns which are subject to co-occurrence restrictions (see *Table 5.20*) or to co-occurrence preferences (see *Tables 6.14 and 7.28.1 to 7.28.3*) occur in both *AR* and *HEB*. However, others are found in only one of these languages. This may be due to the generally rather low observed and expected frequencies of these root patterns.

d) Triliterals with individual labial or coronal sonorants in two root positions
See for this d) for the root patterns based on Manner.

e) *Mediae Geminatae*
Among the root patterns of *Group 8*, only six are avoided (see *Table 5.9*) and five are preferred (see *Table 6.6*). The avoided root patterns are rather scattered among the three languages and the preferred ones occur almost exclusively in *BH*. Because of the small frequencies of the MG's no conclusion can be drawn with respect to similarities or differences between the three languages with respect to the MG's.

f) *Root patterns of the type C1C2C3C3*
   There are few root patterns of this type in *AR*, but in *HEB* a fairly large number is found (see *Tables 6.15 and 6.16*). Almost all are new-formations in *MIH*, originating from a process of reduplication of the consonant in C3 in certain triliterals.

8.12 *Reasons for the differences between AR, BH and HEB*

The comparison in § 8.11 shows that differences do exist between the verbal roots of *AR*, *BH* and *HEB* with respect to the co-occurrence relationships of the consonants. However, the differences are not drastic, but rather in degree. This implies that for Arabic and Hebrew most of the co-occurrence relationships between the consonants which I observed can be generalized for these two languages. The differences between *AR* and *HEB* may be due in part to one or more of the following factors:

1) The relatively low frequencies of certain root patterns which makes the statistical test unreliable.
2) Arabic possesses more coronal stops, coronal fricatives and gutturals than does Hebrew. This is likely to affect the co-occurrence relationships.
3) The occurrence of relatively many denominal triliterals and quadriliterals in *MIH* (and therefore in *HEB*) which are not subject to co-occurrence restrictions.

The differences between *AR* and *HEB* on the one hand, and *BH* on the other may be due to the incomplete lexicon of the written records of *BH*. It represents a selection from a larger corpus that was not preserved, but it sufficed for a description of the subjects in the text of the Bible. Many words from the realm of daily life are missing but must have been in use in the spoken language of this form of Hebrew (see for example Uhllendorff 1971).

SUMMARY

The purpose of my work was to investigate the phonological basis of the co-occurrence relationships between the consonants in the verbal roots of Arabic and Hebrew. I studied Modern Standard Arabic (*AR*), Biblical Hebrew (*BH*) and the whole collection of verbal roots which is attested in the written records of Hebrew from the period of Biblical Hebrew up to present-day Modern Israeli Hebrew (*MIH*). In this book this collection is called *HEB*.

Positional preferences exist for some of the individual consonants and for some of the consonant groups in the files of the triliterals. They were taken into account in the methods of calculation and did not influence the results.

The fa' in Arabic was taken to be a labial fricative and the sade in Hebrew a coronal affricate. The jim in Arabic patterns in its co-occurrence relationships with the velar stop /k/ and was taken to be a velar stop. Since the uvular stop /q/ in Arabic and Hebrew patterns in its co-occurrence relationships with the velars, while in Arabic it does not pattern with the uvular fricatives /x/ and /g/, it was considered to be a member of the group of velars in my study.

Co-occurrence restrictions

The co-occurrence restrictions are never absolute, but always relative (statistical). Triliteral root patterns are subject to combinatory constraints if they contain either the same consonant group classified on the basis of Manner or Place in two adjacent or nonadjacent positions or a pair consisting of an individual consonant and the consonant group to which it belongs and arbitrary consonants in the remaining position. The properties of root patterns with both voiceless and voiced obstruents indicate that Voice does not play a role in the co-occurrence restrictions. Strong co-occurrence restrictions exist on pairs consisting of coronal stops and coronal fricatives, and in *AR* also on pairs which consist of uvular fricatives and velars or pharyngeals/laryngeals.

On the basis of Manner the nasals /m/ and /n/ pattern as a group in the co-occurrence restrictions, but on the basis of Place /m/ patterns with the labials and /n/ with the coronal sonorants /l/ and

/r/. The liquids (coronal sonorants) /l/ and /r/ usually pattern as
a group both on the basis of Manner and on that of Place.

Quadriliteral root patterns in *AR* and *HEB* exhibit combinatory
co-occurrence restrictions on some pairs consisting of the same consonant group classified on the basis of Manner or on that of Place
in adjacent positions.

Triliterals with three specified positions and with either stops or
fricatives in these positions are subject to strong co-occurrence restrictions. This is usually also the case for root patterns with stops
in two positions and fricatives in the remaining position or the reverse or they tend to be avoided. In root patterns with three specified positions classified on the basis of Manner the status of /m/
and /n/ is unclear, but /l/ and /r/ tend to pattern as a group. On
the basis of Place /m/ belongs to the identity class of the labials and
the consonants /r/ and /l/ belong to that of the liquids (coronal
sonorants).

Co-occurrence preferences

Co-occurrence preferences never are absolute, but always relative
(statistical). Combinatory and ordering preferences for triliteral root
patterns with two specified positions on the basis of Manner are found
almost exclusively for consonant pairs which contain nasals or liquids. On the basis of Place they mainly involve consonant pairs which
contain the group of the labials or that of the coronal sonorants.

Individual labial or coronal sonorant in triliteral root patterns do
not pattern clearly as nasals, liquids or coronal sonorants in co-occurrence preferences if they contain, in addition, a consonant group
classified on the basis of either Manner or Place and arbitrary consonants in the remaining position.

In most cases, the preferred quadriliteral root patterns in *AR* or
HEB contain in nonadjacent positions consonants from the same
group classified either on the basis of Manner or on that of Place.

Almost all of the preferred root patterns with three specific positions classified on the basis of Manner contain nasals or liquids. On
the basis of Place they contain labials or coronal sonorants or both.

There is only a limited degree of patterning of the nasals /m/ and
/n/ and of the coronal sonorants /n/, /l/ and /r/ in preferred root
patterns with three specified positions with such a sonorant and, in

addition, two consonant groups classified either on the basis of
Manner or on that of Place.

Quadriliteral root patterns of the type C1C2C3C3 are found almost exclusively in *HEB*. They mainly are new verbs which arose
in *MIH*. The coronal sonorants /r/, /l/ and /n/ are the most frequent consonants in C3 in that order. Altogether they are present
in over one half of this type of root patterns.

Refinement of the observations

Root patterns which have observed frequencies lower (or higher) than
their expected frequencies, but not significantly so, are now also taken
into account. Root patterns with three specified positions are subsets of larger sets which have two specified positions and arbitrary
consonants in the remaining position. A comparison of these subsets with the larger sets made it possible to determine which of the
preferred subsets with nasals or liquids may be preferred for phonological reasons.

Triliteral root patterns are strongly avoided if they contain obstruents classified on the basis of Manner which have the same feature
[α cont] in three positions. This is also the case for root patterns
with such consonants in two positions and with arbitrary consonants
in the remaining position. If obstruents with the opposite feature
[-α cont] are present in the remaining position, the root patterns are
either avoided or tend to be so, but they are preferred with liquids
in the remaining position. This justifies the conclusion that the feature [cont] is not subject to the OCP.

Root patterns with three specified positions on the basis of Place
which have expected frequencies contain adjacent velars and gutturals or coronal obstruents, velars and gutturals and they tend to
contain velars in C2.

It is more difficult to determine which root patterns classified on
the basis of Place are preferred for phonological reasons or rather
by chance than it is in the case of root patterns classified on the basis
of Manner. This is because the number of root patterns on the former
basis is considerably larger than in the latter case. Root patterns with
three specified positions on the basis of Place are also subsets of three
different larger sets of root patterns with two specified positions and
arbitrary consonants in the remaining position. Such subsets which
are preferred for phonological reasons are most likely to be found

among the group of root patterns which belong to two or even three preferred larger sets. In such subsets velars are absent in C1.

Phonological implications

In its co-occurrence relationships the uvular stop /q/ patterns more often with the velar stops than with the uvular fricatives. It does not pattern at all with the emphatic (velarized) consonants. It also lacks a whole set of phonological properties which characterize the gutturals. My proposed representations for the low gutturals, the uvular fricatives, the uvular stop, the velar stop and the emphatics deviate from those proposed by McCarthy. They are based on the crucial difference between the velar and uvular stops both of which are [-cont] and the uvular fricatives and the other gutturals (with the exception of the glottal stop) which are [+cont]. The emphatics behave as coronals and, apparently, [phar] is not involved in their co-occurrence relationships. The feature [cont] is of crucial importance for root patterns classified on the basis of Manner. It also plays a role in preferred root patterns which contain coronal obstruents and three specified positions.

The liquids (coronal sonorants) /l/ and /r/ usually form an identity class in their co-occurrence relationships. The position of /n/ is not clear. It forms an identity class of nasals with /m/ only in certain types of root patterns classified on the basis of Manner. However, in root patterns classified on the basis of Place /m/ tends to pattern with the labials and /n/ with the liquids (coronal sonorants) /l/ and /r/. This shows that the feature [lab] of /m/ and the feature [cor] of /n/ tend to override their common feature [nas] and this suggests that other features may also be of unequal strength.

The variety of models for feature geometry which were proposed in the literature to capture Manner and Sonority are rather divergent. My findings led me to propose geometrical models for the labial and coronal sonorants which are adaptations of other published models. Nasal consonants are represented by an empty SV Node, /l/ by an SV Node specified for either [lat] or /r/ for [rhotic]. Root patterns which contain both nasals and liquids in adjacent positions are neither avoided nor preferred and the root pattern (na)(li)(X) is even avoided. This can be tentatively ascribed to the fact that both nasals and liquids have an SV Node.

I argue that an attempt should be made to design a feature system which will cover the acoustic and perceptual aspects of the segments in a better way. This may result in a more adequate phonological characterization of Manner and Sonority. If acoustic and perceptual features were available, it could also become easier to discuss the phonological implications of some my findings. The lack of such features makes it difficult to decide whether root patterns classified on the basis of Place are preferred for phonological reasons or by chance.

Many root patterns with three specified positions on the basis of Place and with expected frequencies contain adjacent velars and gutturals and tend to have velars in C2, while preferred root patterns of this type tend not to have velars in C1. These facts remain unexplained.

Adjacent consonants from the same group classified on the basis of Manner or Place are avoided in both quadriliteral and triliteral root patterns. But many quadriliteral root patterns are preferred if they contain consonants from the same group classified on the basis of Manner or Place in nonadjacent positions. This suggests that the quadriliterals are not subject to the OCP. The preference may be due to the reduplication not of whole segments, as is the case in root patterns of the type C1C2C1C2, but rather of features. The differences between the triliterals and the quadriliterals may be due in part to the fact that many of the latter are either denominals or are based on loanwords.

McCarthy attributed the co-occurrence restrictions to a version of the OCP or of the NBC which causes the avoidance in the verbal roots of adjacent or non-adjacent consonants pairs with the same Place Node. A critical review of recent publications in which different explanations for this phenomenon were proposed, led me to conclude that the OCP still constitutes the most acceptable explanation of the co-occurrence restrictions on the basis of Place. However, it is not valid for the Manner feature [cont].

Nouns and adjectives are known not to be subject to co-occurrence restrictions. It is justified to assume that many verbs were generated from nouns and adjectives also in the older stages of Hebrew and Arabic. For this reason, the triliterals must have been a mixture of 'pure' and denominal verbs already for a long period. This may be one of the reasons why the co-occurrence restrictions are almost always relative or statistical rather than absolute.

I have compared the co-occurrence restrictions and the co-occurrence preferences in *AR*, *BH* and *HEB*. These languages are rather similar in these respects. Differences between *BH* on the one hand and *AR* and *HEB* on the other hand may be due to the relatively small size of the file of triliterals in *BH* and to its rather incomplete lexicon. *AR* has more coronal stops, coronal fricatives and gutturals than *HEB*. This may be a reason for the differences between these two languages.

REFERENCES

Al-Ani, S. (1970). *Arabic Phonology*, Mouton, The Hague.

Anderson, J.M., Ewen, C.J. (1987). *Principles of Dependency Phonology* , Cambridge University Press, Cambridge.

Baccouche, T. (1974). La structure morphophonologique des verbes trilitères en Arabe Classique, *Comptes rendu du Groupe Linguistique d'Etudes Chamito-semitiques (GLECS)* 19, pp. 33-48.

Bachra, B.N. (1976). Self complementarity in messenger RNA of collagen. I. Possible hairpin structures in the regions coding for oligopeptides of glycine, proline (hydroxyproline) and alanine, *Journal of Molecular Evolution* 8, pp. 155-173.

Bachra, B.N. (1999). The phonological structure of the verbal roots in Arabic and Hebrew, Èlvé, Leiden.

Barkali, Sh. (1972). *Luah ha-pealim ha-shalem*, Ruben Mas, Jerusalem.

Barr, J. (1971). Linguistic Literature, Hebrew, *Enc. Jud.* 16, pp. 1352-1401.

Bat-El, O. (1988). Remarks on Tier Conflation, *Linguistic Inquiry*, 19, pp. 477-485.

Bat-El, O. (1994). Stem Modification and Cluster Transfer in Modern Hebrew, *Natural Language. & Linguistic Theory* 12, pp. 571-596.

Bat-El, O. (1995). Resolving Prosodic Mismatch in Modern Hebrew, in: van der Hulst, H.G., van de Weijer, J.M. (eds.) *Leiden in Last, HIL Phonology Papers I*, pp. 27-40, Holland Academic Graphics, The Hague.

Bauer, H., Leander, P. (1922). *Historische Grammatik der Hebräischen Sprache*, Verlag von Max Niemeyer, Halle an der Saale.

Blau, J. (1981). *The Renaissance of Modern Hebrew and Modern Standard Arabic. Parallels and Diffferences in the Revival of Two Semitic Languages*, University of California Press, Berkeley.

Bohas, G. (1982). *Contribution à l'étude de la méthode de grammairiens arabes en morphologie et phonologie*, Lille III (thèse).

Bohas, G. (1997). *Matrices, Étymons, Racines. Éléments d'une théorie lexicologique du vocabulaire arabe*, Peeters, Leuven-Paris.

Bolozky, S. (1978). Some Aspects of Modern Hebrew Phonology, in Berman, R.A. '*Modern Hebrew structure*, chapter 2, pp. 11-47, Univ. Publ. Projects, Ltd, Tel-Aviv.

Brockelmann, C. (1908). *Grundriss der vergleichenden Grammatik der semitischen Sprachen*, Verlag von Reuther & Reichard, Berlin.

Brovender, Ch. (1971). Hebrew Language. Pre-Biblical, *Encyclopedia Jududaica*, 16, pp. 1560-1568.

Brown, C. (1995). The Feature Geometry of Lateral Approximants and Lateral Fricatives, in: van der Hulst, H.G., van de Weijer, J.: *Leiden in Last, HIL Phonology Papers I*, pp. 41- 88, Holland Academic Graphics, The Hague, 1995.

Benjamins Publishing Company., Amsterdam/Philadelphia.

Cantineau, J. (1946). Esquisse d'une phonologie de l'Arabe Classique, *Bulletin de la. Socociété Linginguistique*, 43, pp. 93-140.

Chomsky, N. (1979). *Morphophonemics of Modern Hebrew*, revised Master's Thesis (1951), Garland Publishing, Inc., New York & London.

Chomsky, N., Halle, M. (1968). *The Sound Pattern of English*, Harper and Row, New York.

Clements, G.N. (1985). The Geometry of Phonological Features, *Phonolgical Yearbook* 2, pp. 225-252.

Clements, G.N. (1990). The Role of the Sonority Cycle in Core Syllabification, in: Kingston, J., Beckman, M. (eds.), *Papers in Lab. Phonol. I: Between the Grammar and the Physics of Speech*, pp. 283-333, Cambridge University Press.

Colin, I.G.S. (1939). *Comptes rendus des séances du groupe linguistique d'études Chamito-Sémitiques*, 3, pp. 61-62.

Conti, G. (1980). *Studi sul Bilitterismo in Semitico e in Egiziano. 1. Il tema verbale N1212.* Istituto di liguistica e di lingue orientali, Università di Firenze.

Davis, S. (1989). The Location of the Feature [continuant] in Feature Geometry, *Lingua*, 78, pp. 1-22.

Den Dikken, M., Van der Hulst, H.G. (1988) Segmental Hierarchitecture in: van der Hulst, H.G., Smith, N. (eds.) *Features and Harmony Processes*, Foris, Dordrecht.

Diakonoff, I.M. (1988). *Afrasian Languages*, NAUKA, Central Department of Oriental Literature, Moscow.

Donner, H., Röllig, W. (1971-1976). *Kanaanäische and aramäische Inschriften*, Otto Harrassowitz, Wiesbaden.

Dor, D. (1995) Deriving the Verbal Paradigm of Modern Hebrew: A Constraints-based Approach, in: van der Hulst, H.G. , van de Weijer, J.: *Leiden in Last, HIL Phonology Papers I*, pp. 105-144, Holland Academic Graphics, The Hague.

Dotan, A. (1971). Masorah, *Encyclopedia Jududaica*, 16, pp. 1401-1482.

Dozy, R. (1881). *Supplement aux Dictionnaires Arabes*, E.J. Brill, Leyden..

Durand, J. (1990). *Generative and Non-linear Phonology*, Longman, London and New York.

Ehret, C. (1989). The Origin of Third Consonants in Semitic Roots: An Internal Reconstruction (Applied to Arabic), *Journal of Afroasiatic Languuages*, 2, pp. 107-202.

Even-Shoshan, A. (1972). *Hamilon Haivri Hamerukaz*, Keren Sefer, Jerusalem.

Even-Shoshan, A. (1968-1970). *Hamilon hehadash*, Keren Sefer, Jerusalem.

Fischer, W-D. (1972). *Grammatik des klassischen Arabisch*, Harrasowitz, Wiesbaden.

Fischer, W-D., Jastrow, O. (eds.) (1980) *Handbuch der arabischen Dialekte*, Harrassowitz, Wiesbaden.

Franzaroli, P. (1973). Statistical Methods in the Study of Ancient Near Eastern Languages, *Orientalia*, 42, pp. 97-113.

Frisch, S., Broe, M. , Pierrehumbert, J. (1997). Similarity and Phonotactics in Arabic, submitted but obtainable from the website: http://ruccs.rutgers.edu/roa.html..

Gibson, J.C.L. (1973). *Textbook of Syrian Semitic Inscriptions*, Clarendon Press, Oxford.

Goldsmith, J.A. (1976). *Autosegmental Phonology*, PhD dissertation, MIT, distributed by IULC, 1979, Garland Press, N.Y.

Goldsmith, J.A. (1990). *Autosegmental & Metrical Phonology*, Basil Blackwell, Cambridge, Masschusetts.

Greenberg, J.H. (1950). The Patterning of Root Morphemes in Semitic, *Word, 6*, pp. 162-181.

Halévy Hurwitz, S.T. (1966) *Root-Determinatives in Semitic Speech. A Contribution to Semitic Philology*, AMS Press, Inc., N.Y.

Hankamer, J., Aissen, J. (1974). The Sonority Hierarchy, in: Bruck, A., Fox, R.A., La Galy (eds.): *Papers from the parasession on natural phonology*, pp. 131-145, Chicago Linguistic Society.

Harris, J. (1990). Segmental Complexity and Phonological Government, *Phonology*, 7, pp. 235-300.

Herdan, G. (1962). The Patterning of Semitic Verbal Roots Subjected to Combinatory Analysis, *Word*, 18, pp. 262-282.

Hoberman, R.D. (1985). Local and Long-distance Spreading in Semitic Morphology, *Natural Language and Linguistic Theory* , 6, pp. 541-550.

van der Hulst, H.G. (1989). Atoms of Segmental Structure. Components, Gestures and Dependency, *Phonology*, 6, pp. 253-284.

van der Hulst, H.G. (1993). Radical CV Phonology, in: Katamba, F., Durand, J. (eds). *Frontiers of Phonology, atoms, structures, derivations*, Longman, London.

van der Hulst, H.G , Smith, N. (1985). The Framework of Nonlinear Generative Phonology, in: van der Hulst, H.G., Smith, N. (eds.). *Advances in Nonlinear Phonology*, pp. 3-58, Foris, Dordrecht.

van der Hulst, H.G., Mous, M. (1992). Transparant Consonants, in: Bok-Bennema, R , van Hour, R. *Linguistics in the Netherlands*, John Benjamins Publishing Company, Amsterdam/Philadelphia.

Jakobson, R , Halle, M. (1956) *Fundamentals of Language*, Mouton, The Hague.

Joüon, P., Muraoka, T. (1991). *A Grammar of Biblical Hebrew*, Editrice Pontificio Istituto Biblico, Roma.

Kaye, J., Lowenstamm, J-R., Vergnaud. (1985). The Internal Structure of Phonological Elements: A Theory of Charm and Government, *Phonological Yearbook*, 2, pp. 303-326.

Kenstowicz, M. (1994). *Phonology in Generative Grammar*, Blackwell Publiahing Company., Cambridge, Massasuchetts.

Knauf, E.A. (1990). War 'Biblisch-Hebräisch' eine Sprache ?, *Zeitschrift für Althebraistik* 3, pp. 11-22.

Koehler, L., Baumgartner, W. (1958). *Lexicon in Veteris Testamenti Libros*, E.J. Brill, Leiden.

Koskinen, K. (1964). Kompatibilität in den dreikonsonantigen hebräischen Wurzeln, *Zeitschrift der Deutschen Morgenländischen Gesellschaft*, 114, pp. 16-58.

Kurylowicz, J. (1972). *Studies in Semitic Grammar and Metrics*, Polska Akademia Nauk, Warshaw.

Kutscher, E.Y. (1971). Hebrew Language, *Enc. Jud.* 16, pp. 1560-1662, Keter Publishing House, Jerusalem.

Kutscher, E.Y. (1982). *A History of the Hebrew Language*, E.J. Brill, Leiden.

LaCharité, D., Paradis, C. (1993). Introduction. The Emergence of Constraints in Generative Phonology and a Comparison of Three Current Constraint-Based Models, *Canadian Journal of Linguinguistics* , 38, pp. 127-153.

Ladefoged, P. (1971). *Preliminaries to Linguistic Phonetics*, The Univ. of Chicago Press, Chicago and London.

Lane, E.W. (1863). *An Arabic-English Lexicon*, Williams and Norgate, London.

Leben, W. (1973). *Suprasegmental Phonology*, doct. diss., MIT, Cambridge, Massasuchetts.

Lindau, M. (1985). The Story of /r/, in: Fromkin, V. (ed.) *Phonetic Linguistics: Essays in Honor of Peter Ladefoged*, pp. 157-168, Acad. Press, N.Y.

McCarthy, J.J. (1979). *Formal Problems in Semitic Phonology and Morphology*, Ph.D. thesis, M.I.T., Boston, published by Garland Publishing, Inc., N.Y. & London, 1985.

McCarthy, J.J. (1981). A Prosodic Theory of Nonconcatenative Morphology, *Linguistic Inquiry*, 12, pp. 373-418.

McCarthy, J.J. (1986). OCP Effects: Gemination and Antigemination, *Linguistic Inquiry*, 17, pp. 207-263.

McCarthy, J.J. (1988). Feature Geometry and Dependency: A Review, *Phonetica*, 45, pp. 84-108.

McCarthy, J.J. (1994). The Phonetics and Phonology of Semitic Pharyngeals, in:Keating, P. (ed.) *Papers in Laboratory Phonology III*, Cambridge University Press.

Monteil, V. (1960). *L'Arabe Moderne*, thèse principale, Librairie C. Klincksieck, Paris.

Morag, Sh. (1971). Pronunciations of Hebrew, *Encyclopedia Judaica* 13, pp. 1120-1145.

Morgenbrod, H., Serifi, E. (1981). The Sound Structure of Verb Roots in Modern Hebrew, *Journal of Linguistics*, 17, pp. 1-16.

Moscati, S., Spitaler, A., Ullendorff, E., von Soden, W. (1969). *An Introduction to the Comparative Grammar of the Semitic Languages*, Otto Harrassowitz, Wiesbaden.

Murray, R., Vennemann, T. (1983). Sound Change and Syllable Structure in Germanic Phonology, *Language*, 59, pp. 514-528.

Odden, D. (1988). Anti Antigemination and the OCP, *Linguistic Inquiry*, 19, pp. 451-476.

Paradis, C. (1993). Ill-formedness in the Dictionary: A Source of Constraint Violations, in: Paradis, C. and LaCharité. D. (eds.) *Constraint-Based Theories of Multilinear Phonology*, Can. J. Lingu. 38, pp. 215-234.

Paradis, C., Prunet, J.-F. (1990). On Explaining Some OCP Violations, *Linguistic Inquiry*, 21, pp. 456-466.

Paradis, C., Prunet, J.-F. (eds.). (1991). *The Special Status of Coronals: Internal and External Evidence*, N.Y., Academic Press.

Paradis, C., Prunet, J.-P. (1993). On the Validity of Morpheme Structure Constraints, *Revue canadienne de linguistique / Canadian Journal of Linguistics*, 38, pp. 235-256.

Petráček, K. (1963). Die Inkompatibiltät in der semitischen Wurzel in Sicht der Informationstheorie, *Rocznik Orientalistyczny*, 27, pp. 133-139.

Piggott, G.L. (1992). Variability in Feature Dependency: The Case of Nasality, *Natural Language and Linguistic Theory*, 10, pp. 33-77.

Prince, A.S. (1987). Planes and Copying, *Linguistic Inquiry*, 18, pp. 491-509.

Pulleyblank, D. (1988). Underspecification, the Feature Hierarchy and the Vowels, *Phonology*, 5, pp. 299-236.

Reiner, E. (1966) *A Linguistic Analysis of Akkadian*, Mouton.

Rice, K.D. (1992) On Deriving Sonority: A Structural Account of Sonority Relationships, *Phonologt*, 9, pp. 61-99.

Rice, K. (1993) A Reexamination of the Feature [Sonorant]: The Status of 'Sonorant Obstruents', *Language*, 69(2), pp. 308-344.

Rice, K., Avery, P. (1991) On the Relationship between Laterality and Coronality, in: Paradis, C., Prunet, J.-F. (eds.) *The Special Status of Coronals: Internal and External Evidence*, pp. 101-124, Academic Press, N.Y.

Sagey, E. (1986) *The Representation of Features and Relations in Nonlinear Phonology*, published by Garland Press, N.Y., 1990 Cambridge, Massasuchetts.

Sagey, E. (1988a) On the Ill-Formedness of Crossing Association Lines, *Linguistic Inquiry.*, 19, pp. 109-118.

Sagey, E. (1988b) Degree of Closure in Complex Segments, in: van der Hulst, H.G., Smith, N. (eds.) *Features, Segmental Structure and Harmony Processes*, pp. 169-208, Foris, Dordrecht.

Schloezer, A.L. (1781), in: Eichhorn, J.G. (ed.) *Repertorium fuer biblische und morgenländische Literatur*, 8, pp.161).

Selkirk, E. (1984) On Major Class Features and Syllable Theory', in: Aronoff, M., Oehrle (eds*). 'Language Sound Structure*, MIT Press, Cambridge, U.S.A.

Spencer, A. (1984) Eliminating the Feature [lateral] *Journal of Linguistics*, 20, pp. 23-43.

Spencer, A. (1991) *Morphological Theory. An Introduction to Word Structure in Generative Grammer*, Basil Blackwell, Oxford.

Steiner, R.C. (1982) Affricated Sade in the Semitic Languages, *The American Acad. for Jewish Research Monograph Series*, no. 3.

Tobin, Y. (1990) A Combinatory Phonology of the Hebrew Triconsonantal (CCC) Root System, *La Linguistique*, 26, pp. 99-114.

Trigo, R.L. (1993) The Inherent Structure of Nasal Segments, in: Huffman, M.K., Krakow, R. (eds.) '*Nasals, Nasalization , the Velum*', pp. 369-400, Acad. Press, Inc., N.Y.

Uhllendorff, E. (1971) Is Biblical Hebrew a Language ?, *Bulletin. of the School of Oriental & African Studies*, 34, pp. 241-255.

Versteegh, K. (1997) *The Arabic Language*, Edinburgh University Press.

Voigt, R.M. (1988). *Die infirmen Verbaltypen des Arabischen und das Biradikalismus-Problem*, Franz Steiner Verlag Wiebaden GMB, Stuttgart.

Wahrmund (1887-1998) *Handwörterbuch der neuarabischen und deutschen Sprache, 2 Bände*, Ricker, Giessen.

Wehr, H., Cowan, J.M. (1974) *A Dictionary of Modern Written Arabic*, Otto Harrassowitz, Wiesbaden.

Weinberg, W. (1966) Spoken Israeli Hebrew: Trends in the Departures from Classical Phonology, *Journal of Semitic Studies*, 11, pp. 40-68.

Weitzman, M. (1987) Statistical Patterns in Hebrew and Arabic Roots, *Journal of the Royal Society*, pp. 15-22.

Yip, M. (1988 a) The Obligatory Contour Principle and phonological rules: a loss of identity, *Linguistic Inquiry*, 19, pp. 65-100.

Yip, M. (1988 b) Template Morphology and the Direction of Association, *Natural Language and Linguistic Theory*, 6, pp. 551-577.

TABLES FOR CHAPTERS 2 TO 8

Explanation for the symbols in the tables

In many cases the actual levels of significance are not shown in the tables, but the root patterns are marked by '-' for avoidance and by '+' for preference. These signs indicate a level of significance of 1-5%. Blanks indicate that there is neither avoidance nor preference. Levels of significance which are smaller than 1% are marked by '*'. In cases that the actual levels of significance are given the following symbols are used:

No = observed frequency.
Ne = expected frequency.
Z = Z-value determined with the test of binomial proportions.
Si = In case No-Ne is significantly different from 0, the Si-column is marked with a '-'sign, which in this case means that the root pattern is avoided. A '+'sign indicates that it is preferred. A blank means that No-Ne is not significantly different from 0 and that the root pattern has an expected frequency.
P = the level of significance is in % and it is rounded off to the nearest whole figure.

TABLE 2.1

The consonants of Arabic and Hebrew, grouped according to Manner[1]

		ARABIC			HEBREW		
		Name	Symbol	N	Name	Symbol	N
Stops (st)	Voiceless (ls)	hamzah	(?)		'aleph	(?)	
		ta'	(t)		taw	(t)	
		Ta'	(T)		tet	(T)	
		qaf	(q)		qof	(q)	
		kaf	(k)	5	kaf	(k)	
					pe	(p)	6
	Voiced (ds)	ba'	(b)		bet	(b)	
		jim	(G)		gimel	(j)	[2]
		dal	(d)		dalet	(d)	3
		Dad	(D)	4			
		Sum		9			9
Fricatives(fr)	Voiceless (lf)	tha'	(F)				
		ḥa'	(H)		ḥet	(H)	
		kha'	(x)				
		sin	(s)		samek	(s)	
					sin	(C)	
		shin	(c)		shin	(c)	5
		sad	(S)				[2]
		fa'	(f)				
		ha'	(h)	8	he	(h)	
	Voiced (df)	dal	(v)				
		za'	(z)		zayin	(z)	
		Za'	(Z)				
		'ayn	(9)		'ayin	(9)	2
		ghayn	(g)	5			
		Sum		13			7
Affricates				0	sade	(S)	1 [2]
Nasals (na)		mim	(m)		mem	(m)	
		nun	(n)	2	nun	(n)	2
Liquids (li)		ra'	(r)		resh	(r)	
		lam	(l)	2	lamed	(l)	2
Glides (gl)		waw	(w)		waw	(w)	
		ya'	(y)	2	yod	(y)	2
Total Number				28			23

[1] The consonants are subdivided into groups according to the sonority scale proposed by Clements (1985 and 1990). See § 2.1.2 for the correspondence between the consonants of Arabic and Hebrew and § 2.1.3 and § 4.5 for the definition of the consonant groups according to Manner. The symbols used in this study for the individual consonants and for the different sonority groups are shown in parentheses. They deviate in part from those commonly used in Semitic studies. See for this footnote 3 in chap. 2. N = the number of different consonants in a group or a subgroup.

[2] See § 2.1.1 and § 2.1.2 for a discussion of the characteristics of the jim, the fa' and the sade.

TABLE 2.2

The consonants of Arabic and Hebrew grouped, according to Place[1]

ARABIC

	Labial	Coronal	Velar	Gutturals		
				Uvular	Pharyngeal	Laryngeal
Stops	b m	t, T d, D	k G	q		?
Fricatives	f	F, s, S v, z, Z c		x g	H 9	h
Sonorants		n, l, r				
Glides	w	y				

HEBREW

	Labial	Coronal	Velar	Gutturals		
				Uvular	Pharyngeal	Laryngeal
Stops	p b m	t, T d	k G	q		?
Fricatives		s z C, c			H 9	h
Affricates		S				
Sonorants		n, l, r				
Glides	w	y				

[1] The consonants are subdivided on the basis of Place. The consonantal Place features are the same as those proposed by McCarthy (1994) and Yip (1988). See § 2.1.3 and § 4.5 for further explanation and *Table 2.1* for an explanation of the symbols used for the individual consonants. The uvular stop /q/ in Arabic and Hebrew patterns with the velars stops /k/ and /G/ in its co-occurrence relationships (see § 5.6.3 and § 8.3).

TABLE 2.3

The verbal roots of Arabic and Hebrew

Numbers of Roots	Language		
	AR	BH	HEB

Triliterals[1]

Nt	2569	1225	2169
Primae Infirmae	158	72	109
Secondae Infirmae	362	169	310
Tertiae Infirmae	280	175	243
MG	278	139	226

Quadriliterals[2]

Nq	336	5	765
C1C2C1C2	130	3	174
C1C2C3C3	4	0	131

[1] The following abbreviations are used:

Nt   =   Number of triliteral verbal roots in *AR, BH* and *HEB,* the roots of the types Primae, Secundae and Tertiae Infirmae are included here, but the Mediae Geminatae are excluded (See § 1.2 and § 4.1 for the definition of *HEB*).

MG =   Number of Mediae Geminatae in which C2 = C3.

The Primae, Secundae and Tertiae Infirmae contain a glide in root position C1, C2 or C3, respectively. Roots which may contain either a high or a low glide with no effect on their meaning are listed only once (see § 2.2).

[2] Nq = Number of quadriliterals with the exclusion of those of those of the types C1C2C1C2 and C1C2C3C3. See § 2.2 for these two special types.

TABLE 3.1

Incompatibility of consonant pairs in Classical Arabic according to Cantineau[1]

First member of pair	Pos	lb	in	si	al	pr	po	ve	ph	lr	li	em
						Second member of pair						
labials (f,b,m)	12	ra										
	23	ra										
interdent. (F,v,Z)	12		-	-	-	-						
	23		-	-	-	-						
sibilants (s,z,S)	12	-	-	-		-						
	23	-	-	-		-						
alveol. (t,d,D,T)	12		-		-							
	23		-		ra							
prepalatals (c,G)	12		-	-				-	-			
	23		-	-				-	-			
postpalatals (k,g)	12				-	-	-					
	23				-	-	-					
velars (x,g)	12				-	-	-	-	-			
	23				-	-	-	-	-			
pharyngeals (H,9)	12						-	-	-			
	23						-	-	-			
laryngeals (h,?)	12						-	-	-			
	23						-	-	-			
liquids (l,n,r)	12										-	
	23										+	
emphatics (S,D,T,V)	12											-
	23											-

[1] Incompatibility of consonants in the verbal roots of *CA* according to Cantineau (1946). The consonant groups which are distinguished by this author (see § 3.2.1) are shown in the leftmost column and abbreviated in the heading of the table. The consonants which belong to these groups are listed in parentheses. The table gives the degrees of incompatibility as noted by Cantineau for the consonants pairs in positions (Pos) in C1 (leftmost column) and C2 (abbreviated in the heading of the table) or positions C2 and C3. Incompatibility is indicated as absolute (-) or rare (ra). Blanks denote compatibility. The '+' sign for the liquids indicates that according to Cantineau pairs of /n/ with /l/ or /r/ occur rather frequently.

TABLE 3.2

Incompatibility of consonant pairs in Classical Arabic according to Greenberg[1]

First member of pair		Pos	Second member of pair								
			la	si	de	in	ve	pv	ph	lr	li
la	(f, b, m)	12	0								
		23	-*								
		13	-*								
fr	si (c, s, z, S)	12		-*	-*	-*					
		23		-*	-*	-*					
		13		-*		-*					
	de (D, t, d, T)	12		-*	0	-*					
		23		-*	-*	-*					
		13			-						
	in (F, v, Z)	12		-*	-*	-*					
		23		-*	-*	-*					
		13		-*	-	-*					
	ve (k, G, q)	12						-*	-*		
		23						-*	-*		
		13									
	pv (x, g,)	12					-*	-*	0	-*	
		23					-*	-*	-*	-*	
		13						-*	-*	-*	
ba	ph (H, 9)	12							0	-*	-*
		23							-*	-*	-*
		13							-*	-*	0
	lr (?, h)	12						-*	-*		
		23						-*	-*		
		13						-*	0		
li	(l, n, r)	12									-*
		23									-*
		13									-*

[1] Incompatibility of consonants in the verbal roots of *CA* according to Greenberg (1950). The consonant groups distinguished by this author (see § 3.2.2) are abbreviated as follows:

la: labials	si: sibilants	ph: pharyngeals
fr: front consonants	ba: back consonants	lr: laryngeals
de: dentals	ve: velars	li: liquids
in: interdentals	pv: postvelars	

The consonant groups distinguished by this author are abbreviated in the leftmost column (first group of the pair) and in the heading of the table (second group of the pair). The consonants which belong to these groups are listed in parentheses. Roots with identical consonants in root positions C2 and C3 are not taken into account. Symbols are used to indicate the levels of significance for the differences between the observed and the expected frequencies for the pairs of consonant groups in positions C1 and C2, C2 and C3 or C1 and C3 (Pos). The symbols used in the table indicate significance according to the χ^2-test:

0	: absence	
-*	: very rare (<1%)	
-	: rare (1%-5%).	
blanks	: compatibility (>5%).	

TABLE 3.3

Incompatibility of consonant pairs in *HEB* according to Morgenbrod and Serifi[1]

	Pos	bl	da	pl	pa	po	la
bl (b, w, m, p)	12	-*	+*				
	23	-					
	13	-*				+*	
da (d, z, T, l, n, s, S, r, C, t)	12	+*	-*			+*	+*
	23		-*			+	+
	13						
pl (c)	12					+	
	23			+*			
	13						
pa (y)	12	-		-			+
	23				-*		
	13						
po (G, H, k, q)	12	+	+*			-*	-
	23						
	13					-*	
la (?, h, 9)	12		+				-*
	23					-	
	13						

[1] Incompatibility of consonants in the verbal roots of *HEB* according to Morgenbrod and Serifi (1981). See § 3.2.6 for details and § 1.2 and § 4.1 for a definition of *HEB*. The consonant groups distinguished by these authors are abbreviated as follows:

    bl: bilabials/labiodentals   pa: palatal
    da: dentals/alveolars   po: postpalatals
    pl: palato-alveolar   la: laryngeals

The consonants which belong to these groups are listed in parentheses in the table. The degrees of incompatibility of the consonant groups are shown in a way similar to that in *Tables 3.1 and 3.2*:

    Avoidance   Preference
    -*, very rare (<1%)   +*, strongly preferred (<1%)
    - , rare   (1%-5%)   + , preferred   (1%-5%)

Blanks indicate that the pair of consonant groups is neither avoided nor preferred.

TABLE 3.4

Incompatibility of consonant pairs in Modern Standard Arabic according to Yip[1]

	la	cs	cf	so	vu	gu
labials (f,b,m)	-					
coronal stops (t,d,T,D)		-	+			
coronal fricatives (F,v,s,z,S,Z,c)		+	-			
coronal sonorants (l,r,n)				-		
velars-uvulars (G,k,q,x,g)					-	
gutturals (x,g,H,9,h,?)						-

[1] Incompatibility according to Yip (1988) of consonant pairs which belong to the same group in the adjacent root positions C1 and C2 or C2 and C3 of the verbal roots of *AR* (see § 3.3.1). The consonant groups distinguished by this author are abbreviated in the heading of the table as follows:

la: labials so: coronal sonorants
cs: coronal stops vu: velars-uvulars
cf: coronal fricatives gu: gutturals

The uvular fricatives /x/ and /g/ appear among both the velars-uvulars and the gutturals. Incompatibility is indicated by a '-' sign. According to Yip, pairs of coronal stops and coronal fricatives are compatible and these pairs are marked by '+' in the table.

TABLE 3.5

Incompatibility of consonant pairs in Modern Standard Arabic according to McCarthy[1]

		la	cs	cf	so	vu	gu
labials	(f,b,m)	-					
coronal stops	(t,d,T,D)		-	-			
coronal fricatives	(F,v,s,z,S,Z,c)		-	-			
coronal sonorants	(l,r,n)				-		
velars	(G,k,q)					-	
gutturals	(g,x,H,9,?,h)						-

[1] The incompatibility of consonants from the same group in the adjacent root positions of the verbal roots of *AR* according to McCarthy (1994). The consonant groups which are distinguished by this author (see § 3.3.2) are abbreviated in the heading of the table. Incompatibility is indicated by a '-' sign. McCarthy lists /q/ as an uvular in the consonant groups based on Place of articulation, but in the sets of consonants which show the co-occurrence restrictions it occurs among the velars. For a discussion of this point see § 5.6.3 and § 8.3. According to McCarthy, coronal stops and coronal fricatives are incompatible.

TABLE 4.1

Verbal roots in Arabic with the consonant /t/ in root position C1 [1])

C3 → C2 ↓	t	d	T	D	b	f	m	k	G	q	F	v	z	s	c	S	Z	x	g	?	H	9	h	n	r	l	w	y
t	0	0	0	0	0	0	0	0	0	0	0	0	0	0	0	0	0	0	0	0	0	0	0	0	0	0	0	0
d	0	0	0	0	0	0	0	0	0	0	0	0	0	0	0	0	0	0	0	0	0	0	0	0	0	0	0	0
T	0	0	0	0	0	0	0	0	0	0	0	0	0	0	0	0	0	0	0	0	0	0	0	0	0	0	0	0
D	0	0	0	0	0	0	0	0	0	0	0	0	0	0	0	0	0	0	0	0	0	0	0	0	0	0	0	0
b	0	0	0	0	1	0	0	0	0	0	0	0	0	0	0	0	0	0	0	0	1	0	0	1	1	0	0	0
f	0	0	0	0	0	1	0	0	0	0	0	0	0	0	0	0	0	0	0	0	0	1	0	0	1	0	0	0
m	0	0	0	0	0	0	1	0	0	0	0	0	0	0	0	0	0	0	0	0	0	0	0	0	0	0	0	0
k	0	0	0	0	0	0	0	1	0	0	0	0	0	0	0	0	0	1	0	0	0	0	0	0	0	0	0	0
G	0	0	0	0	0	0	0	0	0	0	0	0	0	0	0	0	0	0	0	0	0	0	1	0	0	0	0	0
q	0	0	0	0	0	0	0	0	0	0	0	0	0	0	0	0	0	0	0	0	0	0	1	0	0	0	0	1
F	0	0	0	0	0	0	0	0	0	0	0	0	0	0	0	0	0	0	0	0	0	0	0	0	0	0	0	0
v	0	0	0	0	0	0	0	0	0	0	0	0	0	0	0	0	0	0	0	0	0	0	0	0	0	0	0	0
z	0	0	0	0	0	0	0	0	0	0	0	0	0	0	0	0	0	0	0	0	0	0	0	0	0	0	0	0
s	0	0	0	0	0	0	0	0	0	0	0	0	0	0	0	0	0	0	0	0	0	0	0	0	0	0	0	0
c	0	0	0	0	0	0	0	0	0	0	0	0	0	0	0	0	0	0	0	0	0	0	0	0	0	0	0	0
S	0	0	0	0	0	0	0	0	0	0	0	0	0	0	0	0	0	0	0	0	0	0	0	0	0	0	0	0
Z	0	0	0	0	0	0	0	0	0	0	0	0	0	0	0	0	0	0	0	0	0	0	0	0	0	0	0	0
x	0	0	0	0	0	0	1	0	0	0	0	0	0	0	0	0	1	0	0	0	0	0	0	0	0	0	0	0
g	0	0	0	0	0	0	0	0	0	0	0	0	0	0	0	0	0	0	0	0	0	0	0	0	0	0	0	0
?	0	0	0	0	0	0	0	0	0	0	0	0	0	0	0	0	0	0	0	0	0	0	1	0	0	0	0	0
H	0	0	0	0	0	0	0	0	1	0	0	0	0	0	0	0	0	0	0	0	0	0	0	0	0	0	0	0
9	0	0	0	0	1	0	0	0	0	0	0	0	1	0	0	0	0	0	0	0	0	0	0	0	0	0	0	0
h	0	0	0	0	0	0	0	0	0	0	0	0	0	0	0	0	0	0	0	0	0	0	0	0	0	0	0	0
n	0	0	0	0	0	0	0	0	0	0	0	0	0	0	0	0	0	0	0	0	0	0	0	0	0	0	0	0
r	0	0	0	0	1	1	0	1	0	0	0	0	1	0	0	0	0	0	1	1	1	0	0	0	0	0	0	0
l	0	0	0	0	0	1	0	0	0	0	0	0	0	0	0	0	0	0	0	0	1	0	0	0	1	0	0	1
w	0	0	0	0	1	0	0	0	1	1	0	0	0	0	0	0	0	0	0	0	0	0	0	0	0	0	0	0
y	0	0	0	0	0	1	0	0	0	0	0	0	0	0	0	0	0	1	0	1	0	0	1	0	0	1	0	0

[1] This table was produced with a program in PROLOG-2 and is one of the set of tables for the triliteral verbal roots of *AR* which contain a coronal stop in root position C1. The table shows all the verbal roots generated by the program which contain /t/ in root position C1. The leftmost column represents the consonants which occur in position C2 and the top row those in position C3. A root generated by the program which is present in the file is marked by 1 and by 0 if it is absent from it. The Mediae Geminatae which occur in this family of roots are also present in this table. They were omitted from the calculations for the triliterals and are treated as part of a separate file. For an explanation of the symbols used for the consonants see § 2.1.

TABLE 4.2

Frequencies of occurrence of the root patterns in Arabic with the consonant /t/ in root position C1.[1]

(t)(b)(X)	3	(t)(f)(X)	2	(t)(cs)(X)	0	(t)(cf)(X)	0
(t)(ve)(X)	4	(t)(uv)(X)	1	(t)(pl)(X)	4	(t)(m)(X)	0
(t)(n)(X)	0	(t)(r)(X)	7	(t)(l)(X)	3	(t)(q)(X)	2
(t)(X)(b)	3	(t)(X)(f)	2	(t)(X)(cs)	0	(t)(X)(cf)	2
(t)(X)(ve)	4	(t)(X)(uv)	0	(t)(X)(pl)	9	(t)(X)(m)	2
(t)(X)(n)	1	(t)(X)(r)	3	(t)(X)(l)	3	(t)(X)(q)	2

[1] The frequencies of occurrence are shown for the triliteral root patterns of this type in *AR*. The abbreviations which are used for the consonant groups are explained in § 4.5.

TABLE 4.3.1

Consonant distribution on the basis of Manner in the file of the triliterals in Arabic[1]

	C1		C2		C3	
	N	%	N	%	N	%
voiceless stops	388	15.10	347	13.51	370	14.40
voiced stops	343	13.35	390	15.18	390	15.18
voiceless fricatives	796	30.98	579	22.54	540	21.02
voiced fricatives	298	11.60	259	10.08	234	9.11
nasals	329	12.81	246	9.58	307	11.95
liquids	261	10.16	390	15.18	452	17.59
glides	154	6.00	358	13.94	276	10.74
sum	2569	100	2569	100	2569	100
stops	731	28.45	737	28.69	760	29.58
fricatives	1094	42.58	838	32.62	774	30.13

[1] This table shows the observed distribution of the consonants in the three root positions in the whole file of the triliterals in *AR*. The consonants have been grouped on the basis of Manner. For each phonological group (see § 4.5), the number of verbal roots (N) is listed in which it occurs in root position C1, C2 or C3. Also shown are the percentages (%) of the total number of roots in the file represented by N. Frequencies and percentages are given for the stops and the fricatives as such and also for their voiceless and voiced subsets.

TABLE 4.3.2

Consonant distribution on the basis of Manner in the file of triliterals Biblical Hebrew[1]

	C1		C2		C3	
	N	%	N	%	N	%
voiceless stops	282	23.02	274	22.37	273	22.29
voiced stops	137	11.18	162	13.22	147	12.00
voiceless fricatives	299	24.41	185	15.10	167	13.63
voiced fricatives	118	9.63	96	7.84	71	5.80
sade	42	3.43	46	3.76	41	3.35
nasals	169	13.80	104	8.490	123	10.04
liquids	109	8.90	194	15.84	233	19.02
glides	69	5.63	164	13.39	170	13.88
sum	1225	100	1225	100	1225	100
stops	419	34.20	436	35.59	420	34.29
fricatives	417	34.04	281	22.94	238	19.43

[1] Distribution of the consonants observed in the whole file of the triliterals in *BH*. The consonants have been grouped on the basis of Manner. For further explanation see *Table 4.3.1*.

TABLE 4.3.3

Consonant distribution on the basis of Manner in the file of triliterals in *HEB*[1]

	C1		C2		C3	
	N	%	N	%	N	%
voiceless stops	574	26.46	480	22.13	494	22.78
voiced stops	295	13.60	295	13.60	275	12.68
voiceless fricatives	494	22.78	338	15.58	301	13.88
voiced fricatives	187	8.62	151	6.96	143	6.59
sade	71	3.27	63	2.91	67	3.09
nasals	272	12.54	211	9.73	282	13.00
liquids	173	7.98	333	15.35	376	17.34
glides	103	4.75	298	13.74	231	10.65
sum	2169	100	2169	100	2169	100
stops	869	40.06	775	35.73	769	35.45
fricatives	681	31.40	489	22.54	444	20.47

[1] Distribution of the consonants observed in the whole file of the triliterals in *HEB*. The consonants have been grouped on the basis of Manner. For further explanation see *Table 4.3.1*.

TABLE 4.4.1

Consonant distribution on the basis of Place in the file of triliterals in Arabic[1]

	C1		C2		C3	
	N	%	N	%	N	%
labials	340	13.23	458	17.83	493	19.19
coronals	664	25.85	640	24.91	606	23.59
coronal sonorants	477	18.57	480	18.68	578	22.50
velars	322	12.53	248	9.65	215	8.37
uvular fricatives	185	7.20	84	3.27	52	2.02
pharyngeals/laryngeals	427	16.62	301	11.72	349	13.59
glides	154	6.00	358	13.94	276	10.74
sum	2569	100	2569	100	2569	100

	C1		C2		C3	
	N	%	N	%	N	%
b	116	4.52	153	5.96	154	6.00
f	108	4.20	121	4.71	130	5.06
m	113	4.40	156	6.07	181	7.05
cs	217	8.45	281	10.94	300	11.68
cf	447	17.40	359	13.97	306	11.91
k+G	190	7.40	173	6.73	107	4.17
q	127	4.94	93	3.62	126	4.91
n	216	8.41	90	3.50	126	4.91
r	161	6.27	231	8.99	256	9.97
l	100	3.89	159	6.19	196	7.63

[1] This table shows the observed distribution of the consonants in the three root positions in the whole file of the triliterals in *AR*. The consonants have been grouped on the basis of Place. Frequencies and percentages are given for the coronals as such and separately for the coronal stops (cs) and fricatives (cf) and also for certain individual consonants. See *Table 4.3.1* for further explanation.

TABLE 4.4.2

Consonant distribution on the basis of Place in the file of triliterals in Biblical Hebrew[1]

	C1		C2		C3	
	N	%	N	%	N	%
labials	178	14.53	192	15.67	191	15.59
coronals	341	27.84	299	24.41	270	22.04
coronal sonorants	221	18.04	239	19.51	287	23.43
velars	150	12.24	137	11.18	127	10.37
pharyngeals/laryngeals	266	21.71	194	15.84	180	14.69
glides	69	5.63	164	13.39	170	13.88
sum	1225	100	1225	100	1225	100

	C1		C2		C3	
	N	%	N	%	N	%
b	55	4.49	74	6.04	59	4.82
p	66	5.39	59	4.82	63	5.14
m	57	4.65	59	4.82	69	5.63
S	42	3.43	46	3.76	41	3.34
cs	88	7.18	127	10.37	122	9.96
cf	211	17.22	126	10.29	107	8.74
k+G	97	7.92	88	7.18	59	4.82
q	54	4.41	46	3.76	65	5.31
n	112	9.14	45	3.67	54	4.41
l	33	2.69	85	6.94	91	7.43
r	76	6.20	109	8.90	142	11.59

[1] Observed distribution of the consonants in the three root positions in the whole file of the triliterals in *BH*. The consonants in the table have been grouped on the basis of Place. S is sade. See *Table 4.3.1* for further explanation.

TABLE 4.4.3

Consonant distribution on the basis of Place in the file of triliterals in *HEB*[1]

	C1		C2		C3	
	N	%	N	%	N	%
labials	346	15.95	364	16.78	356	16.41
coronals	662	30.52	514	23.70	557	25.68
coronal sonorants	331	15.26	425	19.59	517	23.84
velars	297	13.69	242	11.16	236	10.88
pharyngeals/laryngeals	430	19.82	326	15.03	272	12.54
glides	103	4.75	298	13.74	231	10.65
sum	2169	100	2169	100	2169	100

	C1		C2		C3	
	N	%	N	%	N	%
b	110	5.07	128	5.90	102	4.70
p	122	5.63	117	5.39	113	5.21
m	114	5.26	119	5.49	141	6.50
S	71	3.27	63	2.91	67	3.09
cs	220	10.14	230	10.60	252	11.62
cf	371	17.10	221	10.19	238	10.97
k+G	194	8.94	156	7.19	122	5.63
q	103	4.75	86	3.97	114	5.26
n	158	7.28	92	4.24	141	6.50
l	61	2.81	141	6.50	150	6.92
r	112	5.16	192	8.85	226	10.42

[1] Observed distribution of the consonants in the three root positions in the whole file of the triliterals in *HEB*. The consonants in the table have been grouped on the basis of Place. See *Tables 4.3.1 and 4.3.2* for further explanation.

TABLE 4.5

Results of the calculations for some of the root patterns of *HEB*[1]

C1	C2	C3	No	Ne	Z	P,%
(cs)	(la)	(X)	49	36.92	+2.01	<5
(cs)	(cs)	(X)	7	23.33	-3.40	<1
(cs)	(cf)	(X)	7	22.42	-3.27	<1
(cs)	(ve)	(X)	23	24.55	-0.31	
(cs)	(q)	(X)	7	9.99	-0.95	
(cs)	(pl)	(X)	45	33.07	+2.09	<4
(cs)	(n)	(X)	10	9.33	+0.22	
(cs)	(r)	(X)	25	19.47	+1.28	
(cs)	(l)	(X)	16	14.30	+0.45	

[1] This table shows the values calculated for the root patterns in *HEB* which contain a coronal stop (cs) in root position C1, the same or a different consonant group or a specific consonant in C2 and arbitrary consonants in C3. The symbols which are used for the consonant groups are explained in § 4.5. For an explanation of the abbreviations used in the heading this table see the explanatory page at the beginning of the set of tables.

TABLE 4.6

Distribution of the consonant groups in the files of the Mediae Geminatae in Arabic and Hebrew[1]

A. *Manner*

	AR					BH			
	C 1		C2=C3			C 1		C2=C3	
	N	%	N	%		N	%	N	%
ls	50	17.99	34	12.23	ls	34	24.46	29	20.86
ds	44	15.83	57	20.50	ds	18	12.95	20	14.39
lf	89	32.01	3	26.26	lf	34	24.46	23	16.55
df	44	15.83	27	9.72	df	15	10.79	9	6.48
na	21	7.55	43	15.47	S	4	2.88	7	5.04
l	26	9.35	40	14.39	na	13	9.35	18	12.95
gl	4	1.44	4	1.44	li	18	12.95	28	20.14
					gl	3	2.16	5	3.60
sum	278	100	278	100	sum	139	100	139	100
st	94	33.81	91	32.73	st	52	37.41	49	35.25
fr	133	47.84	100	35.97	fr	49	35.25	32	23.02

	HEB			
	C 1		C2=C3	
	N	%	N	%
ls	60	26.55	53	23.45
ds	32	14.16	37	16.37
lf	51	22.57	37	16.37
df	23	10.18	13	5.75
S	9	3.98	11	4.87
na	20	8.85	30	13.27
li	25	11.06	33	14.60
gl	6	2.66	12	5.31
sum	226	100	226	100
st	92	40.71	90	39.82
fr	74	32.74	50	22.12

TABLE 4.6 (continued)

B. *Place*

	AR					BH			
	C1		C2=C3			C1		C2=C3	
	N	%	N	%		N	%	N	%
ls	50	17.99	34	12.23	ls	34	24.46	29	20.86
la	34	12.23	28	10.07	la	21	15.11	28	20.14
cs	30	10.79	43	15.47	cs	13	9.35	15	10.79
cf	67	24.10	73	26.26	cf	27	19.42	19	13.67
so	35	12.59	61	21.94	S	4	2.88	7	5.04
ve	37	13.31	50	17.99	so	23	16.55	36	25.90
uv	15	5.40	9	3.24	ve	22	15.83	16	11.51
pl	56	20.14	10	3.60	gu	26	18.71	13	9.35
gl	4	1.44	4	1.44	gl	3	2.16	5	3.60
sum	278	100	278	100	sum	139	100	139	100
co	97	34.89	116	41.73	co	44	31.65	41	29.50
gu	71	25.54	19	6.835					

	HEB			
	C1		C2=C3	
	N	%	N	%
la	33	14.60	43	19.03
cs	26	11.50	35	15.49
cf	38	16.81	35	15.49
S	9	3.98	11	4.87
so	33	14.60	49	21.68
ve	34	15.04	26	11.50
gu	47	20.80	15	6.64
gl	6	2.66	12	5.31
sum	226	100	226	100
co	73	32.30	81	35.84

[1] Observed distribution of the consonants groups on the basis of either Manner or Place in the files of the Mediae Geminatae of *AR,* *BH* and *HEB*. Because of the relatively small numbers of MG's with uvulars and laryngeals in *AR*, the combination of uvulars, pharyngeals and laryngeals as the group of the gutturals (gu) is also shown. The gutturals in Hebrew represent the combined groups of pharyngeals and laryngeals. The calculations of the frequencies were performed for the coronal obstruents as such and not for their voiced and voiceless counterparts. The distribution of the coronal affricate /S/ in Hebrew is also shown in the Tables. It was not used in the calculations on the basis of Manner. S is included among the coronals as such on the basis of Place. See § 4.5 and *Table 4.3.1* for further explanation.

TABLE 4.7.1

Distribution of the consonant groups in the quadriliterals of Arabic[1] (Manner)

A. *Quadriliterals not of the types C1C2C1C2 or C1C2C3C3*

	C1		C2		C3		C4	
	N	%	N	%	N	%	N	%
ls	44	21.78	11	5.45	49	24.26	40	19.80
ds	41	20.30	4	1.98	40	19.80	19	9.41
lf	70	34.65	36	17.82	38	18.81	40	19.80
df	22	10.89	17	8.42	10	4.95	16	7.92
na	16	7.92	31	15.35	20	9.90	38	18.81
li	9	4.46	89	44.06	35	17.33	49	24.26
gl	0	0	14	6.93	10	4.95	0	0
Tot	202	100	202	100	202	100	202	100
st	85	42.08	15	7.43	89	44.06	59	29.21
fr	92	45.54	53	26.24	48	23.76	56	27.72

B. *Root patterns of the type C1C2C1C2*

	C1		C2	
	N	%	N	%
ls	29	22.31	20	15.38
ds	19	14.62	15	11.54
lf	34	26.15	34	26.15
df	14	10.77	16	12.31
na	13	10.00	17	13.08
li	16	12.31	28	21.54
gl	5	3.86	0	0
Tot	130	100	130	100
st	48	36.92	35	26.92
fr	48	36.92	50	38.46

C. *Root patterns of the type XYC3C3*

jlbb
bgdd
cxll
zgll

[1] Observed distribution of the consonants groups on the basis Manner in the files of quadriliterals in *AR*. It is shown for the quadriliterals which are not of the types C1C2C1C2 or C1C2C3C3 (A) and also for these two types (B and C). Because of the relatively small numbers of quadriliterals only the values for the stops and fricatives as such (not subdivided into their voiceless and voiced subsets) were used in the calculations and not those for their voiced and voiceless counterparts. For an explanation of the abbreviations used for the consonant groups see *Tables 2.1 and 2.2* and § 4.5.

TABLE 4.7.2

Distribution of the consonant groups in the quadriliterals of *HEB*[1] (Manner)

A. *Quadriliterals not of the types C1C2C1C2 or C1C2C3C3*

	C1		C2		C3		C4	
	N	%	N	%	N	%	N	%
ls	223	48.48	80	17.39	121	26.30	81	17.61
ds	41	8.91	35	7.61	88	19.13	44	9.57
lf	94	20.43	70	15.22	52	11.30	48	10.43
df	29	6.30	27	5.87	31	6.74	28	6.09
S	6	1.30	10	2.17	18	3.91	7	1.52
na	48	10.43	56	12.17	57	12.39	138	30.00
li	16	3.48	179	38.91	71	15.43	111	24.13
gl	3	0.65	3	0.65	22	4.78	3	0.65
Tot	460	100	460	100	460	100	460	100
st	264	201.5	115	87.79	209	159.5	125	95.42
fr	123	93.9	97	74.05	83	63.36	76	58.02

B. *The file of root patterns of the type C1C2C1C2*

	C1		C2	
	N	%	N	%
ls	50	28.74	45	25.86
ds	27	15.52	18	10.34
lf	33	18.97	28	16.09
df	14	8.05	19	10.92
S	8	4.60	8	4.60
na	16	9.20	22	12.64
li	24	13.79	31	17.82
gl	2	1.15	3	1.72
Tot	174	100	174	100
st	77	58.78	63	48.09
fr	47	35.88	47	35.88

C. *The file of root patterns of the type C1C2C3C3*

	C1		C2		C3		C4	
	N	%	N	%	N	%	N	%
ls	40	30.53	42	32.06	25	19.08	25	19.08
ds	16	12.21	15	11.45	14	10.69	14	10.69
lf	35	26.72	26	19.85	10	7.63	10	7.63
df	14	10.69	6	4.58	1	0.76	1	0.76
S	3	2.29	2	1.53	4	3.05	4	3.05
na	10	7.63	12	9.16	22	16.79	22	16.79
li	10	7.63	22	16.79	51	38.93	51	38.93
gl	3	2.29	6	4.58	4	3.05	4	3.05
Tot	131	100	131	100	131	100	131	100
st	56	42.75	57	43.51	39	29.77	39	29.77
fr	49	37.40	32	24.43	11	8.40	11	8.40

[1]) Observed distribution of the consonants groups classified on the basis Manner in the files of quadriliterals in *HEB*. It is shown for the quadriliterals which are not of the types C1C2C1C2 or C1C2C3C3 (A) and also for these two types (B and C). The distribution of the coronal affricate /S/ in Hebrew is also shown in the tables. It was not used in the calculations on the basis of Manner. For further explanation see *Table 4.7.1*.

TABLE 4.8.1

Distribution of the consonant groups in the Quadriliterals of AR[1] (Place)

A. *Quadriliterals not of the types C1C2C1C2 or C1C2C3C3*

	C1		C2		C3		C4	
	N	%	N	%	N	%	N	%
la	55	27.23	17	8.42	49	24.26	27	13.37
cs	20	9.90	4	1.98	40	19.80	23	11.39
cf	38	18.81	14	6.93	19	9.41	36	17.82
so	11	5.45	109	54.00	41	20.30	74	36.63
ve	38	18.81	8	3.96	25	12.38	28	13.86
uv	12	5.94	12	5.94	1	0.50	3	1.49
pl	28	13.86	24	11.88	17	8.42	11	5.45
gl	0	0.00	14	6.93	10	4.95	0	0.00
Tot	202	100	202	100	202	100	202	100
co	58	28.71	18	8.91	59	29.21	59	29.21
gu	40	19.80	36	17.82	18	8.91	14	6.93

B. *The file of root patterns of the type C1C2C1C2*

	C1		C2	
	N	%	N	%
la	18	13.85	26	20.00
cs	19	14.62	8	6.15
cf	21	16.15	16	12.31
so	23	17.69	33	25.39
ve	22	16.92	12	9.23
uv	8	6.15	7	5.38
pl	14	10.77	28	21.54
gl	15	3.85	0	0.00
Tot	130	100	130	100
co	40	30.77	24	18.46
gu	22	16.92	35	26.92

C. *The root patterns of the type XYC3C3*

jlbb
bgdd
cxll
zgll

---

[1] Observed distribution of the consonants groups on the basis Place in the files of the Quadriliterals in AR. It is shown for the Quadriliterals which are not of the types C1C2C1C2 or C1C2C3C3 (A) and also for these two types (B and C). For an explanation of the symbol gu see *Table 4.6*. Because of the relatively small numbers of Quadriliterals the calculations of the frequencies were performed only for the coronal obstruents (not subdivided in their voiceless and voiced subsets). See *Table 4.7.1* for further explanation.

TABLE 4.8.2

Distribution of the consonant groups in the Quadriliterals of *HEB*[1] (Place)

A. *Quadriliterals not of the types C1C2C1C2 or C1C2C3C3*

	C 1		C 2		C 3		C 4	
	N	%	N	%	N	%	N	%
la	98	21.30	59	12.83	109	23.70	67	23.70
cs	104	22.61	31	6.74	60	13.04	50	13.04
cf	67	14.57	57	12.39	55	11.96	54	11.96
S	6	1.30	10	2.17	18	3.91	7	3.91
so	25	5.44	209	45.43	89	19.35	216	19.35
ve	58	12.61	48	10.43	74	16.09	41	16.09
gu	99	21.52	43	9.35	33	7.17	22	7.17
gl	3	0.65	3	0.65	22	4.78	3	4.78
Tot	460	100	460	100	460	100	460	100
co	177	38.48	98	21.30	133	28.91	111	24.10

B. *The file of root patterns of the type C1C2C1C2*

	C 1		C 2	
	N	%	N	%
la	34	19.54	29	16.67
cs	28	16.09	15	8.62
cf	25	14.37	24	13.79
S	8	4.60	8	4.60
so	29	16.67	40	22.99
ve	24	13.79	30	17.24
gu	24	13.79	25	14.37
gl	2	1.15	3	1.72
Tot	174	100	174	100
co	61	35.06	47	27.01

C. *The file of root patterns of the type C1C2C3C3*

	C 1		C 2		C 3 = C 4	
	N	%	N	%	N	%
la	7	5.34	31	23.66	20	15.27
cs	19	14.50	8	6.11	13	9.92
cf	34	25.95	6	4.58	9	6.87
S	3	2.29	2	1.53	4	3.05
so	18	13.74	27	20.61	68	51.91
ve	16	12.21	22	16.79	11	8.40
gu	31	23.66	29	22.14	2	1.53
gl	3	2.29	6	4.58	4	3.05
Tot	131	100	131	100	131	100
co	56	42.75	16	12.21	26	19.85

[1] Observed distribution of the consonants groups on the basis Place in the files of the Quadriliterals in *HEB*. It is shown for the Quadriliterals which are not of the types C1C2C1C2 or C1C2C3C3 (A) and also for these two types (B and C). The calculations of the frequencies were performed for the coronal obstruents (not subdivided in their voiceless and voiced subsets) which also included the coronal affricate /S/. For further explanation see *Table 4.8.1.*

TABLE 4.9

Effects of low actual and expected frequencies on significance[1]

	C1	C2	C3	A				B			
				No	Ne	Z	P	No	Ne	Z	P
1	(li)	(ls)	(df)	7	3.211	+2.12	<5	6	3.211	+1.56	
	(li)	(df)	(ds)	9	3.995	+2.59	<2	7	3.995	+1.51	
	(li)	(df)	(na)	7	3.144	+2.18	<3	6	3.144	+1.61	
2	(li)	(ds)	(li)	1	6.971	-2.26	<3	2	6.971	-1.89	<6
	(li)	(lf)	(li)	4	10.35	-1.98	<5	5	10.35	-1.67	
	(li)	(li)	(ls)	0	5.707	-2.39	<2	2	5.707	-1.55	
	(li)	(li)	(ds)	0	6.015	-2.46	<1	2	6.015	-1.64	
3	(li)	(ds)	(df)	6	3.609	+1.26		8	3.609	+2.31	<3
	(li)	(df)	(gl)	5	2.827	+1.29		7	2.827	+2.48	<2
	(gl)	(df)	(li)	5	2.732	+1.37		6	2.732	+1.98	<5
	(ls)	(li)	(df)	8	5.365	+1.14		10	5.365	+2.00	<5
	(df)	(li)	(gl)	8	4.860	+1.43		10	4.860	+2.33	<2
	(gl)	(li)	(df)	4	2.129	+1.28		5	2.129	+1.97	<5
4	(li)	(ls)	(li)	2	6.203	-1.69		1	6.203	-2.09	<4
	(na)	(li)	(ds)	4	7.582	-1.30		2	7.582	-2.03	<5
	(na)	(li)	(df)	2	4.549	-1.20		0	4.549	-2.13	<4

[1] Examples given are for some of the root patterns with three specified root positions in *AR*.
A = calculations with the observed frequencies of occurrence (No).
B = calculations when these frequencies are raised or lowered artificially by 1 or 2, which values were chosen arbitrarily only for demonstrative purposes. Significantly preferred (1) or avoided (2) root patterns now exhibit expected frequencies and those with expected frequencies have become preferred (3) or avoided (4). See *Table 4.5* for further explanation.

TABLE 5.1

Distribution of the consonants in the three root positions[1]

a) *Consonant groups on the basis of Manner*

	AR			BH			HEB		
	C1	C2	C3	C1	C2	C3	C1	C2	C3
ls									
ds									
st									
lf									
df			-						
fr		-	-			-			
na	+								
li		+*	+*		+	+*		+	+*
gl		+							

b) *Consonant groups on the basis of Place*

	AR			BH			HEB		
	C1	C2	C3	C1	C2	C3	C1	C2	C3
la		+	+*						
cs									
cf		-	-*			-			
co	-	-	-			-			
so	+	+	+*			+*			+*
ve									
gu									
gl		+							

c) *Individual labial and coronal sonorants*

	AR			BH			HEB		
	C1	C2	C3	C1	C2	C3	C1	C2	C3
m									
n	+			+					
r		+*	+*		+	+*		+	+*
l			+						

[1] The distribution of the consonant groups as classified on the basis of Manner and on that of Place in root positions C1, C2 and C3 of the triliteral verbal roots of *AR*, *BH* and *HEB*. Also shown is the distribution of the individual labial and coronal sonorants. The '-' sign and the '+' sign indicate avoidance and preference, respectively. An added '*' means that the avoidance or the preference is at a level of significance <1%. Blanks indicate expected frequencies.

TABLE 5.2

Root patterns in Arabic and Hebrew which exhibit absolute combinatory constraints[1]

a) *Root patterns with two consonant groups*

				AR			BH			HEB		
				No	Ne	P,%	No	Ne	P,%	No	Ne	P,%
Manner	(li)	(li)	(X)	0	39.6	<1	0	17.3	<1	1	26.6	<1
	(gl)	(gl)	(X)	1	21.5	<1	0	9.3	<1	1	14.2	<1
	(X)	(li)	(li)	0	68.6	<1	1	36.9	<1	4	57.7	<1
	(X)	(gl)	(gl)	20	38.5	<1	0	22.8	<1	0	31.7	<1
Place	(la)	(la)	(X)	0	60.6	<1	0	27.9	<1	5	58.1	<1
	(ve)	(ve)	(X)	1	31.1	<1	0	16.8	<1	1	33.1	<1
	(uv)	(uv)	(X)	0	6.0	<2						
	(uv)	(pl)	(X)	0	21.7	<1						
	(gl)	(gl)	(X)	1	21.5	<1	0	9.2	<1	1	14.2	<1
	(X)	(la)	(la)	0	87.9	<1	1	29.9	<1	2	59.7	<1
	(X)	(cf)	(cf)	1	42.8	<1	0	11.1	<1	2	24.3	<1
	(X)	(ve)	(ve)	0	20.8	<1	0	14.2	<1	0	26.3	<1
	(X)	(ve)	(uv)	0	5.0	<3						
	(X)	(pl)	(uv)	0	6.1	<1						
	(X)	(pl)	(pl)	1	40.9	<1	12	28.5	<1	4	40.9	<1
	(X)	(gl)	(gl)	0	38.5	<1	0	22.8	<1	0	31.7	<1
	(ve)	(X)	(ve)	3	27.0	<1	0	15.6	<1	9	32.3	<1

TABLE 5.2 (continued)

b) *Root patterns with one consonant group and a specific consonant*

				AR			BH			HEB		
				No	Ne	P,%	No	Ne	P,%	No	Ne	P,%
	(n)	(na)	(X)	6	20.7	<1	0	9.5	<1	6	15.4	<2
	(X)	(n)	(na)	4	10.8	<4	0	4.5	<4	4	12.0	<3
	(n)	(li)	(X)	0	32.8	<1	1	17.7	<1	1	24.6	<1
	(X)	(n)	(li)	2	15.8	<1	0	8.6	<1	5	16.0	<1
	(X)	(li)	(n)	5	19.1	<1	0	8.6	<1	12	21.7	<4
	(l)	(li)	(X)	0	15.2	<1	0	5.2	<3	1	9.4	<1
	(li)	(l)	(X)	0	16.2	<1	0	7.6	<1	1	11.3	<1
	(X)	(l)	(li)	0	28.0	<1	0	16.2	<1	1	24.4	<1
Manner	(X)	(li)	(l)	0	29.8	<1	0	7.6	<1	3	23.0	<1
	(l)	(X)	(li)	0	17.6	<1	0	6.3	<2	2	10.6	<1
	(r)	(li)	(X)	0	24,4	<1	0	12.0	<1	0	17.2	<1
	(li)	(r)	(X)	0	23.5	<1	0	9.7	<1	0	15.3	<1
	(X)	(r)	(li)	0	40.6	<1	1	20.7	<1	3	33.3	<1
	(X)	(li)	(r)	0	38.9	<1	0	22.5	<1	1	34.7	<1
	(li)	(X)	(r)	0	26.0	<1	1	12.6	<1	2	18.0	<1
	(VE)	(VE)	(X)	0	12.8	<1	0	7.0	<1	1	14.0	<1
	(X)	(VE)	(VE)	0	7.2	<1	0	4.2	<1	0	8.8	<1
	(VE)	(X)	(VE)	0	7.9	<1	0	4.7	<2	6	10.9	-
	(q)	(VE)	(X)	0	8.6	<1	0	6.0	<2	0	11.5	<1
	(VE)	(q)	(X)	0	6.9	<1	0	5.6	<2	0	11.8	<1
	(X)	(q)	(VE)	0	3.9	<5	0	9.1	<1	0	9.4	<1
	(X)	(VE)	(q)	0	8.5	<1	0	7.3	<1	0	12.7	<1
Place	(q)	(uv)	(X)	0	4.2	<5						
	(uv)	(q)	(X)	0	6.7	<1						
	(m)	(la)	(X)	0	20.2	<1	0	8.9	<1	3	19.1	<1
	(la)	(m)	(X)	0	20.7	<1	0	8.6	<1	3	19.0	<1
	(X)	(m)	(la)	0	29.9	<1	0	9.2	<1	0	19.5	<1
	(X)	(la)	(m)	0	32.3	<1	1	10.8	<1	2	23.7	<1
	(m)	(X)	(la)	0	21.7	<1	0	8.9	<1	6	18.7	<1

[1] Listed are the observed and expected frequencies (No and Ne) of the triliteral root patterns in *AR*, *BH* and *HEB* which exhibit absolute combinatory constraints. The consonant groups are classified either on the basis of Manner or on that of Place. The symbol 'VE' is used for the group of the velar stops /k/ and /G/ in order to differentiate these from the uvular stop /q/. Throughout this thesis and in part a of this table, however, the symbol 've' is used for the combined group of these three consonants, because they pattern as a single group in their co-occurrence relationships (see § 5.6.3). Shown here are the cases in which the actual frequency (No) is 0 in at least one language. In these cases the values for No and Ne are also given for the other language(s). The level of significance P for the difference between No and Ne is usually considerably smaller than 1%. There are no uvular fricatives in Hebrew (see *Table 2.2*). For further explanation see § 4.2.

TABLE 5.3

Avoided triliteral root patterns in Arabic and Hebrew[1] (Manner)

		C1C2X											XC2C3											C1XC3										
		ls	ds	st	lf	df	fr	f	S	na	li	gl	ls	ds	st	lf	df	fr	f	S	na	li	gl	ls	ds	st	lf	df	fr	f	S	na	li	gl
ls	AR	-*				-							-											-*										
	BH												-																						
	HEB	-*											-*											-*										
ds	AR	-*												-*					-*												-*				
	BH	-*												-																					
	HEB																																		
st	AR	-*													-*																				
	BH	-													-*					-*							-*								
	HEB	-*													-*					-							-*								
lf	AR				-*											-																			
	BH				-	-										-*	-											-*	-*						
	HEB				-	-										-*	-											-*							
df	AR				-											-	-											-	-						
	HEB				-											-	-*											-							

TABLE 5.3 (continued)

		C1C2X											XC2C3											C1XC3										
		ls	ds	st	lf	df	fr	f	S	na	li	gl	ls	ds	st	lf	df	fr	f	S	na	li	gl	ls	ds	st	lf	df	fr	f	S	na	li	gl
fr	AR						–*											–*											–*					
	BH						–*		–									–*											–*					
	HEB						–*											–*											–*					
f	AR																																	
	BH								–											–											–			
	HEB																																	
S	AR	–																																
	BH	–																			*													
	HEB			–*																	–													
na	AR									–*		–*																						
	BH									–*	–	–*																						
	HEB									–*		–*																						
li	AR									–*		–*											*	–*										–*
	BH									–*		–*											*	–*										–*
	HEB									–*		–*											*	–*										–*
gl	AR								–			–*												–*										
	BH											–*												–*										
	HEB											–*												–*										

---

[1] This table shows the avoided triliteral root patterns of *AR*, *BH* and *HEB* with two specified positions which contain a pair of consonants from groups classified on the basis of Manner. In the remaining position (X) an arbitrary consonant is present. In other avoided root patterns the individual consonant /f/ (fa') in Arabic or /S/ (sade) in Hebrew is present in one position. The consonant group or the consonant in the first root position of the pair is shown in the leftmost column, that which is present in its second position is indicated in the heading of the table. The stops and the fricatives have also been subdivided into their voiced and voiceless subsets. The table shows the root patterns which have actual frequencies of occurrence that are significantly lower than the expected ones. The blanks indicate root patterns with expected requencies.

TABLE 5.4

Avoided triliteral root patterns in Arabic and Hebrew[1] (Place)

		C1C2X												XC2C3												C1XC3										
		la	cs	df	co	so	ve	uv	q	G (k+)	pl	gl	la	cs	df	co	so	ve	uv	q	G (k+)	pl	gl	la	cs	df	co	so	ve	uv	q	G (k+)	G	plgl
la	AR	-*											-*											-*										
	BH	-*											-*											-*										
	HEB	-*											-*											-*										
cs	AR	*-*			-								*-*	*-*											*-*									
	BH	*-*											*-*	*-*											*-*									
	HEB	*-*											-*	*-*											*-*									
df	AR	*-*											*-*	*-*	*-*										*-*									
	BH	*-*											*-*	*-*	*-*										*-*									
	HEB	-*											*-*	*-*	*-*										*-*									
co	AR	*-*											*-*	*-*										*-*									
	BH	*-*											*-*	*-*										*-*									
	HEB	*-*											*-*	*-*										-									
so	AR	*-*											*-*	*-*										*-									
	BH	*-*											*-*	*-*										-									
	HEB	*-*											*-*											-									
ve	AR	-*-*	-*-*	-*										*-	*-*								*-*	*-*	*-*							
	BH	-*-*	-*-*	-*										*-*	*-*								*-*	*-*	*-*							
	HEB	-*	-*-*	-*										*-*	*-*								*-*	*-*	*-*							

TABLE 5.4 (continued)

		C1C2X											XC2C3											C1XC3										
		la	cs	cf	co	so	ve	uv	q	G	pl	gl	la	cs	cf	co	so	ve	uv	q	G	pl	gl	la	cs	cf	co	so	ve	uv	q	G	pl	gl
										k+											k+											k+		
q	AR						-*	-*		-*	-*							-*			-*									-		-*		-*
	BH							-		-	-							-			-									-		-	-	-
	HEB						-*			-*	-*							-*			-*	*								-*		-*	-*	-*
k+G	AR						-*	-*		-*	-*							-*	-*		-*	-*								-*		-*	-*	
	BH						-*	-*		-	-*							-	-		-	-								-*		-*	-	
	HEB						-*	-*		-	-*							-*	-*		-*	-*								-*		-*	-*	-*
uv	AR						-*	-		-*	-*							-				-*												'
	BH									-*	-*																							
	HEB									-*	-*																							
pl	AR						-*				-*										-	-*								-*				-*
	BH										-*											-*								-*				-*
	HEB										-*										-	-*								-*				-*
gl	AR				-*																		-*		-*									
	BH																						-*		-*									
	HEB																						-*		-*									

¹ This table shows the avoided triliteral root patterns of *AR*, *BH* and *HEB* which contain a pair of consonants from groups classified on the basis of Place. In the remaining position (X) an arbitrary consonant is present. In other avoided root patterns the group of the velar stops /k/ and /G/ or the uvular stop /q/ is present. See *Table 5.3* for further explanation.

TABLE 5.5

Avoided triliteral root patterns in Arabic and Hebrew with two labials[1]

		C1C2X			XC2C3			C1XC3		
		m	b	f(p)	m	b	f(p)	m	b	f(p)
m	AR	-*	-*	-		-*	-*	-*	-*	-
	BH		-*	-				-*	-	
	HEB	-*	-	-		-	-*		-	-
b	AR	-*	-*	-	-*		-*	-*	-*	-
	BH									
	HEB	-	-	-	-		-*		-	-
p(f)	AR		-	-	-*	-*			-	-
	BH		-		-*					
	HEB	-*	-*	-*	-				-	-

[1] Shown are the avoided root patterns which contain two labials and have arbitrary consonants in the remaining position. The /f/ in Arabic corresponds to the /p/ in Hebrew (see § 2.1.1). There are no entries in the table for root patterns of the type XC2C3 with identical consonants in C2 and C3, because these root patterns belong to the separate group of the Mediae Geminatae.

TABLE 5.6

Avoided and preferred triliteral root patterns in Arabic and Hebrew with pairs of labial and coronal sonorants[1]

		C1C2X				XC2C3				C1XC3			
		m	n	l	r	m	n	l	r	m	n	l	r
m	AR	-*								-*			
	BH												
	HEB												
n	AR	-*	-	-*	-*			-*	-*		-*	+	
	BH	-	-	-	-*				-				
	HEB	-	-	-*	-*		-						
l	AR		-	-			-*		-*	+	+	-	-*
	BH		-	-			-		-*	+	+	-	-
	HEB								-*				-
r	AR	-*	-*	-*	-*		-*	-*	-*	+	+	-*	-*
	BH		-	-	-*		-	-	-	+*		-	-
	HEB		-*	-*	-*		-*	-*					-

[1] The avoided and preferred root patterns of *AR*, *BH* and *HEB* which contain two labial sonorants, two coronal sonorants or a pair of one of each and arbitray consonants in the remaining position. There are no entries in the table for root paterns of the type XC2C3 which have identical consonants in C2 and C3, because these root patterns belong to the different file of the Mediae Geminatae.

TABLE 5.7

Avoided tiliterals in Arabic and Hebrew with a labial or coronal sonorant[1] (Manner)

a) The sonorant is the first member of the pair

| | | C1C2X | | | | | | | | | XC2C3 | | | | | | | | | C1XC3 | | | | | | | |
	ls	ds	st	lf	df	fr	na	li	gl	ls	ds	st	lf	df	fr	na	li	gl	ls	ds	st	lf	df	fr	na	li	gl
m AR		-					-*																				
m BH		-	-								-																
m HEB																											
n AR							-*	-*								-	-*										
n BH							-*	-*								-	-*										
n HEB						-	-*								-	-*								-			
l AR								-*									-*									-*	
l BH							-*	-								-*	-*									-*	-*
l HEB							-*									-*									-*		
r AR							-*	-*									-*									-*	-*
r BH																	-*								-*		
r HEB							-*									-*									-*		

TABLE 5.7 (continued)

b) *The sonorant is the second member of the pair*

		C1C2X				XC2C3				C1XC3			
		m	n	l	r	m	n	l	r	m	n	l	r
ls	AR												
	BH												
	HEB												
ds	AR												
	BH												
	HEB												
st	AR												
	BH												
	HEB												
lf	AR												
	BH												
	HEB												
df	AR												
	BH												
	HEB												
fr	AR												
	BH												
	HEB												
na	AR	-*	-*	-	-*	-*				-			
	BH	-*			-	-							
	HEB	-		-	-*	-*							
li	AR		-*	-*	-*		-*	-*	-*			-	-*
	BH			-*	-*	-*	-*	-*					-*
	HEB	-		-*	-*			-*	-*			-	-*
gl	AR												
	BH												
	HEB												

[1] The avoided root patterns of *AR*, *BH* and *HEB* which contain in one root position the labial /m/ or one of the coronal sonorants /n/, /l/ or /r/, in another position members from one of the consonant groups classified on the basis of Manner and arbitray consonants in the remaining position.

TABLE 5.8

Avoided tiliterals in Arabic and Hebrew with a labial or coronal sonorant[1] (Place)

a) *The sonorant is the first member of the pair*

		C1C2X									XC2C3									C1XC3								
		la	cs	cf	co	so	ve	uv	pl	gl	la	cs	cf	co	so	ve	uv	pl	gl	la	cs	cf	co	so	ve	uv	pl	gl
m	AR	_*									_*									_*								
	BH	_*									_*									_*								
	HEB	_*									_*									_*								
n	AR	_			_*									_*														
	BH				_*									_*														
	HEB				_*									_*														
l	AR		_	_	_*									_*										_*				
	BH				_*									_*														
	HEB				_*									_*														
r	AR				_*									_*										_*				
	BH				_*									_*										_*				
	HEB				_*									_*										_				

TABLE 5.8 (continued)

b) *The sonorant is the second member of the pair*

		C1C2X				XC2C3				C1XC3			
		m	n	l	r	m	n	l	r	m	n	l	r
la	AR	-*				-*							
	BH	-*				-*							
	HEB	-*				-*							
cs	AR												
	BH												
	HEB												
cf	AR												
	BH												-
	HEB												-*
co	AR												
	BH												-*
	HEB												
so	AR		-	-*	-*	-*	-*	-*					-*
	BH	-	-	-*	-*	-*	-*	-*					-
	HEB		-*	-*	-*	-*	-*	-*					-*
ve	AR												
	BH												
	HEB												
uv	AR												
	BH												
	HEB												
pl	AR												
	BH												
	HEB												
gl	AR												
	BH												
	HEB												

[1] This table shows the avoided root patterns of *AR*, *BH* and *HEB* which contain in one root position the labial sonorant /m/ or one of the coronal sonorants /n/, /l/ or /r/ and in another position members from a consonant group classified on the basis of Place.

TABLE 5.9

Co-occurrence restrictions on the Mediae Geminatae[1] (Place)

		la	cs	cf	co	so	ve	gu	gl
la	AR								
	BH	-							
	HEB	-							
cs	AR								
	BH								
	HEB		-						
cf	AR								
	BH								
	HEB			-					
co	AR				-				
	BH				-*				
	HEB				-				
so	AR					-			
	BH								
	HEB					-			
ve	AR								
	BH								
	HEB						-		
gu	AR								
	BH								
	HEB								
gl	AR								
	BH								
	HEB								

[1] Co-occurrence restrictions on consonant groups classified on the basis of Place in root positions C1 and C2 of the Mediae Geminatae in *AR*, *BH* and *HEB*. The coronal obstruents were also subdivided into coronal stops and fricatives. The pharyngeals/laryngeals and the uvular fricatives in *AR* are combined into the group of the gutturals.

TABLE 5.10

Avoided quadriliterals in Arabic and Hebrew[1] (Manner)

		Adjacent			Nonadjacent		
		C1C2	C2C3	C3C4	C1C3	C2C4	C1C4
(st) (st)	AR		-*				
	HEB		-*				
(st) (na)	AR						
	HEB						-
(st) (li)	AR						
	HEB						
(fr) (st)	AR						
	HEB						
(fr) (fr)	AR						
	HEB		-	-			
(fr) (li)	AR						
	HEB						
(na) (fr)	AR					-	-
	HEB						
(na) (na)	AR						
	HEB	-	-				
(na) (li)	AR						
	HEB	-					
(li) (st)	AR						
	HEB						
(li) (fr)	AR						
	HEB						
(li) (li)	AR	-	-*	-*		-*	
	HEB	-	-*	-*			

[1] Avoided quadriliteral root patterns in *AR* and *HEB* which contain a pair of consonants from groups classified on the basis of Manner in adjacent and nonadjacent positions. Group patterns which are not avoided in either *AR* and *HEB* are not shown.

TABLE 5.11

Avoided quadriliterals in Arabic and Hebrew[1] (Place)

		Adjacent			Nonadjacent		
		C1C2	C2C3	C3C4	C1C3	C2C4	C1C4
(la) (la)	AR	-	-	-*	-*		
	HEB	-	-*	-*			
(co) (co)	AR			-*			
	HEB	-	-*	-*			
(so) (so)	AR	-	-*	-*			
	HEB	-	-*	-*			
(ve) (ve)	AR						
	HEB	-	-	-			
(ve) (gu)	AR						
	HEB	-					
(gu) (ve)	AR						
	HEB						-
(gu) (gu)	AR	-*					
	HEB	-*					
(gl) (co)	AR					-	
	HEB						

[1] Avoided quadriliteral root patterns in *AR* and *HEB* with pairs of consonants from groups which are classified on the basis of Place in adjacent and non-adjacent positions. Group patterns which are not avoided in either *AR* and *HEB* are not shown.

TABLE 5.12

Avoided root patterns of the type C1C2C1C2 in Arabic and Hebrew[1] (Manner)

| C1 | | C2 | | | | | | | | |
		ls	ds	st	lf	df	fr	na	li	gl
ls	AR									
	HEB									
ds	AR									
	HEB									
st	AR									
	HEB									
lf	AR								-	
	HEB									
df	AR									
	HEB									
fr	AR									
	HEB					-				
na	AR									
	HEB									
li	AR									
	HEB								-	
gl	AR									
	HEB									

[1] Avoided quadriliteral root patterns of the type C1C2C1C2 in *AR* and *HEB*. The consonant groups are classified on the basis of Manner. The leftmost column shows the consonant groups which are present in C1 and the heading those in C2. The findings for the consonant pairs which are present in C2 and C3 are exactly the same.

TABLE 5.13

Avoided root patterns of the type C1C2C1C2 in Arabic and Hebrew[1] (Place)

		C2							
	C1	la	cs	cf	co	so	ve	gu	gl
la	AR								
	HEB								
co	AR				-*				
	HEB								
so	AR					-			
	HEB					-			
ve	AR						-		
	HEB								
gu	AR							-	
	HEB								
gl	AR								
	HEB								

[1] Shown are the avoided quadriliteral root patterns of the type C1C2C1C2 in *AR* and *HEB*. The consonant groups are classified on the basis of Place. Since in general the frequencies of occurrence of the different root patterns of this type are rather small, the coronal obstruents were not subdivided into coronal stops and fricatives and in *AR* the uvulars and the pharyngeals/laryngeals were combined as the group of the gutturals. The findings are exactly the same for the consonant pairs which are present in C2 and C3.

TABLE 5.14

Avoided root patterns in Arabic and Hebrew with three specified positions and with nasals in at least one of the three root positions (Manner)[1]

C1 or C2		C1=na C3					C2=na C3					C3=na C2				
		st	fr	na	li	gl	st	fr	na	li	gl	st	fr	na	li	gl
ls	AR															
	HEB															
ds	AR															
	HEB															
st	AR															
	HEB															
lf	AR															
	HEB															
df	AR															
	HEB															
fr	AR															
	HEB															
na	AR	-*	-				-*	-								
	HEB	-*					-*									
li	AR				-*											
	HEB			-	-*		-								-	
gl	AR															
	HEB															

[1] Avoided triliteral root patterns in *AR* and *HEB* with three specified consonant groups classified on the basis of Manner. As is indicated in the table heading, a nasal is present in one of the three root positions. The consonant group which is present in the first of the other two positions is shown in the leftmost column and that which is present in the second of these positions is indicated in the table heading.

TABLE 5.15

Avoided root patterns in Arabic and Hebrew with three specified positions and with a liquid in at least one of the three root positions[1] (Place)

C1 or C2		C1=li / C3									C2=li / C3									C3=li / C2								
		ls	ds	st	lf	df	fr	na	li	gl	ls	ds	st	lf	df	fr	na	li	gl	ls	ds	st	lf	df	fr	na	li	gl
ls	AR																										*	*
	HEB																										*	*
ds	AR																										*	*
	HEB																										-	-
st	AR								-									-									*	*
	HEB								-									-									*	*
lf	AR																	-									*	*
	HEB																	-									-	-
df	AR																										*	
	HEB																											
fr	AR								*									*							-		-	*
	HEB								-								-	-									*	*
na	AR																-											
	HEB																											
li	AR	-		*	*		*						*	*		*							*		*			
	HEB	-		-	*		-						*	*		-							-		-			
gl	AR																											
	HEB																											

[1] Avoided triliteral root patterns in *AR* and *HEB* with three specified consonant groups classified on the basis of Manner. As indicated in the table heading, a liquid is present in one of the three root positions. For further explanation see *Table 5.14*.

TABLE 5.16.1

Avoided root patterns in Arabic and Hebrew with three specified positions and which contain stops in at least one position[1] (Manner)

C1 or C2		C1=st C3					C2=st C3					C3=st C2				
		st	fr	na	li	gl	st	fr	na	li	gl	st	fr	na	li	gl
st	AR	-*	-*				-*	-*				-*				
	HEB	-*	-*				-*	-*				-*				
fr	AR	-	-				-					-	-*			
	HEB	-*	-*					-								
na	AR															
	HEB															
li	AR															
	HEB															
gl	AR															
	HEB															

[1] Avoided triliteral root patterns in *AR* and *HEB* with three specified consonant groups classified on the basis of Manner which contain stops in at least one position (see the heading of the table) and any of the consonant groups in the other two positions. See *Table 5.14* for further explanation.

TABLE 5.16.2

Avoided root patterns in Arabic and Hebrew with three specified positions which contain fricatives in at least one position¹ (Manner)

C1 or C2		C1=fr C3					C2=fr C3					C3=fr C2				
		st	fr	na	li	gl	st	fr	na	li	gl	st	fr	na	li	gl
st	AR	-						-				-*	-			
	HEB		-					-*					-*			
fr	AR	-*	-*				-*	-*				-	-*			
	HEB	-*	-*				-*	-*					-*			
na	AR															
	HEB															
li	AR															
	HEB															
gl	AR															
	HEB															

¹ Avoided root patterns in *AR* and *HEB* with three specified consonant groups classified on the basis of Manner which contain fricatives in at least one position and any of the consonant groups in the other two positions. See *Table 5.14* for further explanation.

TABLE 5.17

Avoided root patterns in Arabic and Hebrew with three specified positions and with labials in at least one of the three root positions (Place)[1]

C1 or C2		C1=la C3								C2=la C3								C3=la C2							
		la	cs	cf	co	so	ve	gu	gl	la	cs	cf	co	so	ve	gu	gl	la	cs	cf	co	so	ve	gu	gl
la	AR	-*	-*	-*	-*	-*	-*	-*		-*	-*	-*	-*	-*	-	-*		-*			-				
	HEB	-*	-*	-*	-*	-*	-	-		-*	-*	-*	-*	-*	-	-		-*		-	-				
cs	AR		-	-						-*								-*		-					
	HEB		-	-						-*								-*		-					
cf	AR			-						-*		-						-*		-					
	HEB									-*								-*							
co	AR				-*					-*								-*			-*				
	HEB				-*					-*								-*			-*				
so	AR					-*		-*		-*				-*				-*				-*			
	HEB					-*		-		-*								-*				-*			
ve	AR						-			-*					-			-*					-		
	HEB						-			-*					-			-*							
gu	AR							-		-*							-	-*						-*	
	HEB									-*								-*						-*	
gl	AR																								
	HEB																								

[1] Avoided triliteral root patterns in AR and HEB with three specified consonant groups classified on the basis of Place. A labial is present in one or more of the three root positions see Table 5.14.

TABLE 5.18

Avoided root patterns in Arabic and Hebrew with three specified root positions and with coronal sonorants in at least one of the three root positions[1] (Place)

C1 or C2		C1=so — C3								C2=so — C3								C3=so — C2							
		la	cs	cf	co	so	ve	gu	gl	la	cs	cf	co	so	ve	gu	gl	la	cs	cf	co	so	ve	gu	gl
la	AR	-*				-				-				-*				-*				-*			
	HEB	-*				-								-*				-*				-*			
cs	AR	-												-*				-				-*			
	HEB	-												-								-			
cf	AR			-										-*						-*		-*			
	HEB			-										-*						-		-*			
co	AR				-*									-*							-*	-*			
	HEB				-*									-*							-*	-*			
so	AR	-*	-*	-*	-*	-*	-	-*	-*	-*	-*	-*	-*	-*	-	-*						-*			
	HEB	-*	-*	-	-*	-*	-*	-*	-*	-*	-*	-	-*	-*	-*	-*		-				-*			
ve	AR						-							-*								-*	-*		
	HEB						-							-								-	-		
gu	AR							-*						-*								-*		-*	
	HEB							-						-*								-*		-*	
gl	AR																								
	HEB																								

[1] Avoided root patterns in *AR* and *HEB* with three specified consonant groups. A coronal sonorant is present in one or more of the three root positions. For further explanation see *Table 5.14*.

TABLE 5.19

Avoided root patterns in Arabic and Hebrew with two specified consonant groups and a labial or coronal sonorant[1] (Place)

a) *Labial sonorant m*

C1 or C2		C1=m					C2=m					C3=m				
		C3					C3					C2				
		st	fr	na	li	gl	st	fr	na	li	gl	st	fr	na	li	gl
st	AR															
	HEB															
fr	AR															
	HEB															
na	AR						-									
	HEB															
li	AR															
	HEB															
gl	AR															
	HEB															

b) *Coronal sonorant n*

C1 or C2		C1=n					C2=n					C3=n				
		C3					C3					C2				
		st	fr	na	li	gl	st	fr	na	li	gl	st	fr	na	li	gl
st	AR							-								
	HEB															
fr	AR							-								
	HEB															
na	AR															
	HEB						-									
li	AR															
	HEB															
gl	AR															
	HEB															

TABLE 5.19 (continued)

c) *Coronal sonorant l*

C1 or C2	C1=l					C2=l					C3=l				
	C3					C3					C2				
	st	fr	na	li	gl	st	fr	na	li	gl	st	fr	na	li	gl
st AR			-				_*								
HEB							_*								
fr AR			-				_*								
HEB							_*								
na AR															
HEB															
li AR						-	-								
HEB															
gl AR															
HEB															

d) *Coronal sonorant r*

C1 or C2	C1=r					C2=r					C3=r				
	C3					C3					C2				
	st	fr	na	li	gl	st	fr	na	li	gl	st	fr	na	li	gl
st AR							_*								
HEB							_*								
fr AR							_*								
HEB							_*								
na AR															
HEB															
li AR						_*	_*				_*	_*			
HEB						-					-	-			
gl AR															
HEB															

[1] Avoided triliteral root patterns in *AR* and *HEB* with three specified positions. A labial or a coronal sonorant is present in one of the three root positions. The other two root positions are occupied by consonant groups classified on the basis of Manner. The stops and fricatives were not subdivided into their voiceless and voiced subsets. See *Table 5.14* for further explanation.

TABLE 5.20

Avoided root patterns in Arabic and Hebrew with two specified consonant groups and a labial or coronal sonorant[1] (Place)

a) *Labial sonorant m*

C1 or C2		C1=m C3						C2=m C3						C3=m C2					
		la	co	so	ve	gu	gl	la	co	so	ve	gu	gl	la	co	so	ve	gu	gl
la	AR	-	-	-				-	-	-				-					
	HEB																		
co	AR	-						-*						-*	-				
	HEB	-						-						-					
so	AR							-						-		-			
	HEB															-			
ve	AR													-					
	HEB																		
gu	AR							-*						-*					-
	HEB							-						-					
gl	AR																		
	HEB																		

b) *Coronal sonorant n*

C1 or C2		C1=m C3						C2=m C3						C3=m C2					
		la	co	so	ve	gu	gl	la	co	so	ve	gu	gl	la	co	so	ve	gu	gl
la	AR	-*																	
	HEB	-																	
co	AR																		
	HEB																		
so	AR																-		
	HEB																		
ve	AR																		
	HEB																		
gu	AR										-								
	HEB										-								-
gl	AR																		
	HEB																		

TABLE 5.20 (continued)

c) *Coronal sonorant l*

C1 or C2		C1=l / C3 — la	co	so	ve	gu	gl	C2=l / C3 — la	co	so	ve	gu	gl	C3=l / C2 — la	co	so	ve	gu	gl
la	AR									-				-					
	HEB									-				-					
co	AR								-*					-*					
	HEB								-*										
so	AR							-	-*										
	HEB							-				-							
ve	AR								-										
	HEB																		
gu	AR								-*									-	
	HEB																		
gl	AR																		
	HEB																		

d) *Coronal sonorant r*

C1 or C2		C1=r / C3 — la	co	so	ve	gu	gl	C2=r / C3 — la	co	so	ve	gu	gl	C3=r / C2 — la	co	so	ve	gu	gl
la	AR	-						-						-					
	HEB		-						-					-					
co	AR	-							-*										
	HEB								-*										
so	AR							-*	-*			-*			-				
	HEB							-	-*										
ve	AR								-										
	HEB																		
gu	AR								-*								-		-
	HEB								-										
gl	AR																		
	HEB																		

[1] Avoided triliteral root patterns in *AR* and *HEB* with three specified positions. A labial or a coronal sonorant is present in one of the three root positions. The other two root positions are occupied by consonant groups classified on the basis of Place. For statistical reasons the coronal obstruents were not subdivided into the corresponding stops and fricatives and the pharyngeals/laryngeals and uvular fricatives and the in *AR* were combined as the group of the gutturals (see *Table 5.14*).

TABLE 6.1

Preferred triliteral root patterns in Arabic and Hebrew[1] (Manner)

C1C2X

		ls	ds	st	lf	df	fr	f	S	na	li	gl
ls	AR											+*
	BH									+		
	HEB									+		+*
ds	AR									+		+
	BH									+		+
	HEB									+		+
st	AR									+*		+*
	BH									+*		+*
	HEB									+*		+*
lf	AR	+*								+		
	BH											
	HEB											
df	AR											
	BH											
	HEB											
fr	AR									+		
	BH									+		
	HEB											

XC2C3

		ls	ds	st	lf	df	fr	f	S	na	li	gl
ls	AR									+	+	
	BH										+	
	HEB										+	+
ds	AR						+					
	BH										+	+
	HEB										+*	+
st	AR									+*	+*	+*
	BH									+*	+*	
	HEB									+*	+*	+
lf	AR	+									+*	
	BH											
	HEB											
df	AR									+	+	+
	BH											
	HEB											
fr	AR									+*	+	
	BH										+	+
	HEB										+	+

C1XC3

		ls	ds	st	lf	df	fr	f	S	na	li	gl
ls	AR				+							
	BH				+*							
	HEB											
ds	AR											
	BH											
	HEB											
st	AR											
	BH											
	HEB						+*					
lf	AR											
	BH	+*										
	HEB											
df	AR										+	+
	BH										+	
	HEB											
fr	AR											
	BH		+	+								
	HEB			+*								

TABLE 6.1 (continued)

	C1C2X											XC2C3											C1XC3										
	ls	ds	st	lf	df	fr	f	S	na	li	gl	ls	ds	st	lf	df	fr	f	S	na	li	gl	ls	ds	st	lf	df	fr	f	S	na	li	gl
f AR	+*																																
f BH																																	
f HEB																																	
S AR																																	
S BH									+																								
S HEB									+																								
na AR					+*	+	+*									+																	
na BH					+*		+									+																	
na HEB			+*		+	+*																											
li AR			+*									+	+*	+	+*	+*	+*																
li BH			+										+*	+	+	+	+										+	+			+		
li HEB					+	+*	+*					+	+*	+	+	+*	+*											+		+	+		
gl AR			+*					+*				+							+*					+									
gl BH				+	+			+*				+*	+						+								+			+*			
gl HEB				+	+			+*					+						+								+			+			

¹ Preferred triliteral root patterns in *AR*, *BH* and *HEB* which contain pairs of consonants from groups classified on the basis of Manner. See *Table 5.3* for further explanation.

TABLE 6.2

Preferred triliteral root patterns in Arabic and Hebrew[1] (Place)

		C1C2X								k +				XC2C3								k +				C1XC3								k +		
		la	cs	cf	co	so	ve	q	j	uv	pl	gl	la	cs	cf	co	so	ve	q	j	uv	pl	gl	la	cs	cf	co	so	ve	q	j	uv	pl	gl
la	AR	+*	+*	+										+*	+*														+	+	+*	+	+*		
	BH	+												+*	+*														+	+	+				
	HEB	+*	+*											+*	+* +*														+	+	+			+*	
cs	AR	+			+*			+				+			+*											+								
	BH	+									+		+																					
cf	AR	+					+*			+* +* +			+*		+*												+		+*					
	BH			+*					+*																									
	HEB			+*					+*		+																							
co	AR	+*			+*					+* +* +* +			+*	+*											+			+		+*				
	BH	+								+* +* +			+	+*																				
	HEB	+								+* +		+	+*	+*					+										+				
so	AR			+					+* +* +* +*			+* +* +		+	+* +* +*			+* +* +		+* +* +*		+			+* +					
	BH								+* +* +					+* +*				+* +*			+* +*					+* +					
	HEB			+					+* +*					+* +* +				+* +*			+* +*					+					

TABLE 6.2 (continued)

C1C2X (sub-columns: la cs cf co so ve q j | k+ | uv pl gl)

	la	cs	cf	co	so	ve	q	j	uv	pl	gl
ve AR			+								
BH			+*								
HEB	+		+*								
q AR											
BH			+								
HEB											
k + j AR			+*								
BH											
HEB	+		+								
uv AR			+*								
BH											
HEB	+										
pl AR		+*	+* +*								
BH			+								
HEB			+								
gl AR			+					+*	+*	+*	
BH			+ +								
HEB											

XC2C3 (sub-columns: la cs cf co so ve q j | k+ | uv pl gl)

	la	cs	cf	co	so	ve	q	j	uv	pl	gl
ve AR			+							+	
BH			+								
HEB			+*								
q AR											
BH											
HEB											
k + j AR				+*							
BH				+*							
HEB				+*							
uv AR				+							
BH											
HEB											
pl AR	+			+							
BH											
HEB											
gl AR			+	+					+		+*
BH			+	+							
HEB	+*		+*	+*					+		

C1XC3 (sub-columns: la cs cf co so ve q j | k+ | uv pl gl)

	la	cs	cf	co	so	ve	q	j	uv	pl	gl
ve AR			+								
BH											
HEB											
q AR											
BH											
HEB		+									
k + j AR											
BH											
HEB											
uv AR											
BH											
HEB											
pl AR	+*										
BH											
HEB											
gl AR											
BH											
HEB											

¹ Preferred triliteral root patterns in *AR*, *BH* and *HEB* which contain pairs of consonants from groups classified on the basis of Place. For further explanation see *Table 5.4*.

TABLE 6.3

Preferred triliterals in Arabic and Hebrew with a labial or coronal sonorant[1] (Manner)

a) *The sonorant is the first member of the pair*

		C1C2X									XC2C3									C1XC3								
		ls	ds	st	lf	df	fr	na	li	gl	ls	ds	st	lf	df	fr	na	li	gl	ls	ds	st	lf	df	fr	na	li	gl
m	AR																			+								
	BH					+								+		+				+								
	HEB				+		+																					
n	AR	+*		+*	+*		+*				+														+			+*
	BH	+		+*	+*																							+*
	HEB	+*		+*																								+
l	AR						+				+		+*	+		+								+*	+			
	BH						+						+			+												
	HEB						+																					
r	AR	+*		+*								+*	+*			+*								+*	+			
	BH					+						+*	+*			+												
	HEB	+				+*					+	+	+*		+	+*								+	+			

TABLE 6.3 (continued)

b) *The sonorant is the second member of the pair*

		C1C2X				XC2C3				C1XC3			
		m	n	l	r	m	n	l	r	m	n	l	r
ls	AR				+								
	BH								+				
	HEB	+*			+				+				
ds	AR	+			+	+							
	BH		+										
	HEB		+						+				
st	AR		+	+	+*	+		+					
	BH		+					+					
	HEB				+*			+*					
lf	AR								+*				
	BH					+							
	HEB					+							
df	AR								+				
	BH	+											
	HEB												
fr	AR							+	+*				
	BH					+		+					
	HEB					+		+					
na	AR												
	BH												
	HEB												
li	AR												
	BH									+			
	HEB												
gl	AR												
	BH												
	HEB												

[1] Preferred root patterns in *AR*, *BH* and *HEB* which contain in one root position the labial sonorant /m/ or one of the coronal sonorants /n/, /l/ or /r/, in one of the other two root positions members from one of the consonant groups classified on the basis of Manner and arbitrary consonants in the remaining root position.

TABLE 6.4

Preferred triliterals in Arabic and Hebrew with a labial or coronal sonorant[1] ('Place)

a) *The sonorant is the first member of the pair*

		C1C2X									XC2C3									C1XC3								
		la	cs	cf	co	so	ve	uv	pl	gl	la	cs	cf	co	so	ve	uv	pl	gl	la	cs	cf	co	so	ve	uv	pl	gl
m	AR								+*				+*	+*											+			
	BH																								+			
	HEB								+				+*	+*											+*			
n	AR			+	+		+*	+*								+			+*									
	BH		+*	+	+*		+												+*									
	HEB			+*	+*		+*												+				+*					
l	AR	+*							+*	+						+*									+			
	BH								+*	+*								+*		+								
	HEB								+*	+*								+*		+*			+*					
r	AR		+*				+*		+				+*	+*		+*		+		+*	+*	+*	+*					
	BH				+*		+						+	+		+*				+	+*							
	HEB				+							+	+*	+*		+*												

TABLE 6.4 (continued)

b) The sonorant is the second member of the pair

		C1C2X				XC2C3				C1XC3			
		m	n	l	r	m	n	l	r	m	n	l	r
la	AR												
	BH			+	+								
	HEB												
cs	AR				+*		+			+*			
	BH							+*					
	HEB					+		+					
cf	AR					+		+*					+
	BH							+*					+*
	HEB					+		+*					+*
co	AR	+			+	+*		+*					+
	BH							+*					+*
	HEB					+*		+*					
so	AR												
	BH												
	HEB												
ve	AR		+										
	BH							+					
	HEB	+	+*				+	+					
uv	AR					+							
	BH												
	HEB												
pl	AR												
	BH	+											
	HEB						+						
gl	AR												
	BH												
	HEB												

¹ Preferred root patterns in *AR*, *BH* and *HEB* which contain in one root position the labial /m/ or one of the coronal sonorants /n/, /l/ or /r/, in one of the other two root positions a member from one of the consonant groups classified on the basis of Place and arbitrary consonants in the remaining position.

TABLE 6.5

Co-occurrence preferences for the Mediae Geminatae[1] (Manner)

		ls	ds	st	lf	df	fr	na	li	gl
ls	AR									
	BH								+	+
	HEB									
ds	AR									
	BH								+*	
	HEB									
st	AR									
	BH								+*	+
	HEB									
lf	AR									
	BH		+					+	+	
	HEB									
df	AR									+*
	BH							+	+	
	HEB									
fr	AR									
	BH			+*				+*	+*	
	HEB									
na	AR									
	BH									
	HEB									
li	AR									
	BH									+*
	HEB									
gl	AR									
	BH		+*							
	HEB									

[1] Co-occurrence preferences for consonant groups classified on the basis of Manner in root positions C1 and C2 of the MG's in *AR*, *BH* and *HEB*. Stops and fricatives are subdivided also into voiceless and voiced consonants.

TABLE 6.6

Co-occurrence preferences for the Mediae Geminatae[1] (Place)

		la	cs	cf	co	so	ve	gu	gl
la	AR								
	BH				+				
	HEB								
cs	AR								
	BH								
	HEB								
cf	AR								
	BH						+		
	HEB								
co	AR								
	BH								
	HEB								
so	AR								
	BH								+
	HEB								
ve	AR								
	BH								+
	HEB								
gu	AR								+
	BH								
	HEB								
gl	AR								
	BH								
	HEB								

[1] Co-occurrence preferences for consonant groups classified on the basis of Place in root positions C1 and C2 of the MG's in *AR*, *BH* and *HEB*. The coronal obstruents were subdivided also in stops and fricatives.

TABLE 6.7

Preferred quadriliterals in Arabic and Hebrew[1] (Manner)

		Adjacent			Nonadjacent		
		C1C2	C2C3	C3C4	C1C3	C2C4	C1C4
(st)(st)	AR				+*		
	HEB						
(st)(na)	AR						
	HEB	+*					
(st)(li)	AR		+*				
	HEB	+*	+*	+			
(fr)(st)	AR						
	HEB				+*		+*
(fr)(fr)	AR				+*		
	HEB						
(fr)(li)	AR		+*				
	HEB						
(na)(fr)	AR						
	HEB	+*					
(na)(na)	AR				+*		
	HEB						
(na)(li)	AR					+*	
	HEB					+*	
(li)(st)	AR			+*			
	HEB	+*	+	+*			
(li)(fr)	AR	+			+	+*	
	HEB						
(li)(li)	AR				+*		
	HEB						
(gl)(na)	AR						
	HEB			+*			

[1] Preferred quadriliteral root patterns in *AR* and *HEB* with two specific consonant pairs classified on the basis of Manner in adjacent or in nonadjacent positions.

TABLE 6.8

Preferred quadriliterals in Arabic and Hebrew[1] (Place)

		Adjacent			Nonadjacent		
		C1C2	C2C3	C3C4	C1C3	C2C4	C1C4
(la)(co)	AR			+*			
	HEB			+			
(la)(so)	AR						
	HEB		+*				
(la)(gu)	AR		+*				+*
	HEB						
(co)(la)	AR						
	HEB		+*	+			
(co)(co)	AR				+*		
	HEB				+*	+*	
(co)(so)	AR		+*				
	HEB		+*				
(co)(ve)	AR						
	HEB						+
(co)(gu)	AR						
	HEB	+*					
(so)(la)	AR		+	+			
	HEB						
(so)(ve)	AR			+*			
	HEB		+*	+*			
(so)(gu)	AR	+*				+	
	HEB		+*				
(ve)(la)	AR						
	HEB					+*	
(ve)(co)	AR						
	HEB				+		
(ve)(so)	AR						
	HEB	+*					
(ve)(gu)	AR			+			
	HEB						
(gu)(la)	AR						+*
	HEB			+			
(gu)(so)	AR		+*				
	HEB						
(gu)(ve)	AR						
	HEB					+	

[1] Preferred quadriliteral root patterns in *AR* and *HEB* with two specific consonant pairs classified on the basis of Place in adjacent or in nonadjacent positions.

TABLE 6.9

Preferred root patterns in Arabic and Hebrew with three specified positions and with nasals in one position[1] (Manner)

C1 or C2		C1=na / C3									C2=na / C3									C3=na / C2								
		ls	ds	st	lf	df	fr	na	li	gl	ls	ds	st	lf	df	fr	na	li	gl	ls	ds	st	lf	df	fr	na	li	gl
ls	AR				+*	+								+*														
	HEB				+*									+*														
ds	AR					+*					+																	
	HEB																											
st	AR						+*									+*												
	HEB						+*									+*												
lf	AR	+									+									+*								
	HEB	+*									+									+*								
df	AR	+																	+									
	HEB																											
fr	AR			+*					+*				+						+						+			
	HEB			+*					+*				+												+*			
na	AR																											
	HEB																											
li	AR																								+			
	HEB																								+*			
gl	AR																								+			
	HEB																											

[1] A nasal is present in one of the three root positions. The other two positions are occupied by specific consonant groups classified on the basis of Manner.

TABLE 6.10

Preferred root patterns in Arabic and Hebrew with three specified positions and with a liquid in one position[1] (Manner)

C1 or C2		C1=na C3									C2=na C3									C3=na C2								
		ls	ds	st	lf	df	fr	na	li	gl	ls	ds	st	lf	df	fr	na	li	gl	ls	ds	st	lf	df	fr	na	li	gl
ls	AR		+			+		+*					+*	+*		+*							+*		+*			
	HEB				+*			+*					+*	+*	+	+*							+*		+*			
ds	AR					+*					+*		+*	+														
	HEB										+		+	+	+										+			
st	AR						+	+*					+*			+*						+*			+*			
	HEB						+*	+					+			+*						+*			+*			
lf	AR	+						+*			+*	+*		+*					+	+	+*							
	HEB							+*			+*	+*							+*	+*	+*							
df	AR		+					+				+											+					
	HEB					+*						+			+													
fr	AR		+					+					+*			+*						+		+				
	HEB		+*					+*					+*									+*		+*				
na	AR																							+	+			
	HEB																							+*	+*			
li	AR																											
	HEB																											
gl	AR					+											+											
	HEB					+																						

[1] A liquid is present in one of the three root positions. The other two positions are both occupied by members of specific consonant groups classified on the basis of Manner.

TABLE 6.11

Preferred root patterns in Arabic and Hebrew with three specified positions and with a labial in one position¹ (Place)

C1=la / C3

C1 or C2		la	cs	cf	co	so	ve	gu	gl
la	AR								
	HEB								
cs	AR					+*	+*	+*	+
	HEB					+	+	+*	
cf	AR				+	+*	+*	+*	
	HEB					+	+*	+*	
co	AR					+*	+*	+*	+
	HEB					+*	+*	+	
so	AR		+		+*		+*	+	
	HEB			+	+*		+		
ve	AR					+			
	HEB								
gu	AR		+*		+*	+*	+*		
	HEB		+*		+	+	+*		
gl	AR								
	HEB								

C2=la / C3

C1 or C2		la	cs	cf	co	so	ve	gu	gl
la	AR								
	HEB								
cs	AR			+*					
	HEB								
cf	AR		+*			+*		+*	
	HEB		+			+*		+	
co	AR								
	HEB								
so	AR			+*	+*	+*		+*	
	HEB			+*	+*	+*		+	
ve	AR			+*	+*	+*		+	
	HEB			+*	+*	+*		+	
gu	AR		+	+*	+*	+*			
	HEB			+*	+*	+*			
gl	AR								
	HEB								

C3=la / C3

C1 or C2		la	cs	cf	co	so	ve	gu	gl
la	AR								
	HEB								
cs	AR							+*	
	HEB							+	
cf	AR							+*	+*
	HEB							+	+
co	AR					+*		+*	+*
	HEB					+*		+	+
so	AR			+	+		+*	+*	+*
	HEB			+	+		+	+*	+*
ve	AR			+*	+		+*		
	HEB			+*	+		+		
gu	AR		+*	+*	+*	+*			
	HEB		+*	+	+*	+			
gl	AR			+*	+*		+		
	HEB			+*	+*				

¹) A labial is present in one of the three root positions. The other two positions are both occupied by members of specific consonant groups classified on the basis of Place.

TABLE 6.12

Preferred root patterns in Arabic and Hebrew with three specified positions and a coronal sonorant in one position[1] (Place)

C1 or C2	AR/HEB	C1=la (C3)								C2=la (C3)								C3=la (C3)							
		la	cs	cf	co	so	ve	gu	gl	la	cs	cf	co	so	ve	gu	gl	la	cs	cf	co	so	ve	gu	gl
la	AR			+*	+*						+*		+*		+*	+*			+*	+	+*		+	+	
	HEB			+*	+*						+	+	+*		+*	+			+	+	+*		+*	+*	
cs	AR	+													+*	+*			+*					+	
	HEB														+*	+*			+*					+	
cf	AR	+					+*	+		+					+*	+*		+*			+*		+*	+*	
	HEB						+*	+							+*	+		+*					+*	+*	
co	AR	+					+	+*		+*					+*	+*		+*	+*		+*		+*	+*	
	HEB	+					+	+*		+*					+*	+		+*	+		+*		+*	+*	
so	AR																								
	HEB																								
ve	AR	+*	+	+*	+*		+*	+		+*		+*	+*		+*	+		+							
	HEB	+		+*	+*		+	+		+*		+*	+*		+	+		+*							
gu	AR	+*		+*	+*			+*		+*		+*	+		+*				+*	+*	+*		+*		
	HEB	+*		+*	+					+		+	+		+				+*	+	+		+*		
gl	AR																								
	HEB																								

[1] A coronal sonorant is present in one of the three root positions. The other two positions are both occupied by members of specific consonant groups classified on the basis of Place.

TABLE 6.13

Preferred root patterns in Arabic and Hebrew with three specified positions and a sonorant in one position[1] (Manner)

a) *Labial sonorant m*

C1 or C2		C1=m — C3					C2=m — C3					C3=m — C2				
		st	fr	na	li	gl	st	fr	na	li	gl	st	fr	na	li	gl
st	AR							+								
	HEB							+*								
fr	AR	+*														
	HEB	+*			+											
na	AR																
	HEB																
li	AR							+				+*					
	HEB												+				
gl	AR																
	HEB											+*					

b) *Coronal sonorant n*

C1 or C2		C1=n — C3					C2=n — C3					C3=n — C2				
		st	fr	na	li	gl	st	fr	na	li	gl	st	fr	na	li	gl
st	AR		+*					+*			+					
	HEB		+*					+*								
fr	AR	+	+			+*	+				+*					
	HEB						+*									
na	AR																
	HEB																
li	AR											+					
	HEB												+*				
gl	AR																
	HEB																

TABLE 6.13 (continued)

c) *Coronal sonorant l*

C1 or C2		C1=l C3					C2=l C3					C3=l C2				
		st	fr	na	li	gl	st	fr	na	li	gl	st	fr	na	li	gl
st	AR				+*			+*									
	HEB							+*					+*				
fr	AR	+					+*					+					
	HEB	+*	+				+*					+					
na	AR													+*			
	HEB													+*			
li	AR																
	HEB																
gl	AR																
	HEB																

d) *Coronal sonorant r*

C1 or C2		C1=r C3					C2=r C3					C3=r C2				
		st	fr	na	li	gl	st	fr	na	li	gl	st	fr	na	li	gl
st	AR	+	+				+*	+*					+*				
	HEB		+*				+*										
fr	AR						+*	+*				+*	+*				
	HEB		+*				+*					+*					
na	AR													+*			
	HEB																
li	AR																
	HEB																
gl	AR																
	HEB																

[1] Triliterals with three specified root positions. A labial or coronal sonorant is present in one of the positions. The other two positions are occupied by specific consonant groups classified on the basis of Manner. For statistical reasons the stops and fricatives were not subdivided into their voiceless and voiced subsets.

TABLE 6.14

Preferred root patterns in Arabic and Hebrew with three specified positions and a sonorant in one position[1] (Place)

a) *Labial sonorant m*

C1 or C2	C1=m C3						C2=m C3						C3=m C2					
	la	co	so	ve	gu	gl	la	co	so	ve	gu	gl	la	co	so	ve	gu	gl
la AR																		
la HEB																		
co AR			+	+					+*		+					+		+*
co HEB			+*						+		+							
so AR																	+*	+*
so HEB																		+*
ve AR									+		+*		+*					
ve HEB									+*		+		+					
gu AR	+*	+*	+*				+*						+*					
gu HEB	+*						+*						+*					
gl AR																		
gl HEB							+*											

b) *Coronal sonorant n*

C1 or C2	C1=n C3						C2=n C3					C3=n C2					
	la	co	so	ve	gu	gl	la	co	so	ve	gu	gl	la	co	so	ve	gu	gl
la AR																		
la HEB																		
co AR		+	+*	+*									+*					+*
co HEB			+*	+*						+*			+					
so AR																		
so HEB																		
ve AR	+*			+*			+*											
ve HEB	+*					+	+*											
gu AR	+*									+*		+*	+					
gu HEB										+*								
gl AR																		
gl HEB																		

TABLE 6.14 (continued)

c) *Coronal sonorant l*

C1 or C2		C1=1						C2=1						C3=1					
		C3						C3						C2					
		la	co	so	ve	gu	gl	la	co	so	ve	gu	gl	la	co	so	ve	gu	gl
la	AR		+*		+							+*	+*		+*				
	HEB	+*						+*			+	+*		+*					
co	AR											+*	+*	+			+	+	
	HEB											+*	+				+		
so	AR																		
	HEB																		
ve	AR	+			+			+	+					+					
	HEB						+				+	+							
gu	AR	+	+*		+*			+*			+*				+*				
	HEB	+*	+*		+*	+		+										+	
gl	AR																		
	HEB																		

d) *Coronal sonorant r*

C1 or C2		C1=r						C2=r						C3=r					
		C3						C3						C2					
		la	co	so	ve	gu	gl	la	co	so	ve	gu	gl	la	co	so	ve	gu	gl
la	AR		+*						+*		+*	+*			+*		+		
	HEB		+*						+*			+*			+*		+	+	
co	AR	+						+*			+*	+*		+*				+	
	HEB	+*			+*						+*						+	+	
so	AR																		
	HEB																		
ve	AR	+	+*		+			+*						+					
	HEB	+						+											
gu	AR	+*					+	+	+*			+*		+*					
	HEB	+*							+			+*		+*				+	
gl	AR																		
	HEB																		

[1] Triliterals with three specified root positions. A labial or coronal sonorant is present in one of the positions. The other two positions are both occupied by specific consonant groups classified on the basis of Place. The coronal obstruents as a group are not subdivided into stops and fricatives and the uvular fricatives and the pharyngeals/laryngeals in *AR* are combined into the group of the gutturals.

TABLE 6.15

The root patterns of the type C1C2C3C3 in *HEB*[1] (Manner)

C3	N		C3 = n		C3 = l		C3 = r	
			C1	C2	C1	C2	C1	C2
ls	25	ls	4	7	9	9	8	11
ds	14	ds	3	3	4	4	2	1
lf	10	lf	4	2	4	6	12	8
df	1	df	2	2	1	0	4	1
S	4	S	0	0	0	0	1	2
na	22	na	1	1	0	1	2	6
li	51	li	3	0	2	1	0	0
gl	4	gl	0	2	1	0	1	1
Total	131	Total	17	17	21	21	30	30

C3	N		C3 = n		C3 = l		C3 = r	
			C1	C2	C1	C2	C1	C2
st	39	st	7	10	13	13	10	12
fr	11	fr	6	4	5	6	16	9

[1] Shown are the frequencies of the different consonant groups classified on the basis of Manner which occur in the 131 root patterns of the type C1C2C3C3 in *HEB*. They are arranged according to the consonant groups in C3. Also shown are the frequencies of the root patterns which have /n/, /l/ or /r/ in C3 and the different consonant groups which are present in C1 and C2. The stops and fricatives are listed as a group and also subdivided into their voiceless and voiced subsets. Because of the small observed frequencies of the different root patterns no statistical calculations were performed.

TABLE 6.16

The root patterns of the type C1C2C3C3 in *HEB*[1] (Place)

C3	N		C3 = n		C3 = l		C3 = r	
			C1	C2	C1	C2	C1	C2
la	20	la	1	3	1	7	0	13
cs	13	cs	1	2	7	1	5	2
cf	9	cf	4	2	4	1	13	1
S	4	S	0	0	0	0	1	2
so	68	so	4	0	2	1	2	1
ve	11	ve	3	5	3	6	2	2
gu	2	gu	4	3	3	5	6	8
gl	4	gl	0	2	1	0	1	1
Total	131	Total	17	17	21	21	30	30

C3	N		C3 = n		C3 = l		C3 = r	
			C1	C2	C1	C2	C1	C2
co	26	co	5	4	11	2	19	5

[1] Shown are the frequencies of the different consonant groups classified on the basis of Place which are present in the 131 root patterns which are of the type C1C2C3C3 in *HEB*. They are arranged according to the consonant groups in C3. Also shown are the frequencies of the root patterns which have /n/, /l/ or /r/ in C3 and the different consonant groups which are present in C1 and C2. The coronal stops and fricatives and the coronal affricate /S/ are listed separately and also combined as the group of coronal obstruents. Because of the small observed frequencies of the different root patterns no statistical calculations were performed.

TABLE 7.1

Root patterns with two labials in Arabic and Hebrew[1]

Left-most column — patterns with the same labial

		No	Ne	Si	P
mmX	AR	0	7	-	<1
	BH	0	3	-	
	HEB	2	6	-	
mXm	AR	0	8	-	<1
	BH	0	3	-	
	HEB	0	7	-	<1
bbX	AR	0	7	-	<1
	BH	0	3	-	
	HEB	0	6	-	<2
bXb	AR	0	7	-	<1
	BH	0	3	-	
	HEB	0	5	-	<3
ppX	AR	0	5	-	<3
	BH	0	3	-	
	HEB	0	7	-	<1
pXp	AR	0	5	-	<2
	BH	0	3	-	
	HEB	0	6	-	<2

Second column (m / b)

		No	Ne	Si	P
mbX	AR	0	7	-	<1
	BH	0	3	-	
	HEB	0	7	-	<1
mXb	AR	0	7	-	<1
	BH	0	3	-	
	HEB	0	5	-	<3
Xmb	AR	0	9	-	<1
	BH	0	3	-	
	HEB	0	6	-	<2
bmX	AR	0	7	-	<1
	BH	0	3	-	
	HEB	1	6	-	<4
bXm	AR	8	8	-	
	BH	1	3	-	
	HEB	6	7	-	
Xbm	AR	0	11	-	<1
	BH	1	4	-	
	HEB	1	8	-	<2

Third column (m / p)

		No	Ne	Si	P
mpX	AR	0	5	-	
	BH	0	3	-	
	HEB	1	6	-	<3
mXp	AR	0	6	-	<4
	BH	0	3	-	
	HEB	3	6	-	<2
Xmp	AR	0	8	-	<1
	BH	0	3	-	
	HEB	0	6	-	<2
pmX	AR	0	7	-	<2
	BH	0	3	-	
	HEB	0	7	-	<1
pXm	AR	9	8	-	
	BH	3	4	-	
	HEB	12	8	-	
Xpm	AR	0	9	-	<1
	BH	0	3	-	
	HEB	1	7	-	<2

Fourth column (b / p)

		No	Ne	Si	P
bpX	AR	0	5	-	<2
	BH	0	3	-	
	HEB	0	6	-	<2
bXp	AR	1	6	-	<5
	BH	1	3	-	
	HEB	1	6	-	<5
Xbp	AR	0	7	-	<1
	BH	0	4	-	
	HEB	0	7	-	<1
pbX	AR	0	6	-	<2
	BH	0	3	-	
	HEB	0	7	-	<1
pXb	AR	0	6	-	<2
	BH	0	3	-	
	HEB	0	6	-	<2
Xpm	AR	0	9	-	<1
	BH	0	3	-	
	HEB	1	8	-	<2

[1] The root patterns with the same labial in two of their root positions appear in the left-most column, those with two different labials in the other three columns. Root patterns with the same labial in root positions C2 and C3 are Mediae Geminatae. They do not belong to the files of triliterals proper and are not listed in the table. For an explanation of the symbols P (=%) and Si which are used in the heading in this and the following tables see § 7.1 and the explanation at the beginning of the section with tables.

TABLE 7.2.1

Root patterns in Arabic and Hebrew with the same coronal sonorant in two positions[1]

		No	Ne	Si	P			No	Ne	Si	P			No	Ne	Si	P
	AR	0	8	-	<1		AR	0	5	-	<3		AR	0	12	-	<1
nnX	BH	0	4	-	<5	llX	BH	0	5	-	<3	rrX	BH	0	14	-	<1
	HEB	1	7	-	<3		HEB	1	5				HEB	0	12	-	<1
	AR	3	12	-	<1		AR	0	5	-	<3		AR	0	5	-	<3
nXn	BH	3	5			lXl	BH	0	5	-	<3	lXl	BH	0	5	-	<3
	HEB	6	10				HEB	1	5				HEB	1	5		

[1] See *Table 7.1* for an explanation of the symbols used.

TABLE 7.2.2

Root patterns in Arabic and Hebrew with the labial /m/ and a coronal sonorant[1]

		No	Ne	Si	P			No	Ne	Si	P			No	Ne	Si	P
	AR	2	5				AR	11	7				AR	13	10		
mnX	BH	2	2			mlX	BH	6	4			mrX	BH	7	5		
	HEB	4	5				HEB	7	7				HEB	11	10		
	AR	11	7				AR	9	8				AR	12	12		
mXn	BH	2	3			mXl	BH	4	4			mXr	BH	8	7		
	HEB	9	7				HEB	8	8				HEB	15	12		
	AR	11	10				AR	16	11				AR	16	16		
Xmn	BH	5	3			Xml	BH	5	4			Xmr	BH	9	7		
	HEB	12	8				HEB	11	8				HEB	15	12		
	AR	6	11				AR	7	4				AR	9	8		
nmX	BH	0	5	-	<2	lmX	BH	1	2			rmX	BH	3	4		
	HEB	5	9				HEB	2	3				HEB	6	6		
	AR	12	13				AR	10	5	+	<3		AR	16	9	+	<3
nXm	BH	7	6			lXm	BH	2	2			rXm	BH	10	4	+	<1
	HEB	9	10				HEB	4	4				HEB	11	7		
	AR	4	8				AR	12	12				AR	17	16		
Xnm	BH	0	3			Xlm	BH	7	5			Xrm	BH	7	6		
	HEB	4	6				HEB	12	9				HEB	12	12		

[1] All of these root patterns contain the labial /m/ and one of the coronal sonorants.

TABLE 7.2.3

Root patterns in Arabic and Hebrew with two different coronal sonorants[1]

		No	Ne	Si	P			No	Ne	Si	P			No	Ne	Si	P
nlX	AR	0	12	-	<1	nrX	AR	0	17	-	<1	lrX	AR	0	6	-	<2
	BH	1	8	-	<2		BH	0	10	-	<1		BH	0	3		
	HEB	1	10	-	<1		HEB	0	14	-	<1		HEB	0	5		
nXl	AR	21	13	+	<3	nXr	AR	21	20			lXr	AR	0	8	-	<1
	BH	10	8				BH	13	13				BH	0	4	-	<5
	HEB	14	11				HEB	17	16				HEB	1	6	-	<4
Xnl	AR	0	8	-	<1	Xnr	AR	2	11	-	<1	Xlr	AR	0	17	-	<1
	BH	0	3				BH	0	5	-	<3		BH	0	10	-	<1
	HEB	0	6	-	<2		HEB	5	10				HEB	1	15	-	<1
lnX	AR	0	3			rnX	AR	6	6			rlX	AR	0	9	-	<1
	BH	0	1				BH	1	3				BH	0	5	-	<3
	HEB	0	3				HEB	1	5				HEB	0	7	-	<1
lXn	AR	10	5	+	<2	rXn	AR	8	9			rXl	AR	10	9		
	BH	4	1	+	<4		BH	3	3				BH	3	6		
	HEB	7	4				HEB	9	7				HEB	4	8		
Xln	AR	1	11	-	<1	Xrn	AR	4	15	-	<1	Xrl	AR	0	16	-	<1
	BH	0	4				BH	0	5	-	<3		BH	1	8	-	<2
	HEB	5	9				HEB	7	12				HEB	3	13	-	<1

[1] All of these root patterns contain two different coronal sonorants.

TABLE 7.3

Preferred root patterns with two specified positions and coronal obstruents[1] (Place)

Pattern		No	Ne	Si	P
(cs) (la) (X)	AR	53	39	+	<3
	BH	18	14		
	HEB	49	37	+	<5
(cs) (so) (X)	AR	60	41	+	<1
	BH	17	17		
	HEB	51	43	+	
(cs) (ve) (X)	AR	12	21	-	<5
	BH	11	10		
	HEB	23	25		
(cs) (uv) (X)	AR	9	7		
(cs) (pl) (X)	AR	34	25	+	<4
	BH	21	14		
	HEB	45	33	+	
(la) (cs) (X)	AR	53	37	+	<1
	BH	19	18		
	HEB	44	37		
(so) (cs) (X)	AR	59	52		
	BH	32	23		
	HEB	45	35		
(ve) (cs) (X)	AR	36	35		
	BH	16	16		
	HEB	29	31		
(uv) (cs) (X)	AR	31	20	+	<2
(pl) (cs) (X)	AR	53	47		
	BH	37	28		
	HEB	56	46		

Pattern		No	Ne	Si	P
(cf) (la) (X)	AR	98	80	+	<4
	BH	40	33		
	HEB	70	62		
(cf) (so) (X)	AR	96	84		
	BH	45	41		
	HEB	74	73		
(cf) (ve) (X)	AR	49	43		<1
	BH	38	24	+	
	HEB	54	41	+	<5
(cf) (uv) (X)	AR	26	15	+	<1
(cf) (pl) (X)	AR	81	52	+	<1
	BH	36	33		
	HEB	63	56		
(la) (cf) (X)	AR	61	48	+	<5
	BH	25	18		
	HEB	53	35	+	<1
(so) (cf) (X)	AR	80	67		
	BH	24	23		
	HEB	45	34	+	<4
(ve) (cf) (X)	AR	60	45	+	<3
	BH	23	15		
	HEB	33	30		
(uv) (cf) (X)	AR	33	26	+	<1
(pl) (cf) (X)	AR	90	60	+	<1
	BH	37	27		
	HEB	55	44		

Pattern		No	Ne	Si	P
(co) (la) (X)	AR	151	118	+	<1
	BH	71	53	+	<2
	HEB	137	111	+	<2
(co) (so) (X)	AR	156	124	+	<1
	BH	71	67		
	HEB	144	130		
(co) (ve) (X)	AR	61	64		
	BH	49	38		
	HEB		77	74	
(co) (uv) (X)	AR	35	22	+	<1
(co) (pl) (X)	AR	115	78	+	<1
	BH	66	54		
	HEB	123	100	+	<2
(la) (co) (X)	AR	114	85	+	<1
	BH	56	53		
	HEB	113	82	+	<1
(so) (co) (X)	AR	139	119		
	BH	69	54		
	HEB	107	123	+	<4
(ve) (co) (X)	AR	96	80		
	BH	44	37		
	HEB	68	70		
(uv) (co) (X)	AR	64	46	+	<1
(pl) (co) (X)	AR	143	106	+	<1
	BH	83	65	+	<3
	HEB	127	102	+	<2

TABLE 7.3 (continued)

Pattern			No	Ne	Si	P
(X) (cs) (la)	AR		62	54	+	<3
	BH		30	20	+	<2
	HEB		52	38		
(X) (cs) (so)	AR		85	63	+	<1
	BH		37	30		
	HEB		68	55		
(X) (cs) (ve)	AR		16	24		
	BH		10	13		
	HEB		25	25		
(X) (cs) (uv)	AR		6	6		
(X) (cs) (pl)	AR		49	38		
	BH		20	19		
	HEB		30	29		
(X) (la) (cs)	AR		69	53	+	<5
	BH		28	19		
	HEB		48	42		
(X) (so) (cs)	AR		59	56		
	BH		24	24		
	HEB		53	49		
(X) (ve) (cs)	AR		27	29		
	BH		14	14		
	HEB		22	28		
(X) (uv) (cs)	AR		13	10		
(X) (pl) (cs)	AR		46	35		
	BH		20	19		
	HEB		46	38		

Pattern			No	Ne	Si	P
(X) (cf) (la)	AR		96	69	+	<1
	BH		25	20		
	HEB		44	36		
(X) (cf) (so)	AR		106	81	+	<1
	BH		39	30		
	HEB		60	53		
(X) (cf) (ve)	AR		33	30		
	BH		18	13		
	HEB		35	24	+	<3
(X) (cf) (uv)	AR		9	7		
(X) (cf) (pl)	AR		48	49		
	BH		18	19		
	HEB		28	28		
(X) (la) (cf)	AR		73	55	+	<2
	BH		25	17	+	<5
	HEB		65	40	+	<1
(X) (so) (cf)	AR		74	57	+	<3
	BH		27	21		
	HEB		61	47	+	<4
(X) (ve) (cf)	AR		42	30	+	<3
	BH		12	12		
	HEB		29	27		
(X) (uv) (cf)	AR		16	10		
(X) (pl) (cf)	AR		36	36		
	BH		16	17		
	HEB		26	36		

Pattern			No	Ne	Si	P
(X) (co) (la)	AR		158	123	+	<1
	BH		64	47	+	<1
	HEB		110	84	+	<1
(X) (co) (so)	AR		191	144	+	<1
	BH		87	70	+	<4
	HEB		148	78	+	<1
(X) (co) (ve)	AR		49	54		
	BH		33	31		
	HEB		65	56		
(X) (co) (uv)	AR		15	13		
(X) (co) (pl)	AR		97	87		
	BH		50	44		
	HEB		71	64		
(X) (la) (co)	AR		142	108	+	<1
	BH		62	42	+	<1
	HEB		131	93	+	<1
(X) (so) (co)	AR		133	113		
	BH		61	53		
	HEB		129	109		
(X) (ve) (co)	AR		69	59		
	BH		28	30		
	HEB		54	62		
(X) (uv) (co)	AR		29	20	+	<4
(X) (pl) (co)	AR		82	71		
	BH		43	43		
	HEB		84	84		

[1] Preferred root patterns in *AR*, *BH* and *HEB* with two specified positions which contain coronal stops, coronal fricatives or coronal obstruents as a group adjacent to one of the other consonant groups and with arbitrary consonants in the remaining position (C1 or C3 and denoted as X).

TABLE 7.4

Preferred triliteral root patterns with a labial or a coronal sonorant and stops or fricatives¹ (Manner)

Left part (labial or coronal sonorant in C1 or C2)

X in		C3				C1			
		No	Ne	Si	P	No	Ne	Si	P
(m) (st)	AR	25	32	-		42	46	-	
	BH	9	20		<2	17	20		
	HEB	37	41			29	42	-	<5
(m) (fr)	AR	46	37			58	47		
	BH	19	13			14	11		
	HEB	36	26	+	<5	35	24	+	<4
(n) (st)	AR	87	62	+	<1	30	27		
	BH	57	40	+	<1	22	15		
	HEB	81	56	+	<1	40	33		
(n) (fr)	AR	102	70	+	<1	33	27	+	<1
	BH	35	26			10	9		
	HEB	45	36			24	19		
(l) (st)	AR	33	29			65	47	+	<1
	BH	11	12	+	<5	33	29	+	<1
	HEB	27	21	+	<2	65	50	+	<4
(l) (fr)	AR	43	33			63	48	+	<3
	BH	13	8	+	<5	25	17	+	<4
	HEB	23	14	+	<2	38	29		
(r) (st)	AR	65	46	+		91	68	+	<1
	BH	35	27			53	37	+	<1
	HEB	53	40	+	<4	89	68	+	<1
(r) (fr)	AR	59	53			97	70	+	<1
	BH	27	17			27	21	+	<1
	HEB	34	25			56	39	+	<1

Right part (labial or coronal sonorant in C2 or C3)

X in		C3				C1			
		No	Ne	Si	P	No	Ne	Si	P
(st) (m)	AR	48	44			57	52		
	BH	21	20			23	25		
	HEB	51	48			49	50		
(fr) (m)	AR	81	66			70	59		
	BH	26	20			24	16	+	<4
	HEB	43	37			43	32	+	<5
(st) (n)	AR	34	26			49	36		<4
	BH	18	15			24	19	+	
	HEB	46	37			60	50		
(fr) (n)	AR	45	38			41	41		
	BH	19	15			14	12		
	HEB	33	29			30	32		
(st) (l)	AR	60	45	+	<3	70	56		
	BH	40	29	+	<5	42	32	+	<5
	HEB	70	56			67	54	+	<4
(fr) (l)	AR	80	68			80	64	+	<5
	BH	33	29			30	21	+	<5
	HEB	49	44			46	34	+	<4
(st) (r)	AR	90	65		<1	91	73	+	<4
	BH	48	37	+		68	51	+	<2
	HEB	100	77	+	<1	109	81	+	<1
(fr) (r)	AR	117	98		<1	117	84	+	<1
	BH	44	37	+		41	33		
	HEB	65	60			62	51		

¹ The preferred root patterns classified on the basis of Manner from *Table 6.3* with stops or fricatives adjacent to a labial or a coronal sonorant and arbitrary consonants in the remaining position (C1 or C3 and denoted as X). Some of the root patterns are avoided rather than preferred. The material has been arranged according to the position of the labial or coronal sonorant: C1 or C2 in the leftmost part of the table and C2 or C3 in its rightmost part.

TABLE 7.5

Preferred triliteral root patterns with a labial or a coronal sonorant and one specific consonant group[1] (Place)

a) *Root patterns with /m/*

Left panel

X	in	C3 No	Ne	Si	P	C1 No	Ne	Si	P
(m)	(co) AR	33	28			58	37	+	<1
	BH	16	14			20	13		
	HEB	35	27			45	31	+	<1
(m)	(so) AR	26	21			43	35		
	BH	15	11			19	14		
	HEB	22	22			38	28		
(m)	(ve) AR	10	11			14	13		
	BH	3	7			5	7		
	HEB	16	13			9	13		
(m)	(uv) AR	5	4			5	3		
(m)	(pl) AR	23	13	+	<1	23	21		
	BH	14	10			9	10		
	HEB	26	17	+	<4	17	15		

Right panel

X	in	C3 No	Ne	Si	P	C1 No	Ne	Si	P
(m)	(co) AR	56	40	+	<2	64	45	+	<2
	BH	23	16			24	17		
	HEB	46	36			49	33	+	<1
(m)	(so) AR	22	29	-		33	34		
	BH	4	11		<4	14	14		
	HEB	13	18			28	28		
(m)	(ve) AR	25	20			24	17		
	BH	9	9	+		7	9		
	HEB	25	16		<4	19	16		
(m)	(uv) AR	17	11			12	6	+	<2
(m)	(pl) AR	31	26			27	21		
	BH	20	15			17	12		
	HEB	30	24			25	21		

TABLE 7.5 (continued)

b) *Root patterns with /n/*

X	in	C3 No	Ne	Si	P	C1 No	Ne	Si	P
(n)	(la) AR	34	39			17	17		
	BH	9	18	-		7	7		
	HEB	24	27		<4	19	15		
(n)	(co) AR	71	54	+	<2	20	21		
	BH	47	27	+	<1	7	10		
	HEB	60	37	+	<1	23	24		
(n)	(ve) AR	41	21	+	<1	13	8	+	<5
	BH	21	13	+	<2	8	5		
	HEB	32	18	+	<1	13	10		
(n)	(uv) AR	14	7	+	<1	2	2		
(n)	(pl) AR	32	25			15	12		
	BH	22	18			10	7		
	HEB	23	24			16	12		

X	in	C3 No	Ne	Si	P	C1 No	Ne	Si	P
(n)	(la) AR	10	12			26	22		
	BH	5	7			11	8		
	HEB	10	15			27	24		
(n)	(co) AR	25	23			35	31		
	BH	15	13			13	13		
	HEB	32	28			37	33		
(n)	(ve) AR	18	11	+	<5	18	12		
	BH	8	6			9	6		
	HEB	22	13	+	<1	21	16		
(n)	(uv) AR	7	6			3	4		
(n)	(pl) AR	21	15			19	15		
	BH	14	10			10	9		
	HEB	24	18			22	21		

TABLE 7.8 (continued)

c) *Root patterns with /l/ or /r/*

X	in		C3 No	C3 Ne	C3 Si	C3 P	C1 No	C1 Ne	C1 Si	C1 P
(l)	(la)	AR	21	11	+		38	31		
		BH	5	5			14	13		
		HEB	13	10		<1	32	23		<1
(l)	(co)	AR	20	25	−		38	38		
		BH	3	17			20	23		
		HEB	9	14		<1	35	36		
(l)	(ve)	AR	15	10			30	13	+	
		BH	4	4			12	9		
		HEB	8	7			20	15		<2
(l)	(uv)	AR	5	3			5	3		
(l)	(pl)	AR	22	12			28	21	+	
		BH	13	5	+	<1	22	12	+	<1
		HEB	22	9	+	<1	33	18		<1
(r)	(la)	AR	30	32			51	44	+	
		BH	12	12			20	17	+	<1
		HEB	21	19			31	32		<1
(r)	(co)	AR	45	40			74	54	+	<1
		BH	19	10	+	<1	34	20	+	<1
		HEB	38	27	+	<3	71	49	+	<1
(r)	(ve)	AR	29	16			33	19	+	<1
		BH	15	9	+	<1	20	11	+	<1
		HEB	19	13	+	<3	35	21	+	<1
(r)	(uv)	AR	8	5			7	5		
(r)	(pl)	AR	21	19			40	31		
		BH	19	12	+		19	16		
		HEB	23	17		<5	28	24		

X	in		C3 No	C3 Ne	C3 Si	C3 P	C1 No	C1 Ne	C1 Si	C1 P
(l)	(la)	AR	29	21			41	35		
		BH	20	12	+		21	14		
		HEB	30	22		<3	34	25		
(l)	(co)	AR	52	42			62	49		
		BH	27	30			26	32		
		HEB	47	38			37	36		
(l)	(ve)	AR	25	20			26	20	+	
		BH	12	10			13	10		
		HEB	25	19			26	17		<3
(l)	(uv)	AR	18	11			6	7		
(l)	(pl)	AR	27	26			31	24	+	
		BH	23	18	+		21	14		
		HEB	31	28		<3	33	23		<3
(r)	(la)	AR	41	31			49	46	+	<1
		BH	25	16	+		25	22	+	<1
		HEB	41	31		<2	42	38	+	<1
(r)	(co)	AR	79	60			94	64	+	<1
		BH	29	24			48	24	+	<1
		HEB	65	59			74	54	+	<1
(r)	(ve)	AR	36	29			30	25	+	<3
		BH	19	13			25	16		<2
		HEB	32	26			38	25	+	
(r)	(uv)	AR	20	17			14	8		
(r)	(pl)	AR	44	38			37	30		
		BH	28	24			27	22		
		HEB	45	38			41	34		

¹ The preferred root patterns classified on the basis of Place from *Table 6.4* are arranged as in *Table 7.4*.

TABLE 7.6

Quadriliterals in Arabic and Hebrew with adjacent and nonadjacent consonant groups[1] (Manner)

Manner		C1C2				C2C3				C3C4				C1C3				C2C4			
		No	Ne	Si	P	No	Ne	Si	P	No	Ne	Si	P	No	Ne	Si	P	No	Ne	Si	P
(st)(st)	AR	5	6			0	7	-	<1	18	26			77	37	+	<1	6	4		
	HEB	67	66			28	52	-	<1	45	57			122	120			40	31		
(fr)(fr)	AR	17	24			9	13			9	13			57	22	+	<1	8	15		
	HEB	22	26		<5	9	18	-	<4	6	14	-	<4	21	22			13	16		
(na)(na)	AR	2	3			0	3			3	4			14	2	+	<1	3	6		
	HEB	1	6	-		1	7	-	<3	10	17			9	6			14	17		
(li)(li)	AR	0	4	-	<5	0	15	-	<1	2	9	-	<3	18	2	+	<1	7	22	-	<1
	HEB	1	6	-	<4	0	28	-	<1	3	17	-	<1	3	2			32	43		
(st)(li)	AR	46	37			11	3	+	<1	29	22			11	15			0	4		
	HEB	116	18	+	<1	40	18	+	<1	67	50	+	<2	37	28			23	28		
(li)(st)	AR	1	1			47	39	+		24	10	+	<1	3	4			22	26		
	HEB	10	4	+	<1	98	81		<5	32	19	+	<1	4	7			50	49		
(li)(na)	AR	1	1			13	9			4	7			1	1			18	17		
	HEB	2	2			23	22			25	21			0	2			57	54		
(na)(li)	AR	4	7			3	5			1	5			3	3			19	8	+	<1
	HEB	9	19	-	<3	7	9			13	14			9	7			23	14	+	<1

[1] Shown are the root patterns which contain the same consonant group in adjacent or nonadjacent positions or either a pair of stops and liquids or a pair of nasals and liquids.

TABLE 7.7

Quadriliterals in Arabic and Hebrew with adjacent and nonadjacent consonants from the same group[1] (Place)

		C1C2				C2C3				C3C4				C1C3				C2C4			
		No	Ne	Si	P	No	Ne	Si	P	No	Ne	Si	P	No	Ne	Si	P	No	Ne	Si	P
(la)	(la) AR	0	5	-	<3	0	4	-	<4	0	7	-	<1	6	13	-	<4	0	2		
	HEB	4	13	-	<2	3	14	-	<1	0	16	-	<1	18	23			3	9		
(co)	(co) AR	1	5	-		3	5	-		4	17	-	<1	53	28	+	<1	1	5	+	<1
	HEB	24	38	-	<2	7	28	-	<1	13	32	-	<1	99	51	+	<1	48	24	+	<1
(so)	(so) AR	1	6	-	<4	4	22	-	<1	2	15	-	<1	3	2			31	40		
	HEB	4	11	-	<3	7	40	-	<1	19	42	-	<1	6	5			95	98		
(ve)	(ve) AR	0	2	-		0	1	-		0	4	-		4	5			1	1		
	HEB	0	6	-	<2	1	8	-	<2	0	7	-	<1	9	9			1	4		
(gu)	(gu) AR	0	7	-	<1	0	3			0	1			0	4			1	2		
	HEB	0	9	-	<1	0	3			0	2			3	7			0	2		

[1] Shown are root patterns which contain consonants from the same group in adjacent or nonadjacent positions.

TABLE 7.8

Avoided root patterns of the type C1C2C1C2[1]

			Manner C1C2/C2C3							Place C1C2/C2C3			
			No	Ne	Si	P				No	Ne	Si	P
(fr)	(fr)	AR	10	13			(co)	(co)	AR	0	7	-	<1
		HEB	5	13	-	<3			HEB	7	16	-	<2
(li)	(li)	AR	0	3			(so)	(so)	AR	0	6	-	<2
		HEB	0	4	-	<4			HEB	1	7	-	<3
							(ve)	(ve)	AR	0	2		
									HEB	0	4	-	<4
							(gu)	(gu)	AR	1	6	-	<4
									HEB	0	3		

[1] Shown in the table are the values for the avoided pairs of adjacent consonants from the same group classified on the basis of Manner or of Place. The values for the consonant pairs in C1C2 and C2C3 are the same (see § 7.4.2).

TABLE 7.9.1

Root patterns with three specified positions and two stops[1] (Manner)

C1

Pos	Pos	Pos		No	Ne	Si	P
(st)	(st)	(st)	AR	26	62	-	<1
			HEB	47	110	-	<1
(fr)	(st)	(st)	AR	70	93	-	<2
			HEB	78	86	-	
(na)	(st)	(st)	AR	24	28		
			HEB	35	34		
(li)	(st)	(st)	AR	31	22		
			HEB	26	22		
(gl)	(st)	(st)	AR	15	13		
			HEB	13	13		
(X)	(st)	(st)	AR	151	218	-	<1
			HEB	199	275	-	<1

C2

Pos	Pos	Pos		No	Ne	Si	P
(st)	(st)	(st)	AR	26	62	-	<1
			HEB	47	110	-	<1
(st)	(fr)	(st)	AR	60	71		
			HEB	63	69		
(st)	(na)	(st)	AR	18	21		
			HEB	26	30		
(st)	(li)	(st)	AR	52	33	+	<1
			HEB	64	47	+	<2
(st)	(gl)	(st)	AR	34	30	-	
			HEB	0	13	-	<1
(st)	(X)	(st)	AR	190	216	-	
			HEB	200	308	-	<1

C3

Pos	Pos	Pos		No	Ne	Si	P
(st)	(st)	(s)t	AR	26	62	-	<1
			HEB	47	110	-	<1
(st)	(st)	(fr)	AR	40	63	-	<1
			HEB	65	64		
(st)	(st)	(na)	AR	21	25		
			HEB	39	40		
(st)	(st)	(li)	AR	45	37	+	<2
			HEB	71	54	+	
(st)	(st)	(gl)	AR	16	23		
			HEB	32	33		
(st)	(st)	(X)	AR	148	210	-	<1
			HEB	254	301	-	<1

[1] Stops are present in two of the three root positions, the consonant group in the third position (C1, C2 or C3) is varied.

TABLE 7.9.2

Root patterns with three specified positions and two fricatives[1] (Manner)

C1 (varied in C1)

C1	C2	C3		No	Ne	Si	P
(fr)	(fr)	(fr)	AR	44	107	-	<1
			HEB	2	31	-	<1
(st)	(fr)	(fr)	AR	52	72	-	<2
			HEB	21	40	-	<1
(na)	(fr)	(fr)	AR	40	32		
			HEB	8	13		
(li)	(fr)	(fr)	AR	29	26		
			HEB	8	8		
(gl)	(fr)	(fr)	AR	14	15		
			HEB	5	5		
(X)	(fr)	(fr)	AR	192	253	-	<1
			HEB	44	100	-	<1

C2 (varied in C2)

C1	C2	C3		No	Ne	Si	P
(fr)	(fr)	(fr)	AR	44	107	-	<1
			HEB	2	31	-	<1
(fr)	(st)	(fr)	AR	79	95	-	
			HEB	33	50	-	<2
(fr)	(na)	(fr)	AR	37	32		
			HEB	12	14		
(fr)	(li)	(fr)	AR	72	50	+	<1
			HEB	22	21		
(fr)	(gl)	(fr)	AR	47	46		
			HEB	20	19		
(fr)	(X)	(fr)	AR	277	330	-	<1
			HEB	89	139	-	<1

C3 (varied in C3)

C1	C2	C3		No	Ne	Si	P
(fr)	(fr)	(fr)	AR	44	107	-	<1
			HEB	2	31	-	<1
(fr)	(fr)	(st)	AR	78	106	-	<1
			HEB	48	54		
(fr)	(fr)	(na)	AR	39	43		
			HEB	15	20		
(fr)	(fr)	(li)	AR	81	63	+	<2
			HEB	22	27		
(fr)	(fr)	(gl)	AR	40	38		
			HEB	16	16		
(fr)	(fr)	(X)	AR	282	357	-	<1
			HEB	103	149	-	<1

[1] Fricatives are present in two of the three root positions, the consonant group in the third position (C1, C2 or C3) is varied.

TABLE 7.10.1

Root patterns with three specified positions; stops followed by fricatives[1] (Manner)

C1

Pattern		No	Ne	Si	P
(st) (st) (fr)	AR	40	63	-	
	HEB	64	64		<1
(fr) (st) (fr)	AR	79	95	-	
	HEB	33	50		<2
(na) (st) (fr)	AR	47	28	+	<1
	HEB	32	20	+	<1
(li) (st) (fr)	AR	34	23	+	
	HEB	26	13		<1
(gl) (st) (fr)	AR	25	13	+	<1
	HEB	17	8	+	<1
(X) (st) (fr)	AR	225	222		
	HEB	172	159		

C2

Pattern		No	Ne	Si	P
(st) (fr) (st)	AR	40	63	-	
	HEB	64	64		<1
(st) (fr) (fr)	AR	52	72	-	<2
	HEB	21	40	-	<1
(st) (fr) (na)	AR	37	21	+	<1
	HEB	35	17	+	<1
(st) (fr) (li)	AR	69	33	+	<1
	HEB	60	27	+	<1
(st) (fr) (gl)	AR	41	31	+	
	HEB	37	24	+	<2
(st) (fr) (X)	AR	239	220	+	
	HEB	217	178	+	<1

C3

Pattern		No	Ne	Si	P
(st) (fr) (st)	AR	60	71		
	HEB	63	69		
(st) (fr) (fr)	AR	52	72	-	<2
	HEB	21	40	-	<1
(st) (fr) (na)	AR	36	29		
	HEB	31	25		
(st) (fr) (li)	AR	66	42	+	<1
	HEB	53	34	+	<1
(st) (fr) (gl)	AR	25	26		
	HEB	28	21		
(st) (fr) (X)	AR	239	238		
	HEB	198	190		

[1] Stops and fricatives are present in two of the three root positions. The consonant group in the third position (C1, C2 or C3) is varied.

TABLE 7.10.2

Root patterns with three specified positions; fricatives followed by stops[1] (Manner)

C1

Pattern		No	Ne	Si	P
(st) (fr) (st)	AR	60	71		
	HEB	63	69		
(fr) (fr) (st)	AR	78	106	-	<1
	HEB	48	54		
(na) (fr) (st)	AR	52	32	+	<1
	HEB	36	22	+	<1
(li) (fr) (st)	AR	36	25	+	<3
	HEB	24	14	+	<1
(gl) (fr) (st)	AR	22	15	+	<5
	HEB	14	8	+	
(X) (fr) (st)	AR	248	248		
	HEB	185	173		

C2

Pattern		No	Ne	Si	P
(fr) (st) (st)	AR	70	93	-	<2
	HEB	78	86		
(fr) (fr) (st)	AR	78	106	-	<1
	HEB	48	54		
(fr) (na) (st)	AR	44	31	+	<2
	HEB	34	23	+	<3
(fr) (li) (st)	AR	72	50	+	<1
	HEB	63	37	+	<1
(fr) (gl) (st)	AR	61	45	+	<2
	HEB	57	24	+	<1
(fr) (X) (st)	AR	340	324	+	<1
	HEB	280	241	+	

C3

Pattern		No	Ne	Si	P
(fr) (st) (st)	AR	70	93	-	<2
	HEB	78	86		
(fr) (st) (fr)	AR	79	95	-	<2
	HEB	33	50		
(fr) (st) (na)	AR	49	38		
	HEB	39	32		
(fr) (st) (li)	AR	83	55	+	<1
	HEB	68	42	+	<1
(fr) (st) (gl)	AR	38	34		
	HEB	35	26		
(fr) (st) (X)	AR	319	314		
	HEB	253	236		

[1] See *Table 7.10.1* for explanation.

TABLE 7.11.1

Root patterns with three specified positions and with nasals or liquids in C1
adjacent to stops or fricatives in C2[1] (Manner)

				No	Ne	Si	P					No	Ne	Si	P
								C3 is varied							
(na)	(st)	(st)	AR	24	28			(li)	(st)	(st)	AR	31	22		
			HEB	35	34						HEB	26	22		
(na)	(st)	(fr)	AR	47	28	+	<1	(li)	(st)	(fr)	AR	34	23		
			HEB	32	20	+	<1				HEB	26	13	+	<1
(na)	(st)	(na)	AR	10	11			(li)	(st)	(na)	AR	20	9	+	<1
			HEB	14	13						HEB	13	8		
(na)	(st)	(li)	AR	21	17			(li)	(st)	(li)	AR	3	13	-	<1
			HEB	23	17						HEB	3	11	-	<2
(na)	(st)	(gl)	AR	10	10			(li)	(st)	(gl)	AR	10	8		
			HEB	12	10						HEB	11	7		
(na)	(st)	(X)	AR	112	94			(li)	(st)	(X)	AR	98	75	+	<1
			HEB	119	97	+	<4				HEB	80	62	+	<2
(na)	(fr)	(st)	AR	52	32	+	<1	(li)	(fr)	(st)	AR	36	25	+	<3
			HEB	36	22	+	<1				HEB	24	14	+	<1
(na)	(fr)	(fr)	AR	40	32			(li)	(fr)	(fr)	AR	29	26		
			HEB	8	13						HEB	8	8		
(na)	(fr)	(na)	AR	10	13			(li)	(fr)	(na)	AR	17	10	+	<3
			HEB	5	8						HEB	13	5	+	<1
(na)	(fr)	(li)	AR	32	19	+	<1	(li)	(fr)	(li)	AR	5	15	-	<1
			HEB	20	11	+	<1				HEB	2	7		
(na)	(fr)	(gl)	AR	14	9			(li)	(fr)	(gl)	AR	15	9		
			HEB	7	7						HEB	7	4		
(na)	(fr)	(X)	AR	148	107	+	<1	(li)	(fr)	(X)	AR	102	85		
			HEB	80	61	+	<2				HEB	57	39	+	<1

[1] The consonant group in root position C3 is varied.

TABLE 7.11.2

Root patterns with three specified positions and with nasals or liquids in C2 adjacent to stops or fricatives in C1[1] (Manner)

				No	Ne	Si	P					No	Ne	Si	P
								C3 is varied							
(st)	(na)	(st)	AR	18	21			(st)	(li)	(st)	AR	52	33	+	<1
			HEB	26	30						HEB	64	47	+	<2
(st)	(na)	(fr)	AR	37	21	+	<1	(st)	(li)	(fr)	AR	69	33	+	<1
			HEB	35	17	+	<1				HEB	60	27	+	<1
(st)	(na)	(na)	AR	7	8			(st)	(li)	(na)	AR	14	13		
			HEB	8	11						HEB	21	17		
(st)	(na)	(li)	AR	11	12			(st)	(li)	(li)	AR	0	20	-	<1
			HEB	12	15						HEB	2	23	-	<1
(st)	(na)	(gl)	AR	9	8			(st)	(li)	(gl)	AR	15	12		
			HEB	13	9						HEB	17	14		
(st)	(na)	(X)	AR	82	70			(st)	(li)	(X)	AR	150	111	+	<1
			HEB	97	85						HEB	172	133	+	<1
(fr)	(na)	(st)	AR	44	31	+	<2	(fr)	(li)	(st)	AR	72	50	+	<1
			HEB	34	23	+	<3				HEB	63	37	+	<1
(fr)	(na)	(fr)	AR	37	32			(fr)	(li)	(fr)	AR	72	50	+	<1
			HEB	12	14						HEB	22	21		
(fr)	(na)	(na)	AR	6	13			(fr)	(li)	(na)	AR	17	20		
			HEB	4	9						HEB	11	14		
(fr)	(na)	(li)	AR	20	18			(fr)	(li)	(li)	AR	0	29	-	<1
			HEB	12	11						HEB	2	18	-	<1
(fr)	(na)	(gl)	AR	19	11	+	<2	(fr)	(li)	(gl)	AR	21	18		
			HEB	10	7						HEB	11	11		
(fr)	(na)	(X)	AR	126	105	+	<4	(fr)	(li)	(X)	AR	197	166	+	<2
			HEB	76	66						HEB	114	105		

[1] The consonant group in root position C3 is varied.

TABLE 7.11.3

Root patterns with three specified positions and with nasals or liquids in C2 adjacent to stops or fricatives in C3[1] (Manner)

				No	Ne	Si	P						No	Ne	Si	P
			C1 is varied													
(st)	(na)	(st)	AR	18	21			(st)	(li)	(st)	AR	52	33	+	<1
			HEB	26	30						HEB	64	47	+	<2
(fr)	(na)	(st)	AR	44	31	+	<2	(fr)	(li)	(st)	AR	72	50	+	<1
			HEB	34	23	+	<3				HEB	63	37	+	<1
(na)	(na)	(st)	AR	1	9	+	<1	(na)	(li)	(st)	AR	11	15		
			HEB	1	9	-	<1				HEB	11	15		
(li)	(na)	(st)	AR	6	7			(li)	(li)	(st)	AR	0	12	-	<1
			HEB	1	6	-	<5				HEB	1	9	-	<1
(gl)	(na)	(st)	AR	3	4			(gl)	(li)	(st)	AR	6	7		
			HEB	1	4						HEB	8	6		
(X)	(na)	(st)	AR	72	73			(X)	(li)	(st)	AR	98	75	+	<1
			HEB	69	75						HEB	154	118	+	<1
(st)	(na)	(fr)	AR	37	21	+	<1	(st)	(li)	(fr)	AR	69	33	+	<1
			HEB	35	17	+	<1				HEB	60	27	+	<1
(fr)	(na)	(fr)	AR	37	32			(fr)	(li)	(fr)	AR	72	50	+	<1
			HEB	12	14						HEB	22	21		
(na)	(na)	(fr)	AR	3	9	-	<4	(na)	(li)	(fr)	AR	10	15		
			HEB	6	5						HEB	3	9		
(li)	(na)	(fr)	AR	12	8			(li)	(li)	(fr)	AR	0	12	-	<1
			HEB	4	3						HEB	0	5	-	<2
(gl)	(na)	(fr)	AR	2	4			(gl)	(li)	(fr)	AR	9	7		
			HEB	1	2						HEB	4	3		
(X)	(na)	(fr)	AR	91	74	+	<5	(X)	(li)	(fr)	AR	160	118	+	<1
			HEB	59	41	+	<2				HEB	94	68	+	<1

[1] The consonant group in root position C1 is varied.

TABLE 7.11.4

Root patterns with three specified positions and with nasals or liquids in C3 adjacent to stops or fricatives in C2[1] (Manner)

				No	Ne	Si	P						No	Ne	Si	P
									Cl is varied							
(st)	(na)	(st)	AR	18	21			(st)	(li)	(st)	AR		52	33	+	<1
(st)	(st)	(na)	AR	21	25			(st)	(st)	(li)	AR		45	37		
			HEB	39	40						HEB		71	54	+	<2
(fr)	(st)	(na)	AR	49	38			(fr)	(st)	(li)	AR		83	55	+	<1
			HEB	39	32						HEB		68	42	+	<1
(na)	(st)	(na)	AR	10	11			(na)	(st)	(li)	AR		21	17		
			HEB	14	13						HEB		23	17		
(li)	(st)	(na)	AR	20	9	+	<1	(li)	(st)	(li)	AR		3	13	-	<1
			HEB	13	8						HEB		3	11	-	<2
(gl)	(st)	(na)	AR	6	5			(gl)	(st)	(li)	AR		9	8		
			HEB	3	5						HEB		8	6		
(X)	(st)	(na)	AR	106	88			(X)	(st)	(li)	AR		161	130	+	<1
			HEB	97	85						HEB		176	134	+	<1
(li)	(fr)	(na)	AR	17	10	+	<3	(na)	(fr)	(li)	AR		32	19	+	<1
			HEB	13	5	+	<1				HEB		20	11	+	<1
(st)	(fr)	(na)	AR	36	29			(st)	(fr)	(li)	AR		66	42	+	<1
			HEB	31	25						HEB		53	34	+	<1
(fr)	(fr)	(na)	AR	39	43			(fr)	(fr)	(li)	AR		81	63	+	<2
			HEB	15	20						HEB		22	27		
(na)	(fr)	(na)	AR	10	13			(li)	(fr)	(li)	AR		5	15	-	<1
			HEB	5	8						HEB		2	7		
(gl)	(fr)	(na)	AR	9	6			(gl)	(fr)	(li)	AR		13	9		
			HEB	7	3						HEB		7	4		
(X)	(fr)	(na)	AR	111	100			(X)	(fr)	(li)	AR		197	147	+	<1
			HEB	73	64						HEB		108	85	+	<2

[1] The consonant group in root position Cl is varied.

TABLE 7.12

Root patterns with three specified positions and with nasals and liquids[1]
(Manner)

li followed by na							na followed by li						
				No	Ne	Si	P					No	Ne	Si	P
(li)	(na)	(st)	AR	6	7			(na)	(li)	(st)	AR	11	15		
			HEB	1	6	-	<5				HEB	11	15		
(st)	(li)	(na)	AR	14	13			(st)	(na)	(li)	AR	11	12		
			HEB	21	17						HEB	12	15		
(li)	(st)	(na)	AR	20	9	+	<1	(na)	(st)	(li)	AR	21	17		
			HEB	13	8						HEB	23	17		
(li)	(na)	(fr)	AR	12	8			(na)	(li)	(fr)	AR	10	15		
			HEB	4	3						HEB	3	9		
(fr)	(li)	(na)	AR	17	20			(fr)	(na)	(li)	AR	20	18		
			HEB	11	14						HEB	12	11		
(li)	(fr)	(na)	AR	17	10	+	<3	(na)	(fr)	(li)	AR	32	19	+	<1
			HEB	13	5	+	<1				HEB	20	11	+	<1

[1] The nasals and liquids are in adjacent or nonadjacent positions. The consonant group in the remaining position is varied.

TABLE 7.13

Preferred root patterns with three specified positions, stops, fricatives and a labial or a coronal sonorant[1] (Manner)

				No	Ne	Si	P					No	Ne	Si	P
(m)	(st)	(fr)	AR	7	10			(n)	(st)	(fr)	AR	40	19	+	<1
			HEB	27	12	+	<1				HEB	5	8		
(st)	(m)	(fr)	AR	22	13	+	<2	(st)	(n)	(fr)	AR	15	8	+	<1
			HEB	20	10	+	<1				HEB	15	8	+	<1
(st)	(fr)	(m)	AR	24	17			(st)	(fr)	(n)	AR	12	12		
			HEB	19	13						HEB	12	13		
(l)	(st)	(fr)	AR	12	9			(r)	(st)	(fr)	AR	22	14	+	<3
			HEB	8	4						HEB	18	8	+	<1
(st)	(l)	(fr)	AR	29	14	+	<1	(st)	(r)	(fr)	AR	40	20	+	<1
			HEB	25	12	+	<1				HEB	37	16	+	<1
(st)	(fr)	(l)	AR	26	18			(st)	(fr)	(r)	AR	40	24	+	<1
			HEB	25	14	+	<1				HEB	28	20		
(m)	(fr)	(st)	AR	20	11	+	<1	(n)	(fr)	(st)	AR	32	21	+	<2
			HEB	17	9	+	<1				HEB	19	13		
(fr)	(m)	(st)	AR	27	20			(fr)	(n)	(st)	AR	17	11		
			HEB	13	13						HEB	21	10	+	<1
(fr)	(st)	(m)	AR	28	22			(fr)	(st)	(n)	AR	21	15		
			HEB	18	16						HEB	21	16		
(l)	(fr)	(st)	AR	17	10	+	<2	(r)	(fr)	(st)	AR	19	16		
			HEB	11	5	+	<1				HEB	13	9		
(fr)	(l)	(st)	AR	38	20	+	<1	(fr)	(r)	(st)	AR	49	29	+	<1
			HEB	27	16	+	<1				HEB	36	21	+	<1
(fr)	(st)	(l)	AR	35	24	+	<3	(fr)	(st)	(r)	AR	48	31	+	<1
			HEB	25	17	+	<5				HEB	43	25	+	<1

[1] An individual labial or coronal sonorant is present in C1, C2 or C3.

TABLE 7.14

Preferred root patterns with three specified positions, two stops or two fricatives and a labial or coronal sonorant[1] (Manner)

				No	Ne	Si	P						No	Ne	Si	P
(m)	(st)	(st)	AR	4	10			(n)	(st)	(st)	AR		20	18		
			HEB	12	14						HEB		23	20		
(st)	(m)	(st)	AR	7	13			(st)	(n)	(st)	AR		11	8		
			HEB	9	17						HEB		17	13		
(st)	(st)	(m)	AR	10	15			(st)	(st)	(n)	AR		11	10		
			HEB	16	20						HEB		23	20		
(l)	(st)	(st)	AR	9	8			(r)	(st)	(st)	AR		22	14	+	<3
			HEB	9	8						HEB		17	14		
(st)	(l)	(st)	AR	19	13			(st)	(r)	(st)	AR		33	19	+	<1
			HEB	27	20						HEB		37	27		
(st)	(st)	(l)	AR	19	16			(st)	(st)	(r)	AR		26	21		
			HEB	28	21						HEB		42	32		
(m)	(fr)	(fr)	AR	8	11			(n)	(fr)	(fr)	AR		32	21	+	<2
			HEB	5	5						HEB		3	7		
(fr)	(m)	(fr)	AR	23	20			(fr)	(n)	(fr)	AR		14	12		
			HEB	8	8						HEB		5	6		
(fr)	(fr)	(m)	AR	23	25			(fr)	(fr)	(n)	AR		16	18		
			HEB	9	10						HEB		6	10		
(l)	(fr)	(fr)	AR	13	10			(r)	(fr)	(fr)	AR		16	16		
			HEB	3	3						HEB		5	5		
(fr)	(lf)	(r)	AR	26	20			(fr)	(r)	(fr)	AR		46	30	+	<1
			HEB	9	9						HEB		13	12		
(fr)	(fr)	(l)	AR	28	27			(fr)	(fr)	(r)	AR		53	36	+	<1
			HEB	5	11						HEB		17	16		

[1] An individual labial or coronal sonorant is present in C1, C2 or C3.

TABLE 7.15.1

Preferred root patterns with three specified positions and coronal obstruents[1]

a) *The coronal obstruent is in C1*

				Cl = X =											
				cs				cf				co			
				No	Ne	Si	P	No	Ne	Si	P	No	Ne	Si	P
(X)	(so)	(la)	AR	13	8			25	16	+	<3	38	24	+	<1
			HEB	11	7			15	12			34	21	+	<1
(X)	(la)	(so)	AR	20	9	+	<1	31	18	+	<1	51	27	+	<1
			HEB	18	9	+	<1	22	15			45	26	+	<1
(X)	(so)	(ve)	AR	10	3	+	<1	15	7	+	<1	25	10	+	<1
			HEB	7	5			15	8	+	<2	24	14	+	<1
(X)	(ve)	(so)	AR	5	5			16	10	+	<5	21	14		
			HEB	12	6	+	<2	20	10	+	<1	32	18	+	<1
(X)	(so)	(gu)	AR	16	6	+	<1	25	13	+	<1	41	19	+	<1
			HEB	12	5	+	<1	13	9			31	16	+	<1
(X)	(gu)	(so)	AR	12	7			39	15	+	<1	51	22	+	<1
			HEB	14	7	+	<2	18	12			39	22	+	<1
(X)	(la)	(ve)	AR	7	3	+	<4	11	7			18	10	+	<1
			HEB	4	4			10	7			16	12		
(X)	(ve)	(la)	AR	1	4			12	8			13	12		
			HEB	3	4			13	7	+	<2	16	12		
(X)	(la)	(gu)	AR	15	6	+	<1	25	12	+	<1	40	18	+	<1
			HEB	10	5	+	<2	13	8			27	14	+	<1
(X)	(gu)	(la)	AR	10	6			30	13	+	<1	40	19	+	<1
			HEB	12	5	+	<1	17	9	+	<1	31	16	+	<1

[1] The consonant groups in C2 and C3 are varied.

TABLE 7.15.2

Preferred root patterns with three specified positions and coronal obstruents[1]

b) *The coronal obstruent is in C2*

| | | | | C2 = X = | | | | | | | | | | | | |
| | | | | cs | | | | cf | | | | co | | | |
				No	Ne	Si	P	No	Ne	Si	P	No	Ne	Si	P
(so)	(X)	(la)	AR	14	10			21	13	+	<3	35	23	+	<2
			HEB	11	6	+	<3	8	6			22	13	+	<2
(la)	(X)	(so)	AR	20	8	+	<1	19	11	+	<2	39	19	+	<1
		`	HEB	16	9	+	<2	14	8			36	20	+	<1
(so)	(X)	(ve)	AR	2	4			16	6	+	<1	18	10	+	<2
			HEB	8	6			10	4	+	<1	22	13	+	<2
(ve)	(X)	(so)	AR	10	8			15	10			25	18		
			HEB	10	8			9	7			21	17		
(so)	(X)	(gu)	AR	15	8	+	<2	17	10	+	<5	32	19	+	<1
			HEB	9	4	+	<3	7	4			21	10	+	<1
(gu)	(X)	(so)	AR	29	15	+	<1	44	19	+	<1	29	15	+	<1
			HEB	17	11			18	10	+	<2	42	24	+	<1
(la)	(X)	(ve)	AR	4	3			11	4	+	<1	15	7	+	<1
			HEB	8	4	+	<5	11	4	+	<1	21	9	+	<1
(ve)	(X)	(la)	AR	14	7	+	<1	21	9	+	<1	35	15	+	<1
			HEB	10	5	+	<3	9	5			21	12	+	<1
(la)	(X)	(gu)	AR	16	6	+	<1	17	7	+	<1	33	13	+	<1
			HEB	8	5			11	4	+	<1	24	11	+	<1
(gu)	(X)	(la)	AR	23	13	+	<1	39	16	+	<1	62	29	+	<1
			HEB	13	7	+	<5	14	7	+	<2	32	17	+	<1

[1] The consonant groups in C1 and C3 are varied.

TABLE 7.15.3

Preferred root patterns with three specified positions and coronal obstruents[1]

c) *The coronal obstruent is in C3*

				C3 = X =											
				cs				cf				co			
				No	Ne	Si	P	No	Ne	Si	P	No	Ne	Si	P
(so)	(la)	(X)	AR	16	10			23	10	+	<1	39	20	+	<1
			HEB	10	6			14	6	+	<1	27	14	+	<1
(la)	(so)	(X)	AR	16	7	+	<1	12	8			28	15	+	<1
			HEB	12	8			15	8	+	<2	32	18	+	<1
(so)	(ve)	(X)	AR	11	5	+	<2	19	5	+	<1	30	11	+	<1
			HEB	7	4			14	4	+	<1	21	9	+	<1
(ve)	(so)	(X)	AR	11	7			20	7	+	<1	31	14	+	<1
			HEB	9	7			16	6	+	<1	27	15	+	<1
(so)	(gu)	(X)	AR	12	8			20	9	+	<1	32	17	+	<1
			HEB	7	6			8	5			21	13	+	<3
(gu)	(so)	(X)	AR	12	13			26	14	+	<1	38	27	+	<4
			HEB	11	10			16	9	+	<3	33	22	+	<2
(la)	(ve)	(X)	AR	5	4			6	4			11	8		
			HEB	4	4			6	4			10	10		
(ve)	(la)	(X)	AR	9	7			14	7	+	<1	23	14	+	<1
			HEB	6	6			18	5	+	<1	28	13	+	<1
(la)	(gu)	(X)	AR	15	6	+	<1	9	6			24	12	+	<1
			HEB	13	6	+	<1	7	6			21	13	+	<4
(gu)	(la)	(X)	AR	20	13	+	<5	25	13	+	<1	45	26	+	<1
			HEB	14	8			16	8	+	<1	38	19	+	<1

[1] The consonant groups in C1 and C2 are varied.

TABLE 7.16

Root patterns with three specified positions and both velars and gutturals¹ (Place)

				No	Ne	Si	P
(la)	(ve)	(gu)	AR	9	5		
			HEB	7	5		
(la)	(gu)	(ve)	AR	8	4		
			HEB	6	6		
(ve)	(la)	(gu)	AR	15	9	+	<5
			HEB	12	6	+	<3
(gu)	(la)	(ve)	AR	11	9		
			HEB	7	8		
(ve)	(gu)	(la)	AR	8	9		
			HEB	4	7		
(gu)	(ve)	(la)	AR	11	11		
			HEB	12	8		

				No	Ne	Si	P
(so)	(ve)	(gu)	AR	18	7	+	<1
			HEB	10	5	+	<2
(so)	(gu)	(ve)	AR	10	6		
			HEB	8	5		
(ve)	(so)	(gu)	AR	16	9	+	<4
			HEB	16	7	+	<1
(gu)	(so)	(ve)	AR	30	10	+	<1
			HEB	21	9	+	<1
(ve)	(gu)	(so)	AR	12	11		
			HEB	14	19		
(gu)	(ve)	(so)	AR	20	13	+	<1
			HEB	22	11	+	

				No	Ne	Si	P
(co)	(ve)	(gu)	AR	10	10		
			HEB	7	9		
(co)	(gu)	(ve)	AR	14	8	+	<5
			HEB	13	11		
(ve)	(co)	(gu)	AR	16	13		
			HEB	8	9		
(gu)	(co)	(ve)	AR	12	13		
			HEB	18	11		
(ve)	(gu)	(co)	AR	13	11		
			HEB	6	11		
(gu)	(ve)	(co)	AR	10	14	+	<4
			HEB	6	12		

¹ Root patterns with three specified positions which contain both velars and gutturals and also labials, coronal sonorants or coronal obstruents as a group.

TABLE 7.17

Root patterns with three specified positions and with expected frequencies[1] (Place)

a) *Root patterns arranged according their common consonant groups in C1 and C3*

				No	Ne	Si	P						No	Ne	Si	P
(la)	(ve)	(co)	AR	11	8			(ve)	(co)	(so)	AR	25	18		
			HEB	10	10						HEB	21	17		
(la)	(ve)	(so)	AR	14	7	+	<2	(ve)	(co)	(gu)	AR	16	13		
			HEB	15	9						HEB	9	7		
(la)	(ve)	(gu)	AR	9	5			(ve)	(gu)	(la)	AR	8	9		
			HEB	8	5						HEB	4	7		
(la)	(gu)	(ve)	AR	8	4			(ve)	(gu)	(co)	AR	13	11		
			HEB	6	6						HEB	6	11		
(co)	(la)	(ve)	AR	18	10	+	<1	(ve)	(gu)	(so)	AR	12	11		
			HEB	16	12						HEB	14	10		
(co)	(ve)	(la)	AR	13	12			(gu)	(la)	(so)	AR	31	25		
			HEB	16	12						HEB	24	17		
(co)	(ve)	(so)	AR	21	14			(gu)	(la)	(ve)	AR	13	9		
			HEB	32	18	+	<1				HEB	7	8		
(co)	(ve)	(gu)	AR	10	10			(gu)	(co)	(ve)	AR	12	13		
			HEB	7	9						HEB	18	11	+	<4
(co)	(gu)	(ve)	AR	14	8			(gu)	(so)	(co)	AR	38	27		
			HEB	13	11						HEB	32	22	+	<2
(so)	(la)	(ve)	AR	10	7			(gu)	(ve)	(la)	AR	11	11		
			HEB	8	6						HEB	12	8		
(so)	(la)	(gu)	AR	19	13			(gu)	(ve)	(co)	AR	10	14		
			HEB	10	7						HEB	6	12		
(so)	(gu)	(ve)	AR	10	6			(gu)	(ve)	(so)	AR	20	13		
			HEB	8	5						HEB	22	11	+	<1

TABLE 7.17 (continued)

b) *Root patterns arranged according their common consonant groups in C2 and C3*

				No	Ne	Si	P					No	Ne	Si	P
(co)	(ve)	(la)	AR	13	12			(co)	(la)	(ve)	AR	18	10	+	<1
			HEB	16	12						HEB	16	12		
(gu)	(ve)	(la)	AR	11	11			(so)	(la)	(ve)	AR	10	7		
			HEB	12	8						HEB	8	6		
(ve)	(gu)	(la)	AR	8	9			(gu)	(la)	(ve)	AR	13	9		
			HEB	4	7						HEB	7	8		
(gu)	(so)	(co)	AR	38	27			(gu)	(co)	(ve)	AR	12	13		
			HEB	32	22	+	<2				HEB	18	11	+	<4
(la)	(ve)	(co)	AR	11	8			(la)	(gu)	(ve)	AR	8	4		
			HEB	10	10						HEB	6	6		
(gu)	(ve)	(co)	AR	10	14			(so)	(la)	(gu)	AR	19	13		
			HEB	6	12						HEB	10	7		
(ve)	(gu)	(co)	AR	13	11			(ve)	(co)	(gu)	AR	16	13		
			HEB	6	11						HEB	9	7		
(gu)	(la)	(so)	AR	31	25			(la)	(ve)	(gu)	AR	9	5		
			HEB	24	17						HEB	8	5		
(ve)	(co)	(so)	AR	25	18			(co)	(ve)	(gu)	AR	10	10		
			HEB	21	17						HEB	7	9		
(la)	(ve)	(so)	AR	14	7	+	<2								
			HEB	15	9										
(co)	(ve)	(so)	AR	21	14										
			HEB	32	18	+	<1								
(gu)	(ve)	(so)	AR	20	13										
			HEB	22	11	+	<1								
(ve)	(gu)	(so)	AR	12	11										
			HEB	14	10										

[1] The 24 root patterns on the basis of Place with three specified positions in *AR* and *HEB* which have expected frequencies in both languages or only in one of them. They have been arranged according to the consonant groups which they have in common either in root positions C1 and C3 (a) or C2 and C3 (b).

TABLE 7.18

Preferred root patterns with three specified positions and both labials and coronal sonorants[1] (Place)

Pattern		No	Ne	Si	P
(co) (la) (so)	AR	51	27	+	<1
	HEB	45	26	+	<1
(co) (so) (la)	AR	38	24	+	<1
	HEB	34	21	+	<1
(la) (co) (so)	AR	39	19	+	<1
	HEB	36	20	+	<1
(so) (co) (la)	AR	35	23	+	<1
	HEB	22	13	+	<2
(la) (so) (co)	AR	28	15	+	<1
	HEB	31	17	+	<1
(so) (la) (co)	AR	39	20	+	<1
	HEB	27	14	+	<1

Pattern		No	Ne	Si	P
(ve) (la) (so)	AR	21	13	+	<3
	HEB	21	12	+	<1
(ve) (so) (la)	AR	20	12	+	<2
	HEB	19	10	+	<1
(la) (ve) (so)	AR	14	7	+	<2
	HEB	15	9	+	
(so) (ve) (la)	AR	18	9	+	<1
	HEB	12	6	+	<2
(la) (so) (ve)	AR	16	5	+	<1
	HEB	17	8	+	<1
(so) (la) (ve)	AR	10	7		
	HEB	8	6		

Pattern		No	Ne	Si	P
(gu) (la) (so)	AR	31	25		
	HEB	24	17		
(gu) (so) (la)	AR	38	22	+	<1
	HEB	22	14	+	<3
(la) (gu) (so)	AR	20	11	+	<2
	HEB	22	12	+	<1
(so) (gu) (la)	AR	29	14	+	<1
	HEB	18	8	+	<1
(la) (so) (gu)	AR	22	10	+	<1
	HEB	16	9	+	<2
(so) (la) (gu)	AR	19	13		
	HEB	10	7		

[1] The remaining root position contains other consonant groups with the exclusion of glides.

TABLE 7.19

Preferred root patterns with three specified positions, coronal obstruents as a group and labials or coronal sonorants[1] (Place)

				No	Ne	Si	P					No	Ne	Si	P
(co)	(la)	(ve)	AR	18	10	+	<1	(co)	(so)	(ve)	AR	25	10	+	<1
			HEB	16	12						HEB	24	14	+	<1
(co)	(ve)	(la)	AR	13	12			(co)	(ve)	(so)	AR	21	14		
			HEB	16	12						HEB	32	18	+	<1
(la)	(co)	(ve)	AR	15	7	+	<1	(so)	(co)	(ve)	AR	18	10	+	<2
			HEB	21	9	+	<1				HEB	15	9	+	<3
(ve)	(co)	(la)	AR	35	15	+	<1	(ve)	(co)	(so)	AR	25	18		
			HEB	21	12	+	<1				HEB	21	17		
(la)	(ve)	(co)	AR	11	8			(so)	(ve)	(co)	AR	30	11	+	<1
			HEB	10	10						HEB	21	9	+	<1
(ve)	(la)	(co)	AR	23	14	+	<1	(ve)	(so)	(co)	AR	31	14	+	<1
			HEB	28	13	+	<1				HEB	27	15	+	<1
(co)	(la)	(gu)	AR	40	18	+	<1	(co)	(so)	(gu)	AR	41	19	+	<1
			HEB	27	14	+	<1				HEB	31	16	+	<1
(co)	(gu)	(la)	AR	40	19	+	<1	(co)	(gu)	(so)	AR	51	22	+	<1
			HEB	24	16						HEB	32	24		
(la)	(co)	(gu)	AR	32	19	+	<1	(so)	(co)	(gu)	AR	32	19	+	<1
			HEB	24	10	+	<1				HEB	21	10	+	<1
(gu)	(co)	(la)	AR	62	29	+	<1	(gu)	(co)	(so)	AR	38	27	+	<4
			HEB	32	17	+	<1				HEB	42	24	+	<1
(la)	(gu)	(co)	AR	23	12	+	<1	(so)	(gu)	(co)	AR	32	17	+	<1
			HEB	19	13	+	<4				HEB	21	13	+	<3
(gu)	(la)	(co)	AR	45	26	+	<1	(gu)	(so)	(co)	AR	38	27	+	<4
			HEB	38	19	+	<1				HEB	33	22	+	<3

[1] The remaining root position contains other consonant groups with the exclusion of glides.

302 TABLES FOR CHAPTER SEVEN

TABLE 7.20.1
Root patterns with three specified positions and consonants from the same groups in C1 and C2[1] (Place)

		No	Ne	Si	P			No	Ne	Si	P
(la) (la) (al)	AR	0	12	-	<1	(co) (co) (co)	AR	1	39	-	<1
	HEB	0	10	-	<1		HEB	1	40	-	<1
(la) (la) (co)	AR	0	14	-	<1	(co) (co) (la)	AR	9	32	-	<1
	HEB	1	15	-	<1		HEB	15	26	-	<4
(la) (la) (so)	AR	0	14	-	<1	(co) (co) (so)	AR	15	37	-	<1
	HEB	1	14	-	<1		HEB	20	37	-	<1
(la) (la) (ve)	AR	0	5	-	<3	(co) (co) (ve)	AR	1	14	-	<3
	HEB	0	6	-	<2		HEB	6	17	-	<1
(la) (la) (gu)	AR	0	9	-	<1	(co) (co) (gu)	AR	8	26	-	<1
	HEB	2	7	-	<5		HEB	10	20	-	<3
(la) (la) (gl)	AR	0	7	-	<2	(co) (co) (gl)	AR	8	18	-	<2
	HEB	2	6				HEB	9	17		
(la) (la) (X)	AR	0	61	-	<1	(co) (co) (X)	AR	42	16	-	<1
	HEB	6	58	-	<1		HEB	61	15	-	<1
(so) (so) (so)	AR	0	20	-	<1	(ve) (ve) (ve)	AR	0	3		
	HEB	0	15	-	<1		HEB	0	4		
(so) (so) (la)	AR	2	17	-	<1	(ve) (ve) (la)	AR	0	6	-	<2
	HEB	1	11	-	<1		HEB	1	5		
(so) (so) (co)	AR	1	21	-	<1	(ve) (ve) (co)	AR	0	7	-	<1
	HEB	1	17	-	<1		HEB	0	9	-	<1
(so) (so) (ve)	AR	1	7	-	<2	(ve) (ve) (so)	AR	1	7	-	<3
	HEB	0	7	-	<1		HEB	0	8	-	<2
(so) (so) (gu)	AR	1	14	-	<1	(ve) (ve) (gu)	AR	0	5	-	<3
	HEB	0	8	-	<1		HEB	0	4	-	<5
(so) (so) (gl)	AR	2	10	-	<2	(ve) (ve) (gl)	AR	0	3		
	HEB	0	7	-	<1		HEB	0	4		
(so) (so) (X)	AR	8	89	-	<1	(ve) (ve) (X)	AR	1	31	-	<1
	HEB	2	65	-	<1		HEB	1	33	-	<1
(gu) (gu) (gu)	AR	0	14	-	<1						
	HEB	0	8	-	<1						
(gu) (gu) (la)	AR	1	18	-	<1						
	HEB	2	11	-	<1						
(gu) (gu) (co)	AR	2	22	-	<1						
	HEB	4	17	-	<1						
(gu) (gu) (so)	AR	3	21	-	<1						
	HEB	4	15	-	<1						
(gu) (gu) (ve)	AR	0	8	-	<1						
	HEB	0	7	-	<1						
(gu)(gu)(gl)	AR	0	10	-	<1						
	HEB	1	7	-	<3						
(gu) (gu) (X)	AR	6	92	-	<1						
	HEB	11	65	-	<1						

[1] The consonant group in position C3 is varied, but the MG's are excluded. Also included are the root patterns which contain arbitrary consonants in C3.

TABLE 7.20.2

Root patterns with three specified positions and consonants from the same groups in C2 and C3[1] (Place)

Pattern		No	Ne	Si	P	Pattern		No	Ne	Si	P
(la) (la) (la)	AR	0	12	-	<1	(co) (co) (co)	AR	1	39	-	<1
	HEB	0	10	-	<1		HEB	1	40	-	<1
(co) (la) (la)	AR	0	23	-	<1	(la) (co) (co)	AR	10	20	-	<3
	HEB	1	18	-	<1		HEB	9	21	-	<1
(so) (la) (la)	AR	0	16	-	<1	(so) (co) (co)	AR	12	28	-	<1
	HEB	0	9	-	<1		HEB	14	20		
(ve) (la) (la)	AR	0	11	-	<1	(ve) (co) (co)	AR	11	19		
	HEB	0	7	-	<2		HEB	8	18	-	<2
(gu) (la) (la)	AR	0	21	-	<1	(gu) (co) (co)	AR	15	36	-	<1
	HEB	0	7	-	<1		HEB	12	26	-	<1
(gl) (la) (la)	AR	0	5	-	<2	(gl) (co) (co)	AR	6	9		
	HEB	1	6	-	<4		HEB	6	6		
(X) (la) (la)	AR	0	88	-	<1	(X) (co) (co)	AR	55	15	-	<1
	HEB	2	60	-	<1		HEB	50	13	-	<1
(so) (so) (so)	AR	0	20	-	<1	(ve) (ve) (ve)	AR	0	3		
	HEB	0	15	-	<1		HEB	0	4		
(la) (so) (so)	AR	1	14	-	<1	(la) (ve) (ve)	AR	0	3		
	HEB	1	13	-	<1		HEB	0	4	-	<5
(co) (so) (so)	AR	3	28	-	<1	(co) (ve) (ve)	AR	0	5	-	<3
	HEB	4	19	-	<1		HEB	0	8	-	<1
(ve) (so) (so)	AR	1	14	-	<3	(so) (ve) (ve)	AR	0	4		
	HEB	5	9				HEB	0	4	-	<5
(gu) (so) (so)	AR	4	26	-	<1	(gu) (ve) (ve)	AR	0	5	-	<3
	HEB	5	12	-	<5		HEB	0	5	-	<3
(gl) (so) (so)	AR	0	6	-	<2	(gl) (ve) (ve)	AR	0	1		
	HEB	1	11	-	<1		HEB	0	1		
(X) (so) (so)	AR	9	108	-	<1	(X) (ve) (ve)	AR	0	21	-	<1
	HEB	16	79	-	<1		HEB	0	26	-	<1
(gu) (gu) (gu)	AR	0	14	-	<1						
	HEB	0	8	-	<1						
(la) (gu) (gu)	AR	1	8	-	<2						
	HEB	5	7								
(co) (gu) (gu)	AR	0	16	-	<1						
	HEB	3	12	-	<1						
(so) (gu) (gu)	AR	0	11	-	<1						
	HEB	3	6								
(ve) (gu) (gu)	AR	0	8	-	<1						
	HEB	4	6								
(gl) (gu) (gu)	AR	0	4								
	HEB	2	2								
(X) (gu) (gu)	AR	1	60	-	<1						
	HEB	17	41	-	<1						

[1] The consonant group in position C3 is varied, but the MG's are excluded. Also included are the root patterns which contain arbitrary consonants in C1.

TABLE 7.20.3

Root patterns with three specified positions and consonants from the samegroups in C1 and C3[1] (Place)

				No	Ne	Si	P					No	Ne	Si	P
(la)	(la)	(la)	AR	0	12	-	<1	(co)	(co)	(co)	AR	1	39	-	<1
			HEB	0	10	-	<1				HEB	1	40	-	<1
(la)	(co)	(la)	AR	6	16	-	<2	(co)	(la)	(co)	AR	29	28		
			HEB	9	13						HEB	36	29		
(la)	(so)	(la)	AR	4	12	-	<2	(co)	(s)	(co)	AR	29	29		
			HEB	6	11						HEB	33	33		
(la)	(ve)	(la)	AR	3	6			(co)	(ve)	(co)	AR	6	15	-	<2
			HEB	5	8						HEB	12	19		
(la)	(gu)	(la)	AR	5	10			(co)	(gu)	(co)	AR	28	23		
			HEB	3	11	-	<2				HEB	21	26		
(la)	(gl)	(la)	AR	1	9	-	<1	(co)	(gl)	(co)	AR	19	22		
			HEB	1	3						HEB	35	23	+	<2
(la)	(X)	(la)	AR	19	65	-	<1	(co)	(X)	(co)	AR	11	156	-	<1
			HEB	23	57	-	<1				HEB	13	170	-	<1
(so)	(so)	(so)	AR	0	20	-	<1	(ve)	(ve)	(ve)	AR	0	3		
			HEB	0	15	-	<1				HEB	0	4		
(so)	(la)	(so)	AR	9	19	-	<2	(ve)	(la)	(ve)	AR	0	5	-	<3
			HEB	8	16	-	<1				HEB	0	5	-	<2
(so)	(co)	(so)	AR	30	27			(ve)	(co)	(ve)	AR	0	7	-	<1
			HEB	21	31						HEB	1	8	-	<2
(so)	(ve)	(so)	AR	12	10			(ve)	(so)	(ve)	AR	2	5		
			HEB	12	14						HEB	2	6		
(so)	(gu)	(so)	AR	12	16			(ve)	(gu)	(ve)	AR	0	4	-	<5
			HEB	8	20	-	<1				HEB	2	5		
(so)	(gl)	(so)	AR	5	15	-	<1	(ve)	(gl)	(ve)	AR	1	4		
			HEB	3	5						HEB	2	4		
(so)	(X)	(so)	AR	73	107	-	<1	(ve)	(X)	(ve)	AR	3	27	-	<1
			HEB	52	101	-	<1				HEB	7	32	-	<1
(gu)	(gu)	(gu)	AR	0	14	-	<1								
			HEB	0	8	-	<1								
(gu)	(la)	(gu)	AR	6	17	-	<1								
			HEB	6	9										
(gu)	(co)	(gu)	AR	5	24	-	<1								
			HEB	2	13	-	<1								
(gu)	(so)	(gu)	AR	6	18	-	<2								
			HEB	8	11										
(gu)	(ve)	(gu)	AR	2	9	-	<1								
			HEB	0	6	-	<2								
(gu)	(gl)	(gu)	AR	3	13	-	<1								
			HEB	0	7	-	<1								
(gu)	(X)	(gu)	AR	22	96	-	<1								
			HEB	16	54	-	<1								

[1] The consonant group in position C2 is varied, but the MG's are excluded. Also included are the root patterns which contain arbitrary consonants in C2.

TABLE 7.21

Source root patterns and subsets with three specified positions which belong to larger sets with two specified positions[1] (Place)

Position		C1 No	C1 Ne	C1 Si	C1 P	Position		C2 No	C2 Ne	C2 Si	C2 P	Position		C3 No	C3 Ne	C3 Si	C3 P
(co) (la) (ve)	AR	18	10	+	<1	(co) (la) (ve)	AR	18	10	+	<1	(co) (la) (ve)	AR	18	10	+	<1
	HEB	16	12				HEB	16	12				HEB	16	12	+	<1
(la) (la) (ve)	AR	0	5	-	<3	(co) (co) (ve)	AR	1	14	-	<1	(co) (la) (la)	AR	0	23	-	<1
	HEB	0	6	-	<2		HEB	6	17	-	<1		HEB	1	18	-	<1
(so) (la) (ve)	AR	10	7			(co) (so) (ve)	AR	25	10	+	<1	(co) (la) (co)	AR	29	28		
	HEB	8	6				HEB	24	14	+	<1		HEB	36	29		
(ve) (la) (ve)	AR	0	5	-	<3	(co) (ve) (ve)	AR	0	5	-	<3	(co) (la) (so)	AR	51	27	+	<1
	HEB	0	5	-	<3		HEB	1	8	-	<1		HEB	45	26	+	<1
(gu) (la) (ve)	AR	13	9			(co) (gu) (ve)	AR	14	8	+	<5	(co) (la) (gu)	AR	40	18	+	<1
	HEB	7	8				HEB	13	11				HEB	27	14	+	<1
(gl) (la) (ve)	AR	3	2			(co) (gl) (ve)	AR	13	8	+	<1	(co) (la) (gl)	AR	13	13		
	HEB	1	2				HEB	26	10				HEB	11	9		
(X) (la) (ve)	AR	42	38			(co) (X) (ve)	AR	71	56	+	<4	(co) (la) (X)	AR	151	118	+	<4
	HEB	32	40				HEB	85	72				HEB	137	111	+	<2

TABLE 7.21 (continued)

Position			No	Ne	Si	P				No	Ne	Si	P				No	Ne	Si	P
			C1							**C2**							**C3**			
(gu) (co)	(so)	AR	73	34	+	<1	(gu) (co)	(so)	AR	73	34	+	<1	(gu) (co)	(so)	AR	73	34	+	<1
		HEB	42	24	+	<1			HEB	42	24	+	<1			HEB	42	24	+	<1
(la) (co)	(so)	AR	39	19	+	<1	(gu) (la)	(so)	AR	31	25			(gu) (co)	(la)	AR	62	29	+	<1
		HEB	36	20	+	<1			HEB	24	17					HEB	32	17	+	<1
(co) (co)	(so)	AR	15	37	-	<1	(gu) (so)	(so)	AR	4	26	-	<1	(gu) (co)	(co)	AR	15	36	-	<1
		HEB	20	37	-	<1			HEB	5	12	-	<5			HEB	12	26	-	<1
(so) (co)	(so)	AR	30	27			(gu) (ve)	(so)	AR	20	13	+	<1	(gu) (co)	(ve)	AR	12	13	+	<4
		HEB	21	31					HEB	22	11					HEB	18	11		
(ve) (co)	(so)	AR	25	18			(gu) (gu)	(so)	AR	3	21	-	<1	(gu) (co)	(gu)	AR	12	24	-	<1
		HEB	21	17					HEB	4	15	-	<1			HEB	2	13	-	<1
(gl) (co)	(so)	AR	11	9	+	<1	(gu) (gl)	(so)	AR	24	19			(gu) (co)	(gl)	AR	33	16	+	<1
		HEB	8	6	+	<1			HEB	13	14					HEB	19	11	+	<1
(X) (co)	(so)	AR	191	144	+	<1	(gu) (X)	(so)	AR	154	138			(gu) (co)	(X)	AR	207	153	+	<1
		HEB	148	78	+	<1			HEB	110	103					HEB	126	102	+	<2

TABLE 7.21 (continued)

Position			C1 No	C1 Ne	C1 Si	C1 P	Position			C2 No	C2 Ne	C2 Si	C2 P	Position			C3 No	C3 Ne	C3 Si	C3 P
(la) (so) (ve)	AR		16	5	+	<1	(la) (so) (ve)	AR		16	5	+	<1	(la) (so) (ve)	AR		16	5	+	<1
	HEB		17	8	+	<1		HEB		17	8	+	<1		HEB		17	8	+	<1
(co) (so) (ve)	AR		25	10	+	<1	(la) (la) (ve)	AR		0	5	-	<3	(la) (so) (la)	AR		4	12	-	<2
	HEB		24	14	+	<1		HEB		0	6	-	<2		HEB		6	11	-	
(so) (so) (ve)	AR		1	7	-	<2	(la) (co) (ve)	AR		15	7	+	<1	(la) (so) (co)	AR		28	15	+	<1
	HEB		0	7	-	<1		HEB		21	9	+	<1		HEB		32	18	+	<1
(ve) (so) (ve)	AR		2	5			(la) (ve) (ve)	AR		0	3	-	<1	(la) (so) (so)	AR		1	14	-	<1
	HEB		2	6				HEB		0	4	-	<5		HEB		1	13	-	<1
(gu) (so) (ve)	AR		30	10	+	<1	(la) (gu) (ve)	AR		8	4			(la) (so) (gu)	AR		22	10	+	<1
	HEB		21	9	+	<1		HEB		6	6				HEB		16	9	+	<2
(gl) (so) (ve)	AR		2	2			(la) (gl) (ve)	AR		3	4			(la) (so) (gl)	AR		9	7		
	HEB		4	2				HEB		8	5				HEB		8	6		
(X) (so) (ve)	AR		76	40	+	<1	(la) (X) (ve)	AR		42	28	+	<2	(la) (so) (X)	AR		80	64	+	<4
	HEB		59	37	+	<1		HEB		52	38	+	<2		HEB		82	68	+	

¹ The table shows 3 different root patterns classified on the basis of Place with three specified root positions which contain labials and/or coronal sonorants. They serve as 'source root patterns' of which one of their three positions C1, C2 or C3 is varied. In each case this yields a family of 6 subsets of root patterns, which include the 'source root pattern'. Each series of 6 subsets is part of a larger set with two specified positions and with arbitrary consonants in the remaning position. These larger sets in the table are either preferred or have expected frequencies.

TABLE 7.22

Preferred source root patterns with three specified root positions with labials and/or coronal sonorants and the larger sets to which they belong[1]

Root patterns with labials

	AR			HEB			AR	HEB
	C1	C2	C3	C1	C2	C3		
(la) (co) (ve)	=	>	>	=	>	>	2	2
(la) (ve) (co)	=	=	=	=	=	=	2	2
(co) (la) (ve)	=	>	=	=	=	>	2	1
(ve) (la) (co)	>	=	>	>	=	>		
(co) (ve) (la)	=	=	=	=	=	=	1	1
(ve) (co) (la)	>	=	=	>	=	>		
(la) (co) (gu)	=	>	>	=	>	>	2	2
(la) (gu) (co)	>	=	=	=	=	=	1	
(co) (la) (gu)	=	>	>	=	=	>	2	1
(gu) (la) (co)	>	=	=	>	=	=	1	
(co) (gu) (la)	=	=	>	=	=	>		
(gu) (co) (la)	>	=	>	>	=	>	2	2
Total								
>	5	4	6	4	3	6		
=	7	8	6	8	11	6		

Root patterns with coronal sonorants

	AR			HEB			AR	HEB
	C1	C2	C3	C1	C2	C3		
(so) (co) (ve)	=	=	=	=	=	=	2	1
(so) (ve) (co)	=	>	>	=	=	>	3	1
(co) (so) (ve)	>	>	>	>	=	=	1	1
(ve) (so) (co)	=	=	>	=	=	>	1	1
(co) (ve) (so)	>	=	=	>	=	=		
(ve) (co) (so)	>	=	=	>	=	=		
(so) (co) (gu)	=	=	=	=	=	=	3	1
(so) (gu) (co)	>	>	>	=	=	>	3	1
(co) (so) (gu)	>	>	>	>	=	=		
(gu) (so) (co)	=	=	=	=	=	>	2	2
(co) (gu) (so)	>	>	>	>	=	>	2	2
(gu) (co) (so)	>	>	>	>	=	>		
Total								
>	7	4	7	6	0	5		
=	5	8	5	6	12	7		

TABLE 7.22 (continued)

Root patterns with both labials and coronal sonorants

			AR			HEB			AR	HEB
			C1	C2	C3	C1	C2	C3		
(la)	(so)	(co)	=	=	>	=	=	=	1	
(la)	(so)	(ve)	>	>	>	>	>	=	3	2
(la)	(so)	(gu)	>	>	>	>	>	=	3	2
(so)	(la)	(co)	>	>	=	>	=	=	2	1
(so)	(la)	(ve)	=	=	=	=	=	=		
(so)	(la)	(gu)	=	=	=	=	=	=		
(la)	(co)	(so)	>	=	>	>	=	>	2	2
(la)	(ve)	(so)	>	=	=	>	=	=	1	1
(la)	(gu)	(so)	>	=	=	>	=	=	1	1
(so)	(co)	(la)	>	=	=	>	=	=	1	1
(so)	(ve)	(la)	=	=	>	=	=	>	1	1
(so)	(gu)	(la)	=	=	>	=	=	>	1	1
(co)	(la)	(so)	=	=	>	=	=	>	1	1
(ve)	(la)	(so)	=	=	=	=	=	=		
(gu)	(la)	(so)	=	=	=	=	=	=		
(co)	(so)	(la)	=	=	>	=	=	=	1	
(ve)	(so)	(la)	=	=	>	=	=	>	1	1
(gu)	(so)	(la)	=	=	=	=	=	=		
Total										
>			7	3	9	7	2	5		
=			11	15	9	11	16	13		

[1] This table shows the preferred 'source root patterns with three specified root positions which contain labials and/or coronal sonorants. Those which contain velars as well as gutturals are shown in *Table 7.23*. The 'source root patterns' are members of three larger sets of root patterns with two specified positions. The subsets arise by varying the consonant groups in position C1, C2 or C3 of the 'source root patterns'. These are not shown in the table ' (see the examples in *Table 7.21* and the text). The symbols used to indicate the co-occurrence properties of the larger sets are: '>' preferred, '=' expected frequency and '<' avoided. The numbers on the right side indicate the number of larger sets which are preferred among the three larger sets to which a particular 'source root pattern' belongs.

TABLE 7.23

'Source root patterns' with three specified root positions with velars as well as gutturals and their larger sets[1]

			AR			HEB			AR	HEB
			C1	C2	C3	C1	C2	C3		
(la)	(so)	(co)	=	=	>	=	=	=	1	1
(la)	(ve)	(gu)	=	>	=	=	>	=	1	1
(la)	(gu)	(ve)	=	>	=	=	>	=		1
(ve)	(la)	(gu)	=	=	=	=	=	>		
(gu)	(la)	(ve)	=	=	=	=	=	=		
(ve)	(gu)	(la)	=	=	<	=	=	=	1	
(gu)	(ve)	(la)	=	=	=	=	=	=		
(so)	(ve)	(gu)	=	=	>	=	=	>	1	1
(so)	(gu)	(ve)	=	=	>	=	=	>	1	1
(ve)	(so)	(gu)	>	=	>	>	=	>	2	2
(gu)	(so)	(ve)	>	=	=	>	=	=	1	1
(ve)	(gu)	(so)	>	=	<	>	=	=	2	1
(gu)	(ve)	(so)	>	=	=	>	=	=	1	1
Total										
>			4	2	3	4	2	4		
=			8	10	7	8	10	8		
<					2					

[1] Shown are all of the 'source root patterns' with three specified root positions which contain both velars and gutturals and also labials or coronal sonorants. Most of these root patterns have expected frequencies, but in *AR* and *HEB* (ve) (la) (gu), (so) (ve) (gu) (ve) (so) (gu) and (gu) (ve) (so) are preferred and so is (gu) (ve) (so) in *HEB*. See *Table 7.22* for further explanation.

TABLE 7.24

Root patterns with three specified positions and coronal obstruents, velars and gutturals[1]

			AR			HEB			AR	HEB
			C1	C2	C3	C1	C2	C3		
(co)	(gu)	(ve)	=	>	>	=	=	>	2	1
(gu)	(co)	(ve)	=	=	>	=	=	>	1	1
(co)	(ve)	(gu)	=	>	=	=	=	=	1	
(ve)	(co)	(gu)	=	=	=	=	=	=		
(ve)	(gu)	(co)	>	=	<	=	=	=	1	
(gu)	(ve)	(co)	=	=	=	=	=	=		
Total										
>			1	1					1	1
=			3	3	3	4	4	4		
<					1					

[1] The root pattern (co) (gu) (ve) is preferred only in *AR* and (gu) (co) (ve) only in *HEB*. They are not included in the totals for the larger subsets. The other types of root patterns have expected frequencies. For further explanation see *Table 7.22*.

TABLE 7.25

Root patterns with three specified positions with expected frequencies and labials and/or coronal sonorants[1]

			AR			HEB			AR	HEB
			C1	C2	C3	C1	C2	C3		
(la)	(ve)	(co)	=	=	=	=	=	=		
(la)	(ve)	(gu)	=	>	=	=	>	=	1	1
(la)	(gu)	(ve)	=	>	=	=	>	=	1	1
(gu)	(la)	(ve)	=	=	=	=	=	=		
(co)	(ve)	(la)	=	=	=	=	=	=		
(ve)	(gu)	(la)	=	=	<	=	=	=	1	
(gu)	(ve)	(la)	=	=	=	=	=	=		
(so)	(gu)	(ve)	=	=	>	=	=	>	1	1
(ve)	(co)	(so)	>	=	=	>	=	=	1	1
(ve)	(gu)	(so)	>	=	=	>	=	<	1	1
(so)	(la)	(ve)	=	=	=	=	=	=		
(so)	(la)	(gu)	=	=	=	=	=	=		
(gu)	(la)	(so	=	=	=	=	=	=		
Total										
>			2	2	1	2	2	1		
=			11	11	11	11	11	11		
<					1			1		

[1] *Tables 7.22 and 7.23* show the preferred root patterns of these types. See *Table 7.22* for further explanation.

TABLE 7.26

Preferred source root pattern which are members of two or more larger sets[1]

Common positions		AR			HEB			AR	HEB
		C1	C2	C3	C1	C2	C3		
C1 and C2	(la) (co) (so)	>	=	>	>	=	>	2	2
	(la) (co) (ve)	=	>	>	=	>	>	2	2
	(la) (co) (gu)	=	>	>	=	>	>	2	2
	(la) (so) (ve)	>	>	>	>	>	=	3	2
	(la) (so) (gu)	>	>	>	>	>	=	3	2
	(co) (la) (ve)	=	>	>	=	>	>	2	2
	(co) (la) (gu)	=	>	>	=	=	>	2	1
	(co) (so) (ve)	>	>	>	>	=	=	3	1
	(co) (so) (gu)	>	>	>	>	=	=	3	1
	(co) (gu) (so)	>	=	>	>	=	>	2	2
	(co) (gu) (ve)	=	>	>	=	=	>	2	1
	(gu) (co) (la)	>	=	>	>	=	>	2	2
	(gu) (co) (so)	>	=	>	>	=	>	2	2
C1 and C3	(la) (co) (ve)	=	>	>	=	>	>	2	2
	(la) (so) (ve)	>	>	>	>	>	=	3	2
	(co) (la) (ve)	=	>	>	=	>	>	2	2
	(co) (gu) (ve)	=	>	>	=	=	>	2	1
	(so) (la) (co)	>	>	=	>	=	=	2	1
	(so) (ve) (co)	=	>	>	=	=	>	2	1
	(so) (gu) (co)	>	>	>	=	=	>	3	1
C2 and C3	(la) (co) (so)	>	=	>	>	=	>	2	2
	(gu) (co) (so)	>	=	>	>	=	>	2	2
	(la) (so) (ve)	>	>	>	>	>	=	3	2
	(co) (so) (ve)	>	>	>	>	=	=	3	1

[1] All of these preferred root patterns serve as 'source root patterns' for the subsets which belong to two or three preferred larger sets in *AR* and/or *HEB*. They have been arranged according to the two positions which they have in common. As a result they may occur more than once in the table. For further explanation see *Table 7.22*.

TABLE 7.27

Preferred root patterns with three specified root positions obstruents and an individual labial or coronal sonorant[1] (Manner)

				No	Ne	Si	P					No	Ne	Si	P
(m)	(st)	(fr)	AR	7	10			(n)	(st)	(fr)	AR	40	19	+	<1
			HEB	27	12	+	<1				HEB	5	8		
(l)	(st)	(fr)	AR	12	9			(r)	(st)	(fr)	AR	22	14	+	<3
			HEB	8	4						HEB	18	8	+	<1
(st)	(m)	(fr)	AR	22	13	+	<2	(st)	(n)	(fr)	AR	15	8	+	<1
			HEB	20	10	+	<1				HEB	15	8	+	<1
(st)	(l)	(fr)	AR	29	14	+	<1	(st)	(r)	(fr)	AR	40	20	+	<1
			HEB	25	12	+	<1				HEB	37	16	+	<1
(st)	(fr)	(m)	AR	24	17			(st)	(fr)	(n)	AR	12	12		
			HEB	19	13						HEB	12	13		
(st)	(fr)	(l)	AR	26	18			(st)	(fr)	(r)	AR	40	24	+	<1
			HEB	25	14	+	<1				HEB	28	20		
(m)	(fr)	(st)	AR	20	11	+	<1	(n)	(fr)	(st)	AR	32	21	+	<2
			HEB	17	9	+	<1				HEB	19	13		
(l)	(fr)	(st)	AR	17	10	+	<2	(r)	(fr)	(st)	AR	19	16		
			HEB	11	5	+	<1				HEB	13	9		
(fr)	(m)	(st)	AR	27	20			(fr)	(n)	(st)	AR	17	11		
			HEB	13	13						HEB	21	10	+	<1
(fr)	(l)	(st)	AR	38	20	+	<1	(fr)	(r)	(st)	AR	49	29	+	<1
			HEB	27	16	+	<1				HEB	36	21	+	<1
(fr)	(st)	(m)	AR	28	22			(fr)	(st)	(n)	AR	21	15		
			HEB	18	16						HEB	21	16		
(fr)	(st)	(l)	AR	35	24	+	<3	(fr)	(st)	(r)	AR	48	31	+	<1
			HEB	25	17	+	<5				HEB	43	25	+	<1

[1] The individual labial or coronal sonorant is present in C1, C2 or C3.

TABLE 7.28.1

Preferred root patterns with three specified positions and an individual labial or coronal sonorants in C1[1] (Place)

				No	Ne	Si	P					No	Ne	Si	P
(l)	(la)	(co)	AR	10	4	+	<1	(l)	(ve)	(la)	AR	5	2	+	<3
			HEB	8	3	+	<1				HEB	1	1		
(r)	(la)	(co)	AR	15	7	+	<1	(r)	(ve)	(la)	AR	7	3	+	<2
			HEB	11	5	+	<1				HEB	5	2	+	<4
(l)	(la)	(ve)	AR	4	1	+	<4	(n)	(ve)	(co)	AR	18	5	+	<1
			HEB	0	1						HEB	11	5	+	<1
(r)	(co)	(la)	AR	14	8	+	<3	(r)	(ve)	(co)	AR	10	4	+	<1
			HEB	11	4	+	<1				HEB	6	3		
(n)	(co)	(so)	AR	19	12			(n)	(ve)	(gu)	AR	8	3	+	<1
			HEB	14	9						HEB	5	2		
(m)	(co)	(ve)	AR	6	2	+	<3	(l)	(ve)	(gu)	AR	4	2	+	<5
			HEB	11	3	+	<1				HEB	1	1		
(n)	(co)	(ve)	AR	10	5	+	<1	(r)	(ve)	(gu)	AR	6	2	+	<3
			HEB	11	4	+	<1				HEB	3	2		
(m)	(co)	(gu)	AR	9	4	+	<3	(l)	(gu)	(la)	AR	7	3	+	<2
			HEB	5	2	+	<1				HEB	5	2	+	<1
(n)	(co)	(gu)	AR	16	8	+	<1	(r)	(gu)	(la)	AR	11	5	+	<1
			HEB	11	5	+	<1				HEB	8	3	+	<1
(r)	(co)	(gu)	AR	10	6			(m)	(gu)	(co)	AR	11	4	+	<1
			HEB	9	3	+	<1				HEB	10	4	+	<1
(m)	(so)	(ve)	AR	1	2			(n)	(gu)	(co)	AR	15	8	+	<1
			HEB	6	2	+	<3				HEB	10	4	+	<1
(m)	(so)	(gu)	AR	9	4	+	<3	(l)	(gu)	(co)	AR	9	4	+	<1
			HEB	6	3						HEB	8	2	+	<1
								(m)	(gu)	(so)	AR	9	4	+	<1
											HEB	8	4		
								(m)	(gu)	(ve)	AR	6	1	+	<1
											HEB	3	2		
								(l)	(gu)	(ve)	AR	6	1	+	<1
											HEB	4	1	+	<1

[1] The preferred root patterns are arranged according to the consonant groups which are present in C2 and C3. The individual labial or coronal sonorant is in C1.

TABLE 7.28.2

Preferred root patterns with three specified positions and an individual labial or coronal sonorants in C2[1] (Place)

		No	Ne	Si	P			No	Ne	Si	P
(co) (r) (la)	AR	21	11	+	<1	(gu) (n) (ve)	AR	6	2	+	<1
	HEB	14	10				HEB	7	2	+	<1
(ve) (n) (la)	AR	4	2			(la) (l) (ve)	AR	7	2	+	<1
	HEB	5	2	+	<5		HEB	6	2	+	<3
(ve) (l) (la)	AR	8	4	+	<3	(la) (r) (ve)	AR	7	3	+	<1
	HEB	7	3	+	<4		HEB	9	3	+	<1
(gu) (l) (la)	AR	15	7	+	<1	(co) (l) (ve)	AR	10	3	+	<1
	HEB	9	5	+	<4		HEB	8	5		
(gu) (r) (la)	AR	17	11	+	<5	(co) (r) (ve)	AR	11	5	+	<1
	HEB	8	6				HEB	13	6	+	<1
(la) (l) (co)	AR	9	5			(gu) (l) (ve)	AR	11	3	+	<1
	HEB	12	6	+	<1		HEB	4	3		
(la) (r) (co)	AR	16	7	+	<1	(gu) (r) (ve)	AR	13	5	+	<1
	HEB	18	8	+	<1		HEB	10	4	+	<1
(ve) (m) (co)	AR	10	5	+	<2	(la) (l) (gu)	AR	8	3	+	<1
	HEB	12	4	+	<1		HEB	8	3	+	<1
(ve) (n) (co)	AR	8	3	+	<1	(la) (r) (gu)	AR	12	5	+	<1
	HEB	9	3	+	<1		HEB	7	4		
(ve) (l) (co)	AR	9	5	+	<5	(co) (m) (gu)	AR	12	6	+	<3
	HEB	6	5				HEB	9	5	+	<4
(ve) (r) (co)	AR	14	7	+	<1	(co) (n) (gu)	AR	7	4		
	HEB	12	7	+	<5		HEB	9	4	+	<1
(gu) (m) (co)	AR	21	9	+	<1	(co) (l) (gu)	AR	14	6	+	<1
	HEB	14	6	+	<1		HEB	13	5	+	<1
(gu) (r) (co)	AR	23	13	+	<1	(co) (r) (gu)	AR	20	9	+	<1
	HEB	16	10	+	<5		HEB	9	7		
(co) (m) (so)	AR	20	9	+	<1	(ve) (m) (gu)	AR	8	3	+	<1
	HEB	17	9	+	<5		HEB	5	2	+	<4
						(ve) (l) (gu)	AR	5	3		
							HEB	6	2	+	<3

[1] The preferred root patterns have been arranged according to the consonant groups which are present in C1 and C3. The individual labial or coronal sonorant is in C2.

TABLE 7.28.3

Preferred root patterns with three specified positions and an individual labial or coronal sonorants in C3[1] (Place)

Pattern		No	Ne	Si	P	Pattern		No	Ne	Si	P
(co) (la) (n)	AR	13	6	+	<1	(la) (ve) (r)	AR	7	3	+	<4
	HEB	13	7	+	<4		HEB	9	4	+	<2
(co) (la) (l)	AR	15	9	+	<5	(co) (ve) (l)	AR	7	5		
	HEB	14	8	+	<3		HEB	10	5	+	<4
(co) (la) (r)	AR	23	12	+	<1	(co) (ve) (r)	AR	9	6		
	HEB	18	12				HEB	14	8	+	<3
(ve) (la) (l)	AR	9	4	+	<2	(so) (ve) (m)	AR	8	3	+	<1
	HEB	8	3	+	<2		HEB	5	2		
(la) (co) (l)	AR	14	6	+	<1	(gu) (ve) (l)	AR	7	5		
	HEB	13	6	+	<1		HEB	7	3	+	<5
(la) (co) (r)	AR	18	8	+	<1	(gu) (ve) (r)	AR	9	6		
	HEB	18	9	+	<1		HEB	10	5	+	<3
(ve) (co) (m)	AR	15	6	+	<1	(la) (gu) (r)	AR	9	5		
	HEB	9	5	+	<4		HEB	10	5	+	<5
(ve) (co) (r)	AR	15	8	+	<2	(co) (gu) (m)	AR	14	7	+	<1
	HEB	11	7				HEB	9	6		
(gu) (co) (m)	AR	24	11	+	<1	(co) (gu) (n)	AR	11	5	+	<1
	HEB	14	7	+	<1		HEB	10	6		
(gu) (co) (n)	AR	14	7	+	<2	(co) (gu) (l)	AR	14	8	+	<2
	HEB	11	7				HEB	11	7		
(gu) (co) (l)	AR	23	12	+	<1	(co) (gu) (r)	AR	26	10	+	<1
	HEB	10	7				HEB	18	10	+	<2
(gu) (co) (r)	AR	36	15	+	<1	(so) (gu) (m)	AR	13	5	+	<1
	HEB	21	11	+	<1		HEB	10	3	+	<1
(co) (so) (m)	AR	8	6								
	HEB	10	8								
(co) (so) (l)	AR	6	9								
	HEB	15	9	+	<5						

[1] The preferred root patterns have been arranged according to the consonant groups which are present in C1 and C2. The individual labial or coronal sonorant is in C3.

TABLE 7.29.1

Mediae Geminatae in Arabic and Hebrew[1] (Manner)

			AR					MH				
			No	Ne	Si	P	+MG	No	Ne	Si	P	+MG
(st)	(st)	(st)	26	62	-	<1	50	47	110	-	<1	76
(fr)	(st)	(st)	70	93	-	<2	116	78	86			112
(na)	(st)	(st)	24	28			33	35	34			43
(li)	(st)	(st)	31	22			42	26	22			39
(st)	(fr)	(fr)	52	72	-	<2	92	21	40	-	<1	46
(fr)	(fr)	(fr)	44	108	-	<1	83	2	31	-	<1	14
(na)	(fr)	(fr)	40	32			48	8	13			14
(li)	(fr)	(fr)	29	26			41	8	8			13
(st)	(na)	(na)	7	8			23	7	8			18
(fr)	(na)	(na)	6	13			26	8	13			19
(na)	(na)	(na)	1	3			3	0	4			1
(li)	(na)	(na)	1	2			4	1	3			4
(st)	(li)	(li)	0	20	-	<1	14	2	23	-	<1	17
(fr)	(li)	(li)	0	29	-	<1	24	2	18	-	<1	15
(na)	(li)	(li)	0	7	-	<1	2	0	9	-	<1	2
(li)	(li)	(li)	0	5	-	<4	0	0	7	-	<1	0

[1] Shown are the numbers of verbal root patterns classified on the basis of Manner in *AR* and *HEB* which contain consonants from the same group in root positions C2 and C3. The values for No, Ne, Si and P are for the root patterns from which the Mediae Geminatae are excluded and +MG denotes the observed frequencies of those in which the corresponding Mediae Geminatae included.

TABLE 7.29.2

Mediae Geminatae in Arabic and Hebrew[1] (Place)

	AR					MH				
	No	Ne	Si	P	+MG	No	Ne	Si	P	+MG
(st) (st) (st)	26	62	-	<1	50	47	110	-	<1	76
(la) (la) (la)	0	12	-	<1	0	0	10	-	<1	0
(co) (la) (la)	0	23	-	<1	23	1	18	-	<1	20
(so) (la) (la)	0	16	-	<1	8	0	9	-	<1	7
(ve) (la) (la)	0	11	-	<1	8	0	7	-	<2	6
(gu) (la) (la)	0	21	-	<1	16	0	7	-	<1	9
(la) (co) (co)	10	20	-	<3	29	9	21	-	<1	24
(co) (co) (co)	1	39	-	<1	9	1	40	-	<1	15
(so) (co) (co)	12	28	-	<1	31	14	20			26
(ve) (co) (co)	11	19			32	8	18	-	<2	24
(gu) (co) (co)	15	36	-	<1	53	12	26	-	<1	36
(la) (so) (so)	1	14	-	<1	10	1	13	-	<1	11
(co) (so) (so)	3	28	-	<1	28	4	19	-	<1	24
(so) (so) (so)	0	20	-	<1	1	0	15	-	<1	2
(ve) (so) (so)	1	14	-	<3	10	5	9			14
(gu) (so) (so)	4	26	-	<1	18	5	12	-	<5	16
(la) (ve) (ve)	0	3			4	0	4	-	<5	6
(co) (ve) (ve)	0	5	-	<3	14	0	8	-	<1	11
(so) (ve) (ve)	0	4			6	0	4	-	<5	3
(ve) (ve) (ve)	0	3			0	0	4			0
(gu) (ve) (ve)	0	5	-	<3	8	0	5	-	<3	3
(la) (gu) (gu)	1	8	-	<2	4	5	7			6
(co) (gu) (gu)	0	16	-	<1	8	3	12	-	<1	10
(so) (gu) (gu)	0	11	-	<1	3	3	6	-	<2	6
(ve) (gu) (gu)	0	8	-	<1	0	4	6			5
(gu) (gu) (gu)	0	14	-	<1	0	0	8	-	<1	0

[1] Shown are the numbers of verbal root patterns classified on the basis of Place in *AR* and *HEB* which have consonants from the same group in root positions C2 and C3. For further explanation see *Table 7.29.1*.

TABLE 8.1

Co-occurrence relationships of the pharyngealized coronals with the uvular stop /q/ and the gutturals in Arabic[1]

Leftmost part:

	No	Ne	Si	P
(em) (em) (X)	0	33	-	<1
(X) (em) (em)	17	32	-	<1
(em) (X) (em)	2	12	-	<1

Midpart:

		No	Ne	Si	P
(q)	(em) (X)	20	9	+	<1
(em)	(q) (X)	5	6		
(X)	(q) (em)	13	6	+	<1
(X)	(em) (q)	4	9		
(q)	(X) (em)	16	8	+	<1
(em)	(X) (q)	10	9		

Rightmost part:

		No	Ne	Si	P
(em)	(gu) (X)	34	27		
(gu)	(em) (X)	60	43	+	<1
(X)	(em) (gu)	30	29		
(X)	(gu) (em)	35	25	+	<5
(em)	(X) (gu)	44	28		
(gu)	(X) (em)	43	39		

[1] The leftmost part of the table table shows the co-occurrence relationships among the emphatic (pharyngealized) coronals /T/, /D/, /S/ and /Z/ (abbreviated here as 'em') and of the emphatics with the uvular stop /q/ (the midpart of the table) and with the gutturals (the rightmost part).

TABLE 8.2.1

Co-occurrence relationships of root patterns with two or three stops or fricatives[1] (Manner)

Pattern	Features	AR	MH	Pattern	Features	AR	MH
(st)(st)	[-con][-con]	-	-	(fr)(fr)	[+con][+con]	-	-
(fr)(st)	[+con][-con]	>	>	(st)(fr)	[-con][+con]	<	=
(na)(st)	[+nas][-con]	>	=	(na)(fr)	[+nas][+con]	>	>
(li)(st)	[+liq][-con]	>	>	(li)(fr)	[+liq][+con]	+	+
(X)(st)	X [-con]	-	-	(X)(fr)	X [+con]	-	-
(st)(st)	[-con][-con]	<	=	(fr)(fr)	[+con][+con]	-	-
(st)(fr)	[-con][+con]	>	>	(fr)(st)	[+con][-con]	<	<
(st)(na)	[-con][+nas]	>	>	(fr)(na)	[+con][+nas]	>	=
(st)(li)	[-con][+liq]	+	+	(fr)(li)	[+con][+liq]	+	+
(st)(X)	[-con] X	>	-	(fr)(X)	[+con] X	-	-
(st)(st)	[-con][-con]	-	-	(fr)(fr)	[+con][+con]	-	-
(st)(fr)	[-con][-con]	<	=	(fr)(st)	[+con][-con]	<	<
(st)(na)	[-con][+nas]	>	=	(fr)(na)	[+con][+nas]	>	>
(li)(st)	[-con][+liq]	>	+	(li)(fr)	[+con][+liq]	+	+
(st)(X)	[-con] X	-	-	(fr)(X)	[+con] X	-	-

[1] Root patterns in *AR* and *HEB* which contain two stops or two fricatives in adjacent or nonadjacent positions and nasals, liquids or arbitrary consonants (X) in the remaining position. Root patterns with glides are not listed. For each of the consonant groups is indicated whether it has the feature [+cont] or [-cont] and whether it is a nasal or a liquid. The symbols used to indicate whether the difference No-Ne is significantly different from 0 are as follows:

+ : No-Ne is significantly larger than 0.   - : No-Ne is significantly smaller than 0.
\> : No-Ne larger than 0, but not significantly so.   < : No-Ne smaller than 0, but not significantly so.
= : No-Ne is not significantly larger or smaller than 0.

TABLE 8.2.2

Co-occurrence behavior of root patterns with adjacent stops and fricatives[1]

Pattern			AR	MH				Pattern		AR	MH
(st)(fr)	[-con]	[+con]	,	=	[-con]	[+con]	[-con]	(st)(st)	(st)	∨	∨
(fr)(st)	[+con]	[-con]	∨	,	[+con]	[+con]	[-con]	(fr)(st)	(st)	,	∨
(na)(st)	[+nas]	[-con]	+	+	[+nas]	[+con]	[-con]	(na)(st)	(st)	+	+
(li)(st)	[+liq]	[-con]	∧	+	[+liq]	[+con]	[-con]	(li)(st)	(st)	+	+
:	:	:	:	:	:	:	:	:	:	:	:
(X)(st)	[-con]	[+con]	∧	∧	X	[+con]	[-con]	(X)(st)	(st)	=	∧
(st)(st)	[-con]	[+con]	,	=	[+con]	[-con]	[-con]	(fr)(fr)	(fr)	,	∨
(st)(fr)	[+con]	[+con]	,	,	[+con]	[+con]	[-con]	(fr)(fr)	(fr)	,	∨
(st)(na)	[+nas]	[+con]	+	+	[+con]	[+nas]	[-con]	(fr)(na)	(fr)	+	+
(st)(li)	[+liq]	[+con]	+	+	[+con]	[+liq]	[-con]	(fr)(li)	(fr)	+	+
:	:	:	:	:	:	:	:	:	:	:	:
(st)(X)	X	[-con]	∧	+	[+con]	X	[-con]	(fr)(X)	(fr)	∧	+
(st)(fr)	[-con]	[+con]	∨	∨	[+con]	[-con]	[-con]	(fr)(st)	(st)	,	∨
(st)(fr)	[+con]	[+con]	,	,	[+con]	[-con]	[+con]	(fr)(st)	(st)	∨	,
(st)(na)	[+con]	[+nas]	∧	∧	[+con]	[-con]	[+nas]	(fr)(na)	(na)	∧	∧
(st)(li)	[+con]	[+liq]	+	+	[+con]	[-con]	[+liq]	(fr)(li)	(li)	+	+
:	:	:	:	:	:	:	:	:	:	:	:
(st)(fr)	[-con]	X	=	∧	[+con]	[-con]	X	(fr)(X)	(X)	∧	∧

[1] All root patterns contain both stops and fricatives in adjacent or nonadjacent positions and nasals, liquids or arbitrary consonants (X) in the remaining position. For further explanation see *Table 8.2.1*.

TABLE 8.3

Root patterns with adjacent nasals and liquids and arbitrary consonants in the remaining position[1]

	AR				BH				HEB			
	Na	Ne	Si	P	Na	Ne	Si	P	Na	Ne	Si	P
naliX	24	50	-	<1	14	27	-	<2	19	42	-	<1
linaX	23	25			5	9			9	17		
Xnali	34	43			14	20			31	37		
Xlina	34	47			14	19			36	43		

[1] X represents the arbitrary consonants.

TABLE 8.4

Adjacent root consonants at the syllable borders of the verbal paradigm[1]

Binyan	ARABIC				Binyan	HEBREW			
	perf	CC	imperf	CC		perf	CC	imperf	CC
faʿala			whole	12	paʿal	3fs	23	whole	12
						3pc	23		
ʾafʿala	whole	12	whole	12					
					nifʿal	whole	12	2pc	23
istafʿala	whole	12	whole	12				3pc	23
					hifʿil	whole	12	whole	12
					hofʿal	whole	12	whole	12

[1] Incidence of adjacent consonants at the syllable borders in positions C1C2 or C2C3 (CC) in the paradigms for the perfect and the imperfect of the binyanim in Arabic and Hebrew. Where required, person, gender and number are mentioned. The meaning of the abbreviations is:

f = feminine, c = masculine and feminine, s = singular, p = plural, whole = all persons, genders and numbers.

TABLE 8.5

Root patterns of the type C1C1X in Arabic and Hebrew[1]

AR	BH	MH
ddy	ddh	ddh
	99r	99r
	cc?	cc?
		bb?
		ddm
		TTp
		TTr
		kkb
		llb
		mmn
		mmc
		pph
		cch
		ccr
		ttH

[1] The root 'ddh' in Hebrew is equivalent to 'ddy' in Arabic. In *BH* 3 roots of this type occur. At least half of the 12 additional roots which occur in *HEB* are denominal (see § 8.10.1).

INDEX

STUDIES IN SEMITIC LANGUAGES AND LINGUISTICS

3. Corré, A.D. *The Daughter of My People*. Arabic and Hebrew Paraphrases of Jeremiah 8.13-9.23. 1971. ISBN 90 04 02552 9

5. Grand'Henry, J. *Les parlers arabes de la région du Mzāb (Sahara algérien)*. 1976. ISBN 90 04 04533 3

6. Bravmann, M.M. *Studies in Semitic Philology*. 1977. ISBN 90 04 04743 3

8. Fenech, E. *Contemporary Journalistic Maltese*. An Analytical and Comparative Study. 1978. ISBN 90 04 05756 0

9. Hospers, J.H. (ed.). *General Linguistics and the Teaching of Dead Hamito-Semitic Languages*. Proceedings of the Symposium held in Groningen, 7th-8th November 1975, on the occasion of the 50th Anniversary of the Institute of Semitic Studies and Near Eastern Archaeology of the State University at Groningen. 1978. ISBN 90 04 05806 0

12. Hoftijzer, J. *A Search for Method*. A Study in the Syntactic Use of the H-locale in Classical Hebrew. With the collaboration of H.R. van der Laan and N.P. de Koo. 1981. ISBN 90 04 06257 2

13. Murtonen, A. *Hebrew in its West Semitic Setting*. A Comparative Survey of Non-Masoretic Hebrew Dialects and Traditions. Part I. *A Comparative Lexicon*.
Section A. *Proper Names*. 1986. ISBN 90 04 07245 4
Section Ba. *Root System: Hebrew Material*. 1988. ISBN 90 04 08064 3
Section Bb. *Root System: Comparative Material and Discussion*. Sections C, D and E: *Numerals under 100, Pronouns, Particles*. 1989.
ISBN 90 04 08899 7

14. Retsö, J. *Diathesis in the Semitic Languages*. A Comparative Morphological Study. 1989. ISBN 90 04 08818 0

15. Rouchdy, A. *Nubians and the Nubian Language in Contemporary Egypt*. A Case of Cultural and Linguistic Contact. 1991. ISBN 90 04 09197 1

16. Murtonen, A. *Hebrew in its West Semitic Setting*. A Comparative Survey of Non-Masoretic Hebrew Dialects and Traditions. Part 2. *Phonetics and Phonology*. Part 3. *Morphosyntactics*. 1990. ISBN 90 04 09309 5

17. Jongeling K., H.L. Murre-van den Berg & L. van Rompay (eds.). *Studies in Hebrew and Aramaic Syntax*. Presented to Professor J. Hoftijzer on the Occasion of his Sixty-Fifth Birthday. 1991. ISBN 90 04 09520 9

18. Cadora, F.J. *Bedouin, Village, and Urban Arabic*. An Ecolinguistic Study. 1992. ISBN 90 04 09627 2

19. Versteegh, C.H.M. *Arabic Grammar and Qur'ānic Exegesis in Early Islam*. 1993. ISBN 90 04 09845 3

20. Humbert, G. *Les voies de la transmission du Kitāb de Sībawayhi*. 1995. ISBN 90 04 09918 2

21. Mifsud, M. *Loan Verbs in Maltese*. A Descriptive and Comparative Study. 1995. ISBN 90 04 10091 1

22. Joosten, J. *The Syriac Language of the Peshitta and Old Syriac Versions of Matthew*. Syntactic Structure, Inner-Syriac Developments and Translation Technique. 1996. ISBN 90 04 10036 9

23. Bernards, M. *Changing Traditions*. Al-Mubarrad's Refutation of Sībawayh and the Subsequent Reception of the Kitāb. 1997. ISBN 90 04 10595 6

24. Belnap, R.K. and N. Haeri. *Structuralist Studies in Arabic Linguistics*. Charles A. Ferguson's Papers, 1954-1994. 1997. ISBN 90 04 10511 5

25. Talmon R. *Arabic Grammar in its Formative Age. Kitāb al-'Ayn* and its Attribution to Ḥalīl b. Aḥmad. 1997. ISBN 90 04 10812 2

26. Testen, D.D. *Parallels in Semitic Linguistics*. The Development of Arabic *la-* and Related Semitic Particles. 1998. ISBN 90 04 10973 0

27. Bolozky, S. *Measuring Productivity in Word Formation*. The Case of Israeli Hebrew. 1999. ISBN 90 04 11252 9

28. Ermers, R. *Arabic Grammars of Turkic. The Arabic Linguistic Model Applied to Foreign Languages & Translation of 'Abū Hayyān al-'Andalusī's* Kitāb al-'Idrāk li-Lisān al-'Atrāk. 1999. ISBN 90 04 113061

29. Rabin, Ch. *The Development of the Syntax of Post-Biblical Hebrew*. 1999. ISBN 90 04 11433 5

30. Piamenta, M. *Jewish Life in Arabic Language and Jerusalem Arabic in Communal Perspective*. A Lexical-Semantic Study. 2000. ISBN 90 04 11762 8

31. Kinberg, N. ; Versteegh, K. (ed.). *Studies in the Linguistic Structure of Classical Arabic*. 2001. ISBN 90 04 11765 2

32. Khan, G. *The Early Karaite Tradition of Hebrew Grammatical Thought*. Including a Critical Edition, Translation and Analysis of the *Diqduq* of 'Abū Ya'qūb Yūsuf ibn Nūḥ on the Hagiographa. 2000. ISBN 90 04 11933 7

33. Zammit, M.R. *A Comparative Lexical Study of Qur'ānic Arabic*. ISBN 90 04 11801 2 (in preparation)

34. Bachra, B.N. *The Phonological Structure of the Verbal Roots in Arabic and Hebrew*. 2001. ISBN 90 04 12008 4